Invisible Architecture in Nineteenth-Century Literature

Edinburgh Critical Studies in Victorian Culture

Recent books in the series:

Home and Identity in Nineteenth-Century Literary London
Lisa C. Robertson

Writing the Sphinx: Literature, Culture and Egyptology
Eleanor Dobson

Oscar Wilde and the Radical Politics of the Fin de Siècle
Deaglán Ó Donghaile

The Sculptural Body in Victorian Literature: Encrypted Sexualities
Patricia Pulham

New Media and the Rise of the Popular Woman Writer, 1832–1860
Alexis Easley

Elizabeth Robins Pennell: Critical Essays
Dave Buchanan and Kimberly Morse-Jones

Plotting the News in the Victorian Novel
Jessica Valdez

Reading Bodies in Victorian Fiction: Associationism, Empathy and Literary Authority
Peter Katz

The Alternative Modernity of the Bicycle in British and French Literature, 1880–1920
Una Brogan

The Gothic Forms of Victorian Poetry
Olivia Loksing Moy

Victorian Fictions of Middle-Class Status: Forms of Absence in the Age of Reform
Albert D. Pionke

Time and Timelessness in Victorian Poetry
Irmtraud Huber

Invisible Architecture in Nineteenth-Century Literature: Rethinking Urban Modernity
Ben Moore

For a complete list of titles published visit the Edinburgh Critical Studies in Victorian Culture web page at www.edinburghuniversitypress.com/series/ECVC

Also Available:
Victoriographies – A Journal of Nineteenth-Century Writing, 1790–1914, edited by Diane Piccitto and Patricia Pulham
ISSN: 2044-2416
www.eupjournals.com/vic

Invisible Architecture in Nineteenth-Century Literature

Rethinking Urban Modernity

Ben Moore

EDINBURGH
University Press

For Ellie, who was there from the start

Edinburgh University Press is one of the leading university presses in the UK. We publish academic books and journals in our selected subject areas across the humanities and social sciences, combining cutting-edge scholarship with high editorial and production values to produce academic works of lasting importance. For more information visit our website: edinburghuniversitypress.com

© Ben Moore 2024, 2025

Edinburgh University Press Ltd
13 Infirmary Street
Edinburgh, EH1 1LT

First published in hardback by Edinburgh University Press 2024

Typeset in 11/13 Adobe Sabon by
IDSUK (DataConnection) Ltd

A CIP record for this book is available from the British Library

ISBN 978 1 3995 0848 3 (hardback)
ISBN 978 1 3995 0849 0 (paperback)
ISBN 978 1 3995 0850 6 (webready PDF)
ISBN 978 1 3995 0851 3 (epub)

The right of Ben Moore to be identified as the author of this work has been asserted in accordance with the Copyright, Designs and Patents Act 1988, and the Copyright and Related Rights Regulations 2003 (SI No. 2498).

Contents

List of Figures	vi
Acknowledgements	viii
Introduction: Mobility, Concealment, Transparency	1

Part I Writers and Cities

1. The Hidden City: James Kay, Friedrich Engels and *Mary Barton*'s Cellars — 37
2. The Unstable City: Rivers, Railways and Houses in *Dombey and Son* and *Our Mutual Friend* — 68
3. The Transparent City: Mansions, Montage and Commodity Architecture in *The Kill* and *The Ladies' Paradise* — 109

Part II Spatial Forms

4. Gothic Architecture and Urban Modernity — 141
5. The Arabesque City — 172
6. The Whiteness of the City — 203

Conclusion: The Invisible Architecture of New York	228
Bibliography	241
Index	259

Figures

1.1	Detail from *A Plan of Manchester and Salford with Vicinities* (1848), Isaac Slater. Manchester Libraries, Information and Archives.	58
2.1	*The New Zealander* (1872), Gustave Doré. Yale Center for British Art.	73
2.2	*Over London by Rail* (1872), Gustave Doré. Yale Center for British Art.	78
2.3	*Watching the Furnace Fire*, Hablot Browne (Phiz). Michael John Goodman, Charles Dickens Illustrated Library.	99
2.4	*Waiting for Father*, Marcus Stone. Michael John Goodman, Charles Dickens Illustrated Library.	100
2.5	*Mr Boffin Does the Honours of the Nursery Door*, Marcus Stone. Michael John Goodman, Charles Dickens Illustrated Library.	101
4.1	Advertising leaflet for Glacier Window Decoration (1880s). Alamy.	144
4.2	Advertisement for Glacier Window Decoration, *The Graphic* (3 May 1890). Look and Learn.	145
4.3	*The Last Day of Pompeii* (1830–3), Karl Bryullov. Wikiart.	147
4.4	*The Skyscraper* (1916), Glyn Philpot. Victoria Art Gallery, Bath and North East Somerset Council/Bridgeman Images.	154
4.5	*Trinity Church and Office Buildings*, New York (between 1910 and 1920), Detroit Publishing Co. Library of Congress, Washington, DC.	165
5.1	Frontispiece to *The Grammar of Ornament* (1856), Owen Jones. The Metropolitan Museum of Art, New York, Gift of Friends of the Thomas J. Watson Library.	180

5.2 *The Alhambra Court* (1854), photograph by Philip Henry
     Delamotte. © Victoria & Albert Museum, London.   182
5.3 Plate 86 from *The Grammar of Ornament* (1856),
     Owen Jones. The Metropolitan Museum of Art, New
     York, Gift of Friends of the Thomas J. Watson Library.   189

Acknowledgements

This book has been a long time in the making. Although a substantial portion was written in 2022, other parts go back almost to the start of my PhD at the University of Manchester in 2010. Over this period many people have contributed, directly or indirectly, to its eventual realisation. My first thanks are due to the AHRC, who funded my original PhD research. I am also deeply grateful to my supervisors at Manchester, Jeremy Tambling and Daniela Caselli, for their encouragement, patience and advice over many years. Among the many others whose comments and feedback helped me develop the project in those early years were Isobel Armstrong, Howard Booth, Barbara Leckie, Michael Sanders, Robert Spencer, Galin Tihanov and Sara Thornton. In particular, the three-year *Arcades Project* reading group I took part in with Jeremy Tambling, Alfie Bown and others in Manchester was the original testing ground for a number of ideas that have found their way into this book.

More recently, I am indebted to those who have listened and responded to parts of the Introduction, including Thomas Manson, Ina Habermann and their students at the University of Basel, as well as the Etcetera student society at the University of Amsterdam. Elena Moschou provided invaluable assistance with the referencing and bibliography. In a more general way, but not less importantly, I am immensely grateful to my colleagues in the UvA English Department for their inspiring conversation and good humour. I thank also all those at Edinburgh University Press who have helped guide the project through to publication, as well as the anonymous reviewers, whose comments were instrumental in sharpening the book during the revision process. I am grateful to the Faculty of Humanities at the University of Amsterdam for an award of sabbatical hours in 2022–3 that gave me the time to complete the manuscript. Last but not least, I thank my family for their support, which takes many different forms, both large and small, and most especially I thank Ellie, to whom I owe more than words can express.

The majority of the material that appears here is new to print, but parts of Chapter 2 are adapted by permission from my contribution to *Dickens and the Virtual City: Urban Perception and the Production of Social Space*, ed. by Estelle Murail and Sara Thornton (Palgrave, 2017).

Introduction: Mobility, Concealment, Transparency

Invisible Architecture

What is invisible architecture? It is what holds the modern city together, but also what prevents it from appearing as a unified and knowable entity, since it means there is always some part of the city which is hidden. It is structure which traverses the transparent, the unseen and the mobile, yet is resistant to interpretation as a totality. Like the psychoanalytic unconscious, it cannot be grasped directly, though its existence can be inferred or projected. It organises city space by limiting and directing perception, especially visual perception. It typically conceals or represses what is unpleasant under capitalism, such as the connections between rich and poor, or wealth and waste, but it can also provide a space for the possible reimagining or reshaping of the city. It brings together the reactionary, paranoid, ideological and molar aspects of the modern city with its capacity for the utopian, fluctuating and destabilising, without simply collapsing or reconciling these things.[1]

The contention of this book is that what I am calling invisible architecture plays a significant role in the literary and cultural imaginary of the years between approximately 1830 and 1910, in ways which only become apparent when the city is analysed as the meeting point of intersecting drives towards mobility, concealment and transparency. This was a period when cities in Britain and elsewhere seemed no longer graspable or comprehensible as a single whole (if they ever were), unless perhaps as a 'mass', a concept which unifies the city's population only to render it more unknowable.[2] William Cook Taylor, whom Asa Briggs calls 'an apologist of the new industrial system', described northern English industrial towns in the 1840s as 'an aggregate of masses, our conception of which clothe themselves in terms which express something portentous and fearful'.[3] Raymond Williams notes that 'the great city was [. . .] so overwhelming, that its people were often seen in a single way: as a crowd, as "masses" or as a "workforce"'.[4] For Charles Baudelaire, the modern city is ungraspable because it disallows totalisation, like modernity itself, which he calls 'the ephemeral, the fugitive, the contingent, the half of art whose other half is the eternal and the immutable'.[5]

Against this backdrop, the concept of invisible architecture has the potential to open up new connections between city spaces that seem otherwise radically separate. For instance, the cellar and the glass department store are two forms of architecture which are both important in the nineteenth century, but which seem to operate in very different ways. The cellar provides invisibility through concealment, as a place for hiding, storing or discarding people and things, while the department store heightens visibility to the point of transparency, threatening to dematerialise architecture completely. Nonetheless, both perform similar ideological work by organising and delimiting the boundaries of different regions of the city, and by providing a repository for conceptual content which cannot be encompassed by dominant modes of thought. This can consist of residual elements of the past, such as rural working-class knowledge in Elizabeth Gaskell's Manchester, or emergent elements of a possible future, like the dreamlike and utopian structures found in Émile Zola's Paris. It is equally vital to recognise that city architecture in this period is not fixed or static, but metaphorically and literally mobile. The instability of Charles Dickens's London, for example, continually turns the visible and the invisible on their heads, bringing within the scope of architecture things that do not at first glance appear architectural at all, such as the river and the railway. Part of my argument is that these mobile features of city space disrupt the conventional stability and monumentality associated with architecture, reframing the limits and capacities of the architectural as a category.

As the above indicates, my use of the term 'architecture' in this book is intentionally broad. I use it in ways that incorporate both the literary and the metaphorical, and which encompass what others might refer to as assemblages or infrastructures.[6] This does not mean I am uninterested in the actual built structures of the city, however. My suggestion is rather that we fail to fully grasp the significance of more straightforwardly architectural structures – Gothic cathedrals for instance – if we do not read them as part of a wider spatial and urban imaginary, within which architecture is ultimately impossible to disentangle from forms of non- or anti-architecture. In taking this broad and speculative approach to architecture, I draw on Anthony Vidler's concept of the 'architectural uncanny', which describes the capacity of buildings to elide 'the boundaries of the real and the unreal in order to provoke a disturbing ambiguity, a slippage between waking and dreaming'.[7] Buildings for Vidler are never uncanny in themselves, but become so when they act as 'representations of estrangement' in cultural and literary texts, which need not necessarily be Gothic or supernatural in nature.[8] Vidler informs my approach to architecture in two main ways: firstly, he shows that the capacity for a building to make and unsettle meanings is thoroughly shaped by its literary and cultural contexts; and secondly, he draws attention to the value of psychoanalysis in reading architecture and its contexts, an idea to which I will return.

The other key concept in my title is the 'invisible', which I understand as related to but not identical with the transparent. At the end of *The Architectural Uncanny*, Vidler discusses the way modernist architects generated a 'myth of transparency: transparency of the self to nature, of the self to the other, of all selves to society'. This myth is manifested in 'a universal transparency of building materials, spatial penetration, and the ubiquitous flow of air, light, and physical movement'.[9] If such transparency is the central ideology of modernism, as Vidler suggests, then it is equally so of the contemporary glass and steel constructions of our own time, those monuments of what Hal Foster calls the 'global style' of architecture, or, more cuttingly, the 'art-architecture complex'.[10] Looking back, the nineteenth century comes to appear as the period of the nascent development of this ideology, which takes shape in reaction to both the dark, cramped and underground spaces of the city and the often stultifying practices of traditional architecture.[11] The architectural theorist Sigfried Giedion argues that this development went largely unrecognised in official culture, since although iron and glass were the most important new building materials of the century, they were consigned to the sphere of the engineer rather than the architect (in bridges, railway stations and so on) with the result that 'construction was, as it were, the subconsciousness of architecture; there lay dormant in it impulses that only later found explicit theoretical statement'.[12] Giedion's work thus offers what Rem Koolhaas in *Delirious New York* calls a 'retroactive manifesto': a reconstructed outline of the unformulated, unconscious logic that lies behind the architectural developments of the nineteenth century.[13]

This suppressed development of transparency took place at the same time as literature was increasingly demanding that things be seen, that the world be opened up. Michel Foucault's description of changes in scientific classification beginning in the late eighteenth century effectively summarises this drive:

> Henceforth, character resumes its former role [from the Renaissance and earlier] as a visible sign directing us towards a buried depth; but what it reveals is not a secret text, a muffled word, or a resemblance too precious to be revealed; it is the coherent totality of an organic structure that weaves back into the unique fabric of its sovereignty both the visible and the invisible.[14]

This reorientation, which Foucault sees as occurring across disciplines, places emphasis not only on the visible, but on the relationship between the visible and invisible. The goal is 'to relate the visible, to the invisible, to its deeper cause, as it were, then to rise upwards once more from that hidden architecture towards the more obvious signs displayed on the surface of bodies'.[15] What is seen in the phenomenal world serves as an index of something deeper that is nonetheless completely incorporated with the 'signs' on the surface, whether this be the shapes of birds' beaks in the Galapagos for Charles Darwin, the details of Venetian Gothic design for John Ruskin, or the patterns of behaviour of ordinary people in a small town for George Eliot. In each case, the visible is not the opposite of the invisible, but combines with it as part of a larger totality: evolution; non-alienated production; the web of humanity. These deeper architectures are simultaneously closed, since they are not immediately available to our perception, and open, since the signs that reveal them proliferate all around us, if only we know how to read them.

In *Invisible Architecture in Nineteenth-Century Literature* I build on these statements by Foucault by proposing that the nineteenth century is the point where two forms of invisibility collide and combine: the hidden or concealed on one hand and the transparent or aethereal on the other. In place of his term 'hidden architecture' I therefore prefer 'invisible architecture', a formulation which allows me to posit a productive co-presence of the transparent and the hidden. The underground cellar-dwellings of Gaskell's Manchester are invisible, but so too is Zola's fantastical glass and iron department store. The crowded arabesque surfaces of the modernising city evoke a sense of the unseen and ineffable, but so too do its blank white walls. In using the term invisible architecture to describe this conjunction I am conscious of echoing the title of Italo Calvino's *Invisible Cities* (1972), a book concerned both with how narratives can organise cities into visibility and knowability, and how it can render them inaccessible, as I am here.

In the readings that follow, the encounters between these different forms of invisibility in the nineteenth century are not simple, nor do they always proceed away from the hidden and towards the transparent, as the 'programmatic' modernist teleology promulgated by Giedion among others would have it.[16] As a result, any appearance of totality they might generate is in the end deceptive. Rather, as the following chapters will show, there is a dynamic interaction between these two categories which involves as many disjunctions as continuities, hence why mobility is my third element of analysis. This requires some reorientation in conventional lines of thought. As I discuss below, this book joins other critics who have begun to question apparently obvious spatial and temporal oppositions, such as the hidden and the transparent, the medieval and the modern, or the whole and the ruined. Such distinctions are still often persistent and persuasive in accounts of the nineteenth-century city, as in one critic's remark that during the improvement of London's roads between 1830 and 1856, 'the new, wide, straight streets cross-sectioning the prior street plan were the spatial opposite of "Old London", which was imagined as dark, unsanitary and labyrinthine'.[17] This is not a false statement by any means, but it tells only part of the story. What is also needed is to go beyond the concept of opposition and to enter into a closer consideration of the particular kinds of invisibility these two forms of architecture – wide streets and labyrinthine alleyways – produce, where they intersect as well as where they diverge, and what ideological formations this combination supports. In order to demonstrate how reading through invisible architecture can offer answers to these questions, the next section provides both an example of my approach and an elucidation of the categories of the mobile, concealed and transparent, by way of a close reading of George Gissing's *The Nether World* (1888).

A Visit to Sydenham: *The Nether World*

Invisible architecture can be understood as a combination of three interrelated elements, or moments, of urban architecture: mobility, concealment and transparency, which together lie at the core of my readings of the interface between architecture and literature. To demonstrate, I want to discuss in some detail chapter 12 of Gissing's *The Nether World*, in which the newly married couple Bob and Pennyloaf Hewett take an August bank-holiday trip to the Crystal

Palace at Sydenham, where the building had stood since its removal from Hyde Park in 1854.[18]

The first moment I want to consider is mobility, evident in the train journey Bob and Pennyloaf take at the start of the chapter, as part of a crowd of day-trippers. As they depart from Holborn Viaduct station in the City of London, they witness 'a perpetual rush of people for the trains to the "Paliss"' (NW 105). The slightly mocking term 'Paliss' hints at a transformation of the Crystal Palace from a national spectacle into a degraded place of working-class entertainment, an impression the rest of the chapter deepens. The 'perpetual rush' of the people foregrounds movement as a feature of bodies and crowds, but this movement is also mechanical and architectural, since the passengers speed away on rails that pass 'over the roofs of South London, about them the universal glare of sunlight, the carriage dense with tobacco-smoke' (NW 106). Although the train passes over London's rooftops, the panoptical railway view of urban architecture imagined by Dickens in *Dombey and Son* (1846–8) or Gustave Doré in the engraving 'Over London by Rail' (1872), discussed further in Chapter 2, is not a feature of these passengers' sensorium. The 'universal glare of sunlight' on the one hand and the smog-like tobacco smoke on the other make this instead an experience of disorientation and confusion. The carnivalesque confusion of the scene is redoubled by a temporary dissolution of social order; there is 'no distinction between "classes" to-day; get in where you like, where you can' (NW 105). Such a lack of distinction is itself a form of movement, a jumbling of the structures that usually secure social hierarchy even amid the upheaval of rail travel.

It is important to recognise that the mobility evident in this passage, exaggerated by the August bank-holiday atmosphere, is not external to the Crystal Palace at Sydenham but an integral part of its architecture. An 1854 *Guide to the Crystal Palace and Park* by Samuel Phillips opens with instructions on how to arrive at the building by railway or road, explaining that as part of the building's relocation the Brighton Railway Company

> undertook to lay down a new line of rails between London and Sydenham, to construct a branch from the Sydenham station to the Crystal Palace garden, and to build a number of engines sufficiently powerful to draw heavy trains up the steep incline to the Palace.[19]

The railway line is not an afterthought, but is fully incorporated into the new design for the building. It is connected with 'Sir Joseph

Paxton's Tunnel', a 'capacious horizontal brick shaft, twenty-four feet wide, extending the whole length of the building', which is 'used as a roadway for bringing into, and taking from, the Palace all objects of art and of industry', as well as providing access to the building's heating apparatus.[20] Indeed, Phillips's introduction imagines a reader already onboard a train to the Palace: 'we will presume that the visitor has taken his railway ticket, which, for his convenience, includes admission within the Palace, and that his short ten minutes' journey has commenced'.[21] The railway journey is presented as part of the Crystal Palace experience, registering a new mobility in how architecture was able to be understood in the mid-nineteenth century.[22]

Added to this is the fact that the entire building had been relocated after the Great Exhibition of 1851. In being moved, it was substantially redesigned, its nave raised 'forty-four feet higher than the nave in Hyde park – and three transepts [. . .] introduced into the structure instead of one'.[23] As the rapid construction of the original structure in Hyde Park had already begun to show, architecture no longer needed to be fixed in place, but could become modular and customisable. This reorientation laid the ground for the dreams of later architects, such as Mies van der Rohe's Core House of 1951, designed with a flexible structure that could be reshaped by its inhabitants. Mobility was also embedded in the ongoing life of the Crystal Palace, with one of Philips's footnotes observing that 'the entire covering of glass may be renewed again and again without in any way interfering with the construction it covers'.[24] Phillips names the new style of the building 'Modern English', evoking Early English Gothic as both a point of contrast and a model to be emulated. Like the ancient Gothic cathedrals, the Palace's glass and iron manufacture is said to 'defy the effects of time', making it paradoxically both temporary and eternal.[25] As it turned out, the guide's optimism was misplaced. Not only because the Crystal Palace burned down in 1936, but also because by the 1870s, when *The Nether World* is set, the building had become a distinctly downmarket attraction. For Gissing, it provides the perfect setting to symbolise the disappointing failure of Pennyloaf's dreams of marriage, culminating in her reflection that 'on the morrow it would be necessary to pawn her wedding-ring' (NW 113). This rapid descent is signified by the couple's two train journeys: they travel to the Palace in a first-class carriage, but return in a 'long third-class coach' (NW 112).

The impermanence and mobility of Gissing's Crystal Palace is redoubled by its grounds. These are described by Phillips as a mix of English and Italian styles, 'combining the formality of the one school with the freedom and natural grace of the other', but in *The Nether World* they have been taken over by a fairground which parodies the grand historical and geographical sweep of the Crystal Palace's exhibits, where visitors can throw a stick at a 'wooden model of the treacherous Afghan or the base African' (NW 107), so unveiling (but then reframing as entertainment) the violent underside of the palace's imperial pretensions.[26] The scene is one of constant motion, with 'swing-boats and merry-go-rounds' that 'soared and dipped and circled' (NW 106). While this fairground is a culturally degraded contrast to the Palace in terms of content, its nomadic and temporary architecture is not so much an inversion of the building it stands next to as an appropriate mirroring of it.

The second architectural moment is concealment. Concealment is already present on the train journey, where blinding sunlight and tobacco-smoke make any view into or out of the train carriage impossible. It is continued by the 'thick white wavering cloud of dust' (NW 106) that rises above Bob and Pennyloaf's heads in the fairground, choking and whitening them 'from head to foot' (NW 107). The experience causes Pennyloaf to wish 'that they might go into the "Paliss" and find a shadowed seat' (NW 108), but this hope is only partly satisfied by the 'Shilling Tea-room' (NW 108), which turns out to be a place of bawdy entertainment, filled with 'a spirit of imbecile joviality' (NW 108) that echoes the fair outside.

More generally, the entire chapter explores the transformation of a place of high culture into something much lower, as the Crystal Palace is brought down into, and by, the 'nether world' of the novel's title. The building's original purpose and meaning have become obscured, as all horizons are obscured in this novel. This process disgusts the narrator, who observes, ventriloquising the crowd:

> away to the west yonder the heavens are afire with sunset, but at that we do not care to look; never in our lives did we regard it. We know not what is meant by beauty or grandeur. Here under the glass roof stand white forms of undraped men and women – casts of ancient statues – but we care as little for the glory of art as for that of nature. (NW 110)

The disconnection between the visitors on the one hand and the 'beauty and grandeur' of both nature and classical art on the other undoes the apparent openness of the Crystal Palace, casting a barrier between people and environment. Nature and art are both effectively withdrawn, rendered invisible by the limited perspectives of the day-trippers.

Gissing's disdain exceeds that of an earlier literary scene he echoes and reinvents, whether consciously or not: the visit to the Louvre in Émile Zola's *L'Assommoir* (1877).²⁷ In Zola's novel, Gervaise's marriage to Coupeau is celebrated with the working-class wedding party visiting Paris's most famous museum. Yet the visitors are more stunned by the 'gold of the frames' and the floor in the Gallery of Apollo, which is 'clear and shiny like a mirror', than by great works of art like Géricault's *Raft of the Medusa* (1818–19) or Murillo's *The Birth of the Virgin* (1661).²⁸ The museum becomes to them a labyrinth, as the region of the Rue de la Goutte-d'Or where they live is for the middle classes, causing them to end up in 'total despair [. . .] roam[ing] haphazardly through the galleries'.²⁹ Although the Coupeau wedding party is portrayed as ludicrously incongruous in the Louvre, the building itself remains fundamentally untouched by their presence, unlike the Crystal Palace for Gissing, which is dragged down to the level of its philistine invaders. Pennyloaf ends the chapter by groping her way 'blindly up to the black hole which was her wedding-chamber' (NW 113), but this 'black hole' is not so much a contrast to the Crystal Palace as an extension of it. The Palace has also become a black hole, or a whirlpool (the title of another of Gissing's novels), since it generates frantic excitement but finally sucks its victims down into the darkness of poverty and alcoholism.

The final architectural moment is transparency. Despite being taken over by anarchic revelry and cultural deprivation, the Palace retains its famous glass and iron architecture. The 'glass canopy' (NW 108) creates a sweltering heat, like the greenhouses on which its design was originally based by Joseph Paxton, while in the centre of the building there is 'a vast amphitheatre, filled with thousands of faces' (NW 109), indicating that this openness is not antithetical to the crowd but magnifies it. The combination of openness and massed bodies is repeated in the tea-room, where paying guests can 'feed freely on all that lay before them' (NW 108), so long as they can fight their way through the enormous crowd of other customers. Like the fairground, this petit-bourgeois Cockaigne parodies the original purpose of the Crystal Palace, in this case its lavish display of produce from around the world. As with the fairground, the spatial form of the Palace is repeated even while the content is inverted, here by replacing the contemplation of modern industrial society with the animalistic consumption of its products. Like the colonial elements of the fairground, the scene functions as an opening up of the historical unconscious of the Great Exhibition, whose civilised elegance was always based on the violently consumptive drives of industrial and imperial capitalism.³⁰

The transparency present in Gissing's chapter is not only architectural but narrative. As they swarm through the Palace, the visitors are opened up to display and interpretation by the narrator. Gissing calls it 'a great review of the People', asking, 'since man came into being did the world ever exhibit a sadder spectacle?' (NW 110). The glorious spectacle of 1851 has become a tragic display of ugly humour and uglier passions in 1878, but a spectacle it nonetheless remains. We are presented with an openness and transparency that is not simply opposed to the hidden, underground and concealed parts of society, but emphasises these things. The bank-holiday outing brings to light men with 'visages so deformed by ill-health that they excite disgust; their hair is cut down to within half an inch of the scalp; their legs are twisted out of shape by evil conditions of life from birth upwards' (NW 109), while young women are revealed to be 'worn-out', with 'listless eyes' (NW 109).

I have dwelt on Gissing's bank-holiday outing at some length because it demonstrates two important features of my approach to architecture and literature. Firstly, it presents mobility, transparency and concealment not as mutually exclusive features of architectural space, but coextensive, intermingled and reciprocally determining. They are not held apart but combine together, even turn into one another, dialectically producing new forms of space. Secondly, these architectural modes also turn out to be features of literary representation. When Gissing writes of the crowd on the train, 'ho for the bottle of muddy ale, passed round in genial fellowship from mouth to mouth!' (NW 106), motion is implicitly signalled as a feature of the writing as well as of the train, the crowd, and the bottle itself. This moving bottle is both closed and open: closed in the sense that it is 'muddy', and hence dirty, hidden and obscure; but also open, both literally and symbolically, in the way it connects the mouths of the drinkers, and in its generating of a 'genial fellowship' that serves to synecdochally crystallise working-class sociality.

To put it another way, the bottle acts as a mobile element that is metaphorically and metonymically open to the chapter around it, and to the social world the chapter describes. In this sense the scene represents the central idea of the chapter: the failure of the utopian promise of the Crystal Palace's glass architecture (which, to stretch the point, is symbolised by the glass bottle) to produce any genuine 'fellowship' with other people and places. But at the same time the bottle acts as a point of semantic resistance, through its meaninglessness, superfluity and disposability. It is, after all, only a bottle of muddy ale, an ultimately unnecessary detail whose removal would not change the chapter in any significant way. This duality of the symbolic and arbitrary, the meaningful and meaningless, the visible and invisible, has long been acknowledged as central to literary realism by critics such as Roland Barthes, Peter Brooks, Fredric Jameson and Jacques Rancière.[31] Yet such dichotomies of realism are not usually read as deeply enmeshed with architecture, as I propose to do.

Undoing Oppositions

In this book I invite readers to think together two terms which are more commonly placed in opposition: transparency and concealment. Central to my readings is the task of undoing the sense of opposition between these terms, and instead seeing them as mutually comingling, mobile and interpenetrating tendencies within both architectural practice and literary representation. In doing so I build on several critics who have made similar moves in this direction.

Barbara Leckie argues that Sigfried Giedion offers a model of architecture in the nineteenth century that acknowledges the comingling of forms, and which can also be taken as a 'model of knowledge', namely '*Durchdringung* or interpenetration'.[32] For Giedion, the architectural style of the Crystal Palace and other exhibition buildings 'engenders floating relations'.[33] In *Open Houses*, Leckie argues that the houses of the poor, though 'in every way the antithesis of the new architecture', also give rise to such interpenetration, generating 'a sense of transparency' despite their cramped and poor conditions.[34] She proposes that despite the obvious differences between the two, such houses serve a similar function to Baron Haussmann's boulevards in Paris, sending a 'jolt into received ways of experiencing space and profoundly alter[ing] such orientations to the point of bringing about a new sensibility'. Hovels and boulevards should then be opposed not to each other, but to the 'closed and protected bourgeois interiors' with which the realist novel is frequently concerned.[35] Such rethinking of oppositions is also a feature of my approach, but for me the central concern is not the houses of poor per se, but rather the interaction between two drives – a drive to concealment and a drive to transparency – which are at once literary and architectural. These drives are manifested across a range of urban texts and spaces in the nineteenth century, so for this reason my objects are more varied than Leckie's: industrial cellar-dwellings; the railway and river; the department store; the Gothic cathedral; arabesque decoration; and urban whiteness.

Leckie's book title alludes to Sharon Marcus's *Apartment Stories*, Part One of which is named 'Open Houses'. Here, as Marcus puts it, she

> shows discourses promoting urban mobility and legibility at work in Paris from 1820 to 1848, extending the visibility and legibility of all urban space even to the homes and women who, in an ideology of separate spheres, would have been associated with sequestered private space.[36]

For Marcus, Paris displays a desire to 'make the apartment building continuous with the street, where everything and everyone was visible and within reach'.[37] Such visibility-making is often associated with Asmodeus, 'the devilish hero of Lesage's *le Diable boiteux* (1707)', including in *Paris, ou Le livre des cent-et-un* (1831), a multi-author encyclopaedic account of the city. Here and elsewhere Asmodeus represents the fantasy of a bird's-eye view of Paris (and of other cities, including London) that is also able to penetrate its private houses. In one text of 1847, for instance, Asmodeus simply 'makes a gesture, and the walls that hid the interior from you have become transparent'.[38] As Sambudha Sen observes, Marcus shows that by around the 1840s, 'Asmodeus's eye begins to approximate the elasticity as well as the alienated nature of the truly modern vision'.[39]

This work of visibility-making operates across cities, since Leckie identifies a fantasy of London that is remarkably similar to Marcus's 1847 Parisian example, in the 1851 article 'The Houses of London Crystallized; or the Great Transparency'. The author evokes Asmodeus, asking 'what [. . .] if all these massive walls were suddenly to become transparent, and London converted into one vast glass bee-hive!'[40] This comment relies on the widespread perception that the Crystal Palace resembled a beehive, as evident in George Cruikshank's 'The Opening of the Great Hive of the World, May 1, 1851, or the Industrial Exhibition of All Nations' (published in *1851: or, The Adventures of Mr and Mrs Sandboys*, a collaboration with Henry Mayhew). In both Paris and London, the fantasy is that of the city transformed into an exhibition, or of the exhibition transformed into a city. But as Walter Benjamin was already aware in the *Arcades Project*, such an opening up of the city cuts two ways: 'the street becomes room and the room becomes street. The passerby who stops to look at the house stands, as it were, in the alcove.'[41] Benjamin's point is that the desire for opening up is also, at the same time, a desire for enclosure. In Leckie's example, the desire is to make London transparent, certainly, but also to make it a 'bee-hive', which means roofing it over and separating it from the outside world. If this is interpenetration in Giedion's sense, then that concept must be recognised as including not only the breaking down of distinctions but also the multiplication of boundaries and thresholds within the city. The associated process of enclosure and transparency increasing simultaneously, in mutually enforcing ways, is one of the tendencies which invisible architecture is an attempt to name.

Another critic who has questioned accepted architectural oppositions is Stephen Eskilson, who in *The Age of Glass* treats the nineteenth-century revival of stained glass not as a Pugin-esque resistance to modernity that retreated to medieval building styles, but a 'core part' of the 'emerging aesthetic' of modern architects.[42] Eskilson challenges the majority of commentators on the topic, who 'seem convinced that stained glass in the nineteenth century represented a dying vestige of a medieval art', by contending that 'in fact the opposite was true and a critical mass of cutting-edge architectural reformers invested in and promoted the newly revived practice'.[43] The nineteenth-century development of stained glass, Eskilson argues, culminates with figures such as Frank Lloyd Wright, who created geometric, almost arabesque, window decorations for the Luxfer Prism Company and in the Prairie houses he designed in the early 1900s.[44] Theo van Doesburg, influenced by design movement De Stijl, similarly used stained glass as a tool of modernity in the Netherlands, treating it as a 'form of intermedia that could connect painting, architecture, and décor in a contemporary *Gesamtkunstwerke*'.[45] In questioning this common assumption about architectural modernity's relationship to the medieval, Eskilson opens the way to one of my topics: rethinking the place of the Gothic cathedral within urban modernity. Rather than interpreting the Gothic cathedral as a superseded contrast to the emerging iron and glass architecture of the nineteenth century, I argue in Chapter 4 that we should follow those writers who recognise a peculiar modernity to the Gothic cathedral itself.

Douglas Murphy also challenges the separation of the modern and the outmoded in his reading of the Crystal Palace, by proceeding in an almost opposite direction to Eskilson. For Murphy, following a line of thought established by Walter Benjamin, the Crystal Palace and other exhibition palaces of the nineteenth century should be read against the grain of their promoters, not as glorious successes but as ruins. These structures were 'built in a rush of optimism' but turn out mostly to be 'pathetic failures', riven by contradictions.[46] Though 'designed by the most stringently rational minds, they were also confusing, contradictory, obscure and fragmented places'.[47] Whereas Eskilson shows that an apparently anti-modern form could become modern in the course of the nineteenth century, Murphy shows that apparently modern exhibition buildings were, even at the height of their success, sites of failure and ruin. His book functions as an extended explication of Benjamin's observation, at the end of the 1935 version of 'Paris, the Capital of the Nineteenth Century', that 'with the destabilising of the market economy, we begin to recognise the monuments of the bourgeoisie as ruins even before they have crumbled'.[48]

Murphy's analysis also casts further light on my reading of the Crystal Palace at Sydenham. As Murphy points out, the second iteration of the building was consciously conceived as a 'Palace of the People', in the Victorian spirit of rational recreation, so that outings such as the one Gissing describes were part of the intention from the start, though the outcome was supposed to be the improvement of the cultural and physical health of the poor rather than debauchery.[49] Yet the Sydenham building ended up containing a stranger set of spaces than its Hyde Park predecessor, becoming 'an eerie collage of strange spatial juxtapositions', so that the main effect was one of fragmentation, what Murphy calls a 'logic of incompleteness', rather than the formation of coherent, rational subjects. [50] The building ends up becoming allegorical in Benjamin's sense of the term, as a 'melancholy space of contradictory meaning, simultaneously remembering and forgetting itself'.[51] It is this process that *The Nether World* begins to capture.

Crystal Palaces and Underground Voices

The opposition between the hidden and the transparent which I am challenging was a feature of nineteenth-century discourse itself as well as later criticism, but one of the most famous literary examples of this antagonism also acts as its undoing, as this section will show. I refer to Chernychevsky's visionary 1863 text *What Is to Be Done?* and Dostoevsky's response to it in *Notes from Underground* (1864), which turn on two alternative attitudes towards the Crystal Palace. In this intertextual encounter, we find nineteenth-century literature already complicating conceptions of architectural modernity even as it helps to create them.

Nikolai Chernychevsky's text, written partly in response to the nihilism of Turgenev's *Fathers and Sons* (1862), takes the Crystal

Palace as an optimistic symbol of a new utopian and socialist order of society. Describing a fantastical building that stands 'amid fields of grain, meadows, gardens, and groves', which produce supernaturally abundant crops, the narrator apostrophises his readers:

> But this edifice! what is it? what style of architecture? There is nothing like it now; no, but there is one that points towards it. – the palace which stands on Sydenham Hill, built of cast-iron and glass – cast-iron and glass, and that is all. No, not all; that is only the integument of an edifice, – the outside walls. But inside of this palace is a real house, a tremendous house! This integument of cast-iron and glass only covers it as by a sheath; it forms around it wide galleries on all the floors. How simple is the architecture of the inward house![52]

Part of the fantasy here is the domestication of an architecture originally built for exhibition display. This involves a retreat back to familiarity that perhaps marks the limits to which Chernychevsky was able to push his imaginative gesture; the glass and iron architecture is in the end only a 'sheath' covering a more conventional house with 'stone walls'.[53] On the other hand, the wonderfully simple design of this interior house represents a rejection of bourgeois ornamentation, anticipating modernist aesthetics. In any case, this vision clearly takes the openness of the Crystal Palace as a blueprint for the future, both architecturally and socially. The inhabitants of the new Russia 'all have sufficient room', building these grand crystalline palaces 'three versts apart, like numberless, great chessmen on a mighty chessboard'.[54] Such an arrangement anticipates, as Marshall Berman points out, Le Corbusier's plan for the *ville radieuse*, a network of skyscrapers separated by vast gardens.[55]

Dostoevsky, however, mistrusts this appropriation of the Crystal Palace. Articulating a critique that could perhaps be levelled at all utopias, the underground man protests:

> You believe in the Palace of Crystal, eternally inviolable, that is in something at which one couldn't furtively put out one's tongue or make concealed gestures of derision. But perhaps I fear this edifice just because it is made of crystal and eternally inviolable, and it will not be possible even to put one's tongue out in secret.[56]

This voice from the underground criticises the Crystal Palace, and the dreams it engenders, as 'a castle in the air', finding them too totalising, too rationalising and too simplistic in their view of human nature.[57] Dostoevsky gives us something like the voice of the unconscious, which can never say simply yes or no: 'don't pay any attention to the fact that just now I rejected the palace of crystal for the sole reason that one won't be able to stick one's tongue out at it', he says a little later.[58] This voice is radically dialogic in Mikhail Bakhtin's terms.[59] It speaks against a building that it takes to represent an absolutely unified and inviolable ego, and hence to deny difference. At the same time, it expresses a revolt by the body, which wants to put out its tongue against any intellectual or architectural system that claims to stand for pure rationality. What it is not, though, is a rejection of modernity in any simple way. While the underground man might appear regressive compared to the transparency of the Crystal Palace, Marshall Berman shows that what Dostoevsky is critiquing is an anti-urban strain of utopianism in Chernychevsky, which makes society something static and stale, rather than the Crystal Palace itself, which after all began as an urban phenomenon. The underground man, says Berman, is 'attacking the modernity of the suburbs and exurbs – still, in the 1860s, only an ideal – in the name of the modernity of the city'. The city is, by contrast, able to encompass 'doubt, negation, desire, struggle of every kind'.[60]

The apparent chronology here, which would move from the hidden underground cellar to the transparent display of the exhibition, and after that the garden city and the skyscraper, is undermined, since the underground that rejects the Crystal Palace turns out also to be on the side of modernity, just a different kind of modernity. Following Berman's reading again, it is precisely the urban setting that allowed the Crystal Palace to become something more than static transparent modernity, and this is what the underground man's protest insists on restoring. It is for this reason that my focus in this study is on urban architectural modernity. The city is the place where contradictions lie side by side, where the transparent and the underground cannot be mobilised as simple opposites.

In Dickens's *Bleak House* (1853), for instance, Mr Snagsby at one point finds himself unexpectedly passing along a street in Tom-All-Alone's, probably in Holborn, which is 'reeking with such smells and sights that he, who has lived in London all his life, can scarcely believe his senses'.[61] Though he is only a stone's throw from the respectable Gray's Inn Square, the contrast to Snagsby's own sense of gentility is dramatic and extreme. It is, however, not unusual. Snagsby's journey is an early instance of the trend of taking East London as a 'symbolic example' of 'the darkness and poverty of the city', which culminated in the conventional use of 'Darkest London' as a descriptive term in the 1880s and 1890s.⁶² Not coincidentally, this was also the period that saw an explosion of colonial adventure stories, led by H. Rider Haggard's *King Solomon's Mines* (1885). The capital becomes another kind of colonial frontier, as it is in the opening of Conrad's *Heart of Darkness* (1899), where Marlow tells his audience that London has also 'been one of the dark places of the earth'.⁶³

Another example comes from Théophile Gautier, quoted by Benjamin in the *Arcades Project*, who remarks that the 'running board' of a Parisian carriage marks the threshold between radically different worlds: 'it is the point of departure from one country to another, from misery to luxury, from thoughtlessness to thoughtfulness. It is the hyphen between him who is nothing and him who is all'.⁶⁴ Gautier makes the city the *sine qua non* of extreme contrast, a place where narrow but immense chasms in wealth and social position are part of the structure of everyday life. As such, the city has a unique potential to transform conservative, outmoded or static forms into modern, emergent or mobile configurations, even while it gives rise to some of the greatest suffering of the industrial period. One of my presumptions in this book is that literature is a – perhaps the – pre-eminent site where these transformative tensions become evident, and where they are worked through imaginatively.

From Visible Cities to Mute Speech

In addition to the hidden and the transparent, the other opposition I seek to challenge in this book is that between literature and architecture. I maintain a double focus on both domains in the chapters that follow, with the aim of showing that they are deeply integrated with one another, to the extent that they transform in parallel throughout the nineteenth century. In this section, I begin to formulate a theoretical account of this dual movement of architecture and literature, by way of a reading of Jacques Rancière.

Rancière has developed in detail the concept of the 'aesthetic regime', which, he argues, comes to prominence in literature and other arts in the nineteenth century.⁶⁵ The aesthetic regime is said to abolish hierarchy and structure, these being associated with the earlier representative regime, and to instead allow the free combination of heterogeneous elements: 'a product identical with something not produced, knowledge transformed into non-knowledge, *logos* identical with pathos, the intention of the unintentional, etc.'⁶⁶ While Rancière most often conceptualises this regime in terms of speaking or writing, as in the title of his book *Mute Speech*, or in the claim that literature in the nineteenth century begins to say 'we are nothing, let us be everything', it can also be understood as a lifting of the barrier between the visible and invisible.[67] In *Aisthesis*, Rancière quotes a passage from Ralph Waldo Emerson's 'The Poet' (1844), taken to represent 'the epitome of German idealist philosophy', which includes the line: 'as the eyes of Lyncæus were said to see through the earth, so the poet turns the world to glass, and shows us all things in their right series and procession'.[68] Rancière links this idea with lines from Schelling:

> the meaning we seek glimmers through the sensible world, as it does through words, and through the dissolving mists which alone reveal the land of fantasy where our desires are headed. Each beautiful painting is born, as it were, when an invisible barrier dividing the real from the ideal world is removed.[69]

In both cases, the intention is to reveal the world as alive, to undo a false dichotomy between the material world (the visible) and the ideal world (the invisible), and to do so through the force of aesthetic experience (poetry or painting). As Rancière puts it, the modern thought that we can see in formation here believed that 'the contemporary world is structured by a separation that must be abolished'.[70] In the quotation from Emerson especially it is clear that this is a process whereby the buried and hidden is transformed by the transparency of the aesthetic gaze. Every artist becomes an Asmodeus.

Rancière partially echoes Foucault in *The Order of Things* by finding in what is usually called modernity a new connection between visible and invisible. In *Mute Speech* he acknowledges, as Foucault does, that the shift from a 'representative poetics' to an 'expressive poetics' cuts across disciplines, putting 'on the same side the adepts of pure literature and the historians and sociologists who see it as the expression of a society'.[71] In both cases, the principles to be followed are 'first, to find beneath words the vital force that is the cause of their utterance; second, to find in the visible the sign of the invisible'.[72] Rancière follows Victor Hugo in *Notre Dame de Paris,* from the chapter 'This Will Kill That' (which I discuss further in Chapter 4), in seeing this development as proceeding out of architecture, specifically the Gothic cathedral, but he argues that 'the cathedral here is a scriptural model, not an architectural one', meaning that 'the poet can make, in a cathedral of words, the novel of the cathedral of stone because the latter is in itself already a book'.[73] Rancière dissolves the cathedral into words, or rather he proposes that Hugo's gaze has already done so, by seeing architecture as language and language as architecture. Moreover, Hugo's writing about the cathedral already anticipates the cathedral's opposite, which is later articulated in Flaubert's desire for 'a work without substance: no longer the work as cathedral, but the work as desert, the "book about nothing" that makes word and thought adhere to one another by the force of style alone'.[74] The course of the nineteenth century thus witnesses a dissolving of the cathedral into words without content: a becoming invisible of architecture. Flaubert indeed seems to see art in this way, as a movement from density to weightlessness, and implicitly from architecture to poetry, in a letter Rancière quotes:

> The finest works are those that contain the least matter; the closer expression comes to thought, the closer language comes to coinciding and merging with it, the finer the result. I believe the future of art lies in this direction. I see it, as it has developed from its beginnings, growing progressively more ethereal, from Egyptian pylons to Gothic lancets, from the 20,000-line Hindu poems to the effusions of Byron.[75]

A slightly different way to read Flaubert's letter is not as describing literature replacing architecture, as Hugo's 'This Will Kill That' would have it, but as architecture and literature progressing in parallel, both gradually transforming into forms of nothingness.

This idea of architecture and literature transforming in parallel is the approach I take, although I also seek to unsettle Flaubert's idea of a straightforward progression towards ethereality. Rancière's work is valuable here firstly because it provides the conceptual tools to dissolve the dichotomy between architecture and literature, as it does between literature that says everything and literature that says nothing, or, what is for him the same thing, between truth as visible and truth as invisible. Secondly, Rancière consistently rejects the supposed rupture between realism and modernism, which a remark in the Prelude to *Aisthesis* makes a matter of architecture as much as literature: 'one would be hard pressed to perceive the paradoxical "spirituality" of functionalist architecture without referring to Ruskin's "gothic" reveries'.[76] Ruskinian Gothic is not then simply the superseded detritus of an architectural tradition which modernism must reject; rather, modernism transforms the aspirations of the Gothic into another form, dialectically concealing and preserving what it apparently discards. It is in this spirit of interaction and encounter, rather than only supersession, that I approach the literary texts analysed in this book.

Above and Below

In the following two sections I show how *Invisible Architecture in Nineteenth-Century Literature* speaks to two influential and related traditions in urban literary studies, each of which centres on an opposition that has been taken to be particularly significant: 'above and below' and 'visible and invisible'. Such work is valuable, but my aim is ultimately to shift away from these oppositions in favour of the tripartite structure of the hidden, mobile and transparent I have outlined above.

Critics working on the nineteenth-century city have often taken its dominant contrast to be that between the overground and the underground, the view from above and the view from below, sometimes inspired by Michel de Certeau's distinction between the voyeur who 'reads' the city and the walker who 'writes' it.[77] For instance, David Pike suggests that nineteenth-century Paris and London are both organised by a 'vertical framework' which 'serves two distinct functions: it allows those it places underground to give expression to their own unfulfilled desires, and it allows persons placed aboveground to make some manner of sense out of those desires'.[78] This topographic structure approximates the psychoanalytic division between conscious and unconscious, with the underground/unconscious as the space of desire and disorder, and the overground/conscious as the site of a rationality that attempts to organise these disordered desires. Asmodeus is again an important figure for Pike, representing the possibility of a new kind of social awareness that would cut across classes. Haewon Hwang takes a similar approach, but comes closer to Certeau's alignment of walking and writing when she conceives of the underground as a 'fluid discursive space that tells the history of powers through the history of the disempowered'.[79] Asa Briggs's classic study of Victorian cities also conceptualised their topography in this way, taking the view from a hot-air balloon as symbolic of the growing aspiration to produce a 'new and more ordered vision' of the city.[80]

For my readings, the most important feature of Certeau's approach to city space is that like Dostoevsky he takes the hidden voices of the city, which in a Benjaminian manner he calls 'stories about place [. . .] composed with the world's debris', as sites where modern mythology is generated:

> It is through the opportunity they offer to store up rich silences and wordless stories, or rather through their capacity to create cellars and

garrets everywhere, that local legends (*legenda*: what is *to be read*, but also what *can be read*) permit exits, way of going out and coming back in, and thus habitable spaces.⁸¹

This recalls Gaston Bachelard's *Poetics of Space*, where the most basic of habitable spaces, the house, is described as the place that 'shelters daydreaming' and 'allows one to dream in peace'.⁸² For Bachelard, however, unlike for Certeau, the cellar and garret are opposed. In the cellar, 'darkness prevails both day and night, and even when we are carrying a lighted candle, we see shadows dancing on the walls', whereas the 'solid geometry' of the attic represents 'rationality'; it is a room where 'the day's experiences can always efface the fears of night'.⁸³ Cellars are one of the topics of Chapter 1, where they are shown to represent by turns domesticity, preservation of the rural, and absolute horror. Such cellar-dwellings are generated by the forces of modernity, but can also be forms of resistance to them. They become sources of anxiety for the new social scientists who seek, like a statistically inclined Asmodeus, to render the working-class spaces of the industrial city seeable and knowable.

Certeau emphasises that mobility can also be a form of resistance to the stasis of urban planning. Such planning can be aligned with Henri Lefebvre's 'representations of space', defined as 'the space of scientists, planners, urbanists, technocratic subdividers and social engineers'.⁸⁴ The unfolding of personal stories and histories that occurs when individuals traverse the city, particularly when their movement reactivates the playful experiences of childhood, undoes its 'readable surfaces' and 'creates within the planned city a "metaphorical" or mobile city, like the one Kandinsky dreamed of: "a great city built according to all the rules of architecture and then suddenly shaken by a force that defies all calculation"'.⁸⁵ As the underground man also shows, mobility of thought and language can resist architectural inertia, though in his case this is a mobility riven with repetition and self-negation, coupled ironically with physical immobility, rather than the joyful, *dérive*-like wanderings imagined by Certeau.⁸⁶ Another well-known example of conceptual movement reacting upon static architecture is the panorama, a mode of seeing the city first exhibited in London in the 1780s and 90s. As Sen argues, the panorama plays a key role in generating a new mobility in urban writing for Dickens and others, thanks to its 'capacity to produce potentially mobile details even as it focused on the city as a whole'.⁸⁷ Such transformative mobility is most explicitly the topic of Chapters 2 and 5, on Dickens and the arabesque respectively, but it informs my readings throughout.

Visible and Invisible

Related to readings of the city that divide it between above and below is a critical tradition which takes the visible surface of the city, and of modernity in general, as the key to an invisible world behind or beyond it. For Tanya Agathacleous, this invisible world can be variously termed the global, the universal, the cosmopolitan or the utopian. In her view, literary texts from Wordsworth to Woolf 'struggle in different ways to read the visible face of the city as the sign of an invisible world of solidarity to come'.[88] For Certeau, by contrast, as for Bachelard, city surfaces often signify absence and memory:

> It is striking here that the places people live in are like the presences of diverse absences. What can be seen designates what is no longer there: 'you *see*, here there used to be ...', but it can no longer be seen. Demonstratives indicate the invisible identities of the visible: it is the very definition of a place, in fact, that it is composed by these series of displacements and effects among the fragmented strata that form it and that it plays on these moving layers.[89]

The possible future or the lost past: both are kinds of invisible architecture that hover spectrally behind the visible city. Modern vision can itself can be interpreted in these terms, as by Graham MacPhee, who has written of 'the invisible architecture of the visible', defined as 'the transcendental conditions of perceptual experience'.[90] He focuses on how new visual technologies impacted on Western thought and culture in the nineteenth and twentieth centuries, offering an archaeology of modern vision that builds on Jonathan Crary's ground-breaking work in *Techniques of the Observer* (1992). Similar in its focus is Jonathan Potter's *Discourses of Vision in Nineteenth-Century Britain*, which explores 'the reciprocal influences of technological and empirical perception upon imaginative and psychological acts of perception'.[91]

Behind much of this literature on the invisible architecture of the visible lies the work of Walter Benjamin. The *Arcades Project* is intensely interested in the surfaces of the modern capitalist city – its shells, facades, coverings and commodities – but it reads these things in part as clues to an unseen historicity of the city. They reveal it to be both a site where utopian dreams of the future are generated (in the *passages*, in exhibition halls, in Jugendstil, in the schemes of Saint-Simon, Fourier and Louis-Auguste Blanqui) and one where the past continues to haunt the present (in the allegorical poetry of

Baudelaire, in Parisian street names, in half-forgotten advertising posters, in underground catacombs). Berman identifies a tension in Benjamin's attitude, however:

> His heart and his sensibility draws him irresistibly toward the city's bright lights, beautiful women, fashion, luxury, its play of dazzling surfaces and radiant scenes; meanwhile his Marxist conscience wrenches him insistently away from these temptations, instructs him that this whole glittering world is decadent, hollow, vicious, spiritually empty, oppressive to the proletariat, condemned by history.[92]

This is a Benjamin torn between the visible urban surface and the invisible work of history, hoping perhaps to reconcile the two. The desire outlined here is arguably what Adorno berates him for in their famous letter exchange of 1935, when he critiques Benjamin's use of the epigraph 'each epoch dreams the one to follow.'[93] Adorno writes:

> The dialectical image could not be located as dream in consciousness; rather dream should be turned out [*entäussert*] through dialectical interpretation, and immanent consciousness itself understood as a constellation of the real. Just as if it were the astronomical phase in which hell moves among mankind.[94]

Benjamin's desire to read the surface of the dreamworld that is the capitalist city as the place where the dialectical image becomes present to consciousness, and thus the place where the backdrop of history becomes fleetingly visible, is for Adorno an impossible proposition, since the dream itself cannot be the key to its own analysis. The surface of the city is what needs to be explained, Adorno argues, not what provides explanation. For Benjamin, though, there is no position from which to approach the historicity of the city that would be separate from the contingent and fleeting objects within it. Like art for Baudelaire, history for Benjamin is composed of two halves: the eternal and the ephemeral.[95] Referring to Schopenhauer, he writes that 'to seize the essence of history, it suffices to compare Herodotus and the morning newspaper'.[96] These two halves have their counterpart in experience, expressed by the two terms *Erfahrung* (experience as progression or duration) and *Erlebnis* (isolated or momentary experience). He is interested, for example, in 'how lyric poetry can be grounded in experience [*einer Erfahrung*] for which exposure to shock [*Chockerlebnis*] has become the norm'.[97]

As Irving Wohlfarth observes, Benjamin confronts the topic of historiography explicitly in 'On the Concept of History' (1940) (also known as 'Theses on the Philosophy of History'), where he places in opposition the view from above and the view from below, so anticipating the critical trend mentioned above. For Benjamin, the conventional historicist writes history 'from some phantasmagorical vantage point above the fray', empathising with the victors: something that 'invariably benefits the rulers' according to Thesis VII.[98] Benjamin's response, as described by Wohlfarth, is an allegorical one: 'to the bird's-eye view of the soaring imperial eagle Benjamin implicitly opposes that of a subterranean "hunchback", who is his theologico-political counterpart to Marx's "old mole". It is from below that history is to be made and written, unmade and unwritten.'[99] The hunchback is the figure who operates the chess-playing mechanical Turk that represents historical materialism in Thesis I:

> There was once, we know, an automaton constructed in such a way that it could respond to every move by a chess player with a countermove that would ensure the winning of the game. A puppet wearing Turkish attire and with a hookah in its mouth sat before a chessboard placed on a large table. A system of mirrors created the illusion that this table was transparent on all sides. Actually, a hunchbacked dwarf – a master at chess – sat inside and guided the puppet's hand by means of strings. One can imagine a philosophic counterpart to this apparatus. The puppet, called 'historical materialism', is to win all the time. It can easily be a match for anyone if it enlists the services of theology, which today, as we know, is small and ugly and has to keep out of sight.[100]

Benjamin does not, as Wohlfarth implies, put himself in the position of the hunchback, who stands for theology, but rather the puppet which represents the historical materialist, or perhaps the whole apparatus. While its implications are ambiguous, we might detect a self-critique in this opening thesis, as Benjamin reflects on his own combination of historical materialism and theology. He shows an awareness that, as is often remarked, he deploys theological concepts in the service of Marxist goals, which explains why his legacy has been contested between Jewish-Messianic and Marxist-materialist readings (as represented by Gershom Scholem and Theodor Adorno/Bertolt Brecht respectively).[101] Thesis XVII provides an example of this combination, when the historical materialist is said to recognise a rather non-materialist 'messianic arrest of happening' that will 'blast a specific era out of the homogeneous course of history'.[102]

Thesis I can therefore be read as a veiled admission by Benjamin of the sleight of hand that underpins his own unorthodox method of historical analysis.

The scene described in Thesis I serves also as an image of invisible architecture as I conceive it. The automaton combines transparency (the table appears open on all sides), concealment (the hidden hunchback), and mobility (the shifting chess pieces). Concealment and transparency are not mutually exclusive here, but work together to produce a fantastical illusion. The oriental Turkish puppet with its hookah redoubles this effect by hinting at the mind- and space-altering effects of hashish, the subject of Benjamin's 'Hashish in Marseilles' (1932). He there quotes Baudelaire's observation (from *Les Paradis artificiels*, 1860) that under the drug's influence, 'space can expand, the ground tilt steeply, atmospheric sensations occur', producing an experience typified by 'a continual alternation of dreaming and waking states, a constant and finally exhausting oscillation between different worlds of consciousness'.[103] This disorientating confusion of sleeping and waking returns us to Vidler's uncanny architecture, and provides an example of what Benjamin calls 'awakening'.[104] Awakening, he suggests, might be 'perhaps the synthesis of dream consciousness (as thesis) and waking consciousness (as antithesis)', creating a moment in which 'things put on their true – surrealist – face'.[105] Certainly the Turkish automaton with the hunchback crouching inside it is a suitably surreal image. Awakening is an experience of crossing boundaries, and Benjamin comments that 'nowhere, unless perhaps in dreams, can the phenomenon of the boundary be experienced in a more originary way than in cities'.[106] It is in cities, then, that the surreal, uncanny, oscillating effects of awakening, which is a perceptual counterpart to both Giedion's interpenetration and Vidler's uncanny architecture, are most strongly felt. As Patricia McKee notes, the 'interpenetration and interruption of moments usually kept distinct' is one of Benjamin's most characteristic strategies.[107] In such moments, what is hidden and what is transparent collide, on the terrain that I am calling invisible architecture.

Architecture and Literature: Writers, Cities, Forms

In addition to what has been said above, this book contributes to the growing subfield of architecture and literature studies. Philippe Hamon's *Expositions: Literature and Architecture in Nineteenth-Century France*, first published in 1989, is an important milestone in this area. Hamon argues that 'architecture would become the obsession of the nineteenth century', including in its literature, where writers exhibit a 'growing sensitivity to the symbolic power of architectural frameworks'.[108] Drawing on Benjamin, he proposes that literature has a particular interest in four kinds of architectural object: the ruin, 'in which the interior is exposed to the exterior and the eye can penetrate through cracks in the walls'; the arcade and its variants; the phalanstery, the invention of Charles Fourier which Hamon sees as anticipating Le Corbusier's 'machines for living'; and the big city, especially London and Paris, the latter of which 'not only hosts expositions but [. . .] along with its inhabitants becomes an object of exposition'.[109] Hamon takes the ruin not just as a Romantic symbol which modern literature and architecture must break from, but as anticipating strains within modernism. He, like Rancière, rejects the modernist supposition of a sudden break at the end of the century. In this book I maintain a focus on the fourth of his architectural objects – the big city – though the arcade and phalanstery are also present in altered forms in Zola's department store, discussed in Chapter 3. To Hamon's objects I add the cellar, important in itself but also symbolic of a wider array of hidden spaces found in nineteenth-century urban literature, as well as the architectures of mobility – the railway and the river pre-eminently, but also the arabesque. I propose also that the Gothic cathedral operates as a meeting point between literature and architecture in the urban context.

More recently, Nicole Reynolds has reflected on the relation between architecture and literature in *Building Romanticism*, where she seeks to show how 'architecture and architectural tropes impelled Romanticism's dramatic reconceptualizations of the individual subject and of the world the subject inhabits'.[110] Oriented towards the other end of the nineteenth century is David Spurr's *Architecture and Modern Literature*, which takes 'dwelling' and its opposite, Heideggerean homelessness – 'not just lacking shelter but not being at home in the world' – as the points of organising focus.[111] Gothic architecture plays a key role for Spurr in the modern reorientation of literature towards modernity and away from classicism:

> the nineteenth century literary interest in Gothic architecture signals, in important writers, both a break with classical values and an estrangement from what these writers perceive as the objective and subjective conditions of modernity. Against these conditions stands the purity of spirit that is thought to lie at the origin of the great medieval cathedrals.[112]

This is the Gothic as a sign both of modernity and of resistance to it. Spurr's shift towards thinking about how Gothic contributes to modern literature is valuable, but lacking here is the possibility that Gothic can itself provide conceptual resources for thinking about modernity, as I argue it does.

Hamon, Reynolds and Spurr all write from literary backgrounds, but there has also been increasing interest in the topic from architecture scholars. Klaske Havik's *Urban Literacy* reads literature as providing 'another way of *thinking* about architecture and the city', one which can 'connect architectural and urban research to the lived experience of place' in writers such as Proust, Pessoa, Joyce and Kafka.[113] The collection *Reading Architecture* similarly notes that if 'orality is primary, analogous to our experience of living in buildings, then we have much to learn from literature and architecture and the cities we live in'.[114] Other essay collections have consciously attempted to bring together literary and architectural scholars, including *Writing the Modern City* (2012), *Writingplace: Investigations in Architecture and Literature* (2016) and *The Routledge Companion on Architecture, Literature and the City* (2018),[115] the introduction of which cites Zola's *The Kill* (1871), which I discuss in Chapter 3, as a preeminent nineteenth-century example of how literature can 'illustrate the phenomenological character of a city in an immediate and pressing way'.[116]

The rest of this book is divided into two sections that speak to this developing field in different but related ways. Part I, Writers and Cities, is arranged around three cities that have all been proposed as capitals of the nineteenth century, most prominently Paris by Benjamin, but also London by Evan Horowitz and Steve Dillon, and Manchester by Janet Wolff.[117] Its three chapters move approximately from concealment in Manchester, to mobility in London, to transparency in Paris, but in each case they also interrogate and complicate that chronology.

Chapter 1 looks at James Kay, Friedrich Engels and Elizabeth Gaskell's writing on industrial Manchester, paying particular attention to *Mary Barton* (1848). It argues that Manchester's underground spaces, which are associated particularly with the working class, operate as a form of invisible architecture in the sense of the unseen or hidden, and considers how Kay's 1832 pamphlet on Manchester cotton-workers seeks to bring the city into greater visibility for the middle classes. Chapter 2 reads the railway and the river in Charles Dickens's *Dombey and Son* (1846–8) and *Our Mutual Friend* (1864–5) as mobile conduits that simultaneously break apart and connect the city of London, undoing the conventional role of architecture to secure and stabilise city space. It considers the uncanny mobility of Dickens's houses in these novels, as they shift between visibility and invisibility. Chapter 3 examines how new vistas of space and glass in Émile Zola's *The Kill* and *The Ladies' Paradise* (1883) seem to open the city up, offering absolute visibility, while in fact also suppressing, concealing or destroying parts of the city and its social life. Transparency aligns here with the ideological phantasmagorias of the commodity.

Part II, Spatial Forms, turns to three topics which have been under-considered in the context of nineteenth-century urban modernity. These chapters range across cities and authors, seeking to build a typography of how each spatial form contributes to the literary and architectural imaginary of the period. The order of discussion approximately repeats the pattern of Part I, moving from the concealed (the Gothic cathedral), to the mobile (the arabesque), to the transparent (urban whiteness), whilst also once again complicating these categorisations.

Chapter 4 considers the Gothic cathedral through Gogol, Hugo, Zola and Henry James, alongside Frank Lloyd Wright and Ernst Bloch. I propose that Gothic cathedrals are not simply superseded by the modern architecture of the nineteenth century, but also provide a conceptual resource for literary writers to represent modernity and the modern city. Chapter 5 takes the arabesque as a case of crossover between the architectural and literary, articulated through an interest in spatial and temporal movement. The arabesque is shown to be a form of decoration that both draws attention to the surface and points beyond that surface, and which lies on the border between order and disorder, making it an appropriate model for the modern city. The discussion takes in readings of Owen Jones, George Eliot, Edgar Allan Poe, Charlotte Perkins Gilman and Nikolai Gogol. Chapter 6 considers nineteenth-century city whiteness, which is shown to be both opposed to, and in some measure to anticipate, the white walls of modernist buildings. Such whiteness acts as if it is invisible, yet also promotes visibility. It is read as a cleansing and a blankness that both reveals and represses, drawing on texts including *Dombey and Son*, *Alton Locke* (1850), *Moby-Dick* (1851) and *North and South* (1854).

The Conclusion reflects on how the features of invisible architecture discussed in this book continue to circulate after the end of the nineteenth century, using as a case study literary depictions of New York from the twentieth and twenty-first centuries by Willa Cather, John Dos Passos, Teju Cole and Colson Whitehead.

Notes

1. For Gilles Deleuze and Felix Guattari, the molar is the 'rigid', in contrast to the 'molecular', which is 'supple'. *A Thousand Plateaus*, trans. by Brian Massumi (London: Continuum, 2001), pp. 234–44.
2. For a reading that puts the mass at the centre of British nineteenth-century fiction, see Emily Steinlight, *Populating the Novel: Literary Form and the Politics of Surplus Life* (Ithaca, NY: Cornell University Press, 2018).
3. Asa Briggs, *Victorian Cities* (London: Odhams Press, 1963), p. 59.
4. Raymond Williams, *The Country and the City* (London: Hogarth Press, 1985), p. 222.
5. Charles Baudelaire, *The Painter of Modern Life and Other Essays*, trans. by Jonathan Mayne (London: Phaidon, 1995), p. 13.
6. The concept of the assemblage is developed by Deleuze and Guattari across *A Thousand Plateaus*. It was consciously brought into relation with architecture in the journal *Assemblage* (1986–2000). On the significance of this journal see C. Greig Crysler, *Writing Spaces: Discourses of Architecture, Urbanism and the Built Environment* (New York: Routledge, 2003), pp. 48–70. For an introduction to infrastructure studies in the social sciences and humanities, see Susan Leigh Star, 'The Ethnography of Infrastructure', *American Behavioral Scientist*, 43.3 (1999), 377–91, and Brian Larkin, 'The Politics and Poetics of Infrastructure', *Annual Review of Anthropology*, 42 (2013), 327–43.
7. Anthony Vidler, *The Architectural Uncanny: Essays in the Modern Unhomely* (Cambridge, MA: MIT Press, 1992), p. 11.
8. Vidler, p. 12.
9. Vidler, p. 217.
10. Hal Foster, *The Art-Architecture Complex* (London: Verso, 2011).
11. On the links between nineteenth-century modernity and early twentieth-century modernism, see James Donald, *Imagining the Modern City* (Minneapolis: University of Minnesota Press, 1999) and, on the role of glass in particular, the Conclusion of Isobel Armstrong, *Victorian Glassworlds: Glass Culture and the Imagination, 1830–1880* (Oxford: Oxford University Press, 2008).
12. Sigfried Giedion, *Space, Time and Architecture: The Growth of a New Tradition*, 5th edn (Cambridge, MA: Harvard University Press, 1967), p. 183. Benjamin modifies Giedion's statement in the *Arcades Project*: 'Attempt to develop Giedion's thesis: '"In the nineteenth century", he writes, "construction plays the role of the subconscious". Wouldn't it be better to say "the role of bodily processes" – around which "artistic" architectures gather, like dreams around the framework of physiological processes?' Walter Benjamin, *The Arcades Project*, trans. by Howard Eiland and Kevin McLoughlin (Cambridge, MA: Belknap Press, 1999), p. 391. Benjamin attempts here to reconcile Giedion, for whom

engineering was something like the dream of the modernist future, with his own analysis of nineteenth-century bourgeois art and design as a dreamworld. Susan Buck-Morss comments of this passage that 'Benjamin resurrects an image of the body politic, out of fashion in political discourse since the baroque era, in which the nineteenth-century dream elements register the collective's vital signs'. Susan Buck-Morss, *The Dialectics of Seeing: Walter Benjamin and the Arcades Project* (Cambridge, MA: MIT Press, 1989), p. 272.
13. Rem Koolhaas, *Delirious New York: A Retroactive Manifesto for Manhattan* (New York: Monacelli Press, 1994).
14. Michel Foucault, *The Order of Things*, trans. by Alan Sheridan (Abingdon: Routledge, 1989), p. 249.
15. *The Order*, p. 249.
16. Hilde Heynen argues that Giedion's programmatic, rather than transitory, concept of modernity assumes that 'a single vast evolutionary pattern underlies the history of architecture and that this evolution develops more or less in a linear fashion, culminating in twentieth-century modern architecture'. Hilde Heynen, *Architecture and Modernity: A Critique* (Cambridge, MA: MIT Press, 1999), p. 29.
17. Joanna Hofer-Robinson, *Dickens and Demolition: Literary Afterlives and Mid-Nineteenth-Century Urban Development* (Edinburgh: Edinburgh University Press, 2018), p. 30.
18. The novel is set 'ten years ago' according to Gissing's opening chapter, placing it around 1878. George Gissing, *The Nether World* (Oxford: Oxford University Press, 1992), p. 1. Further references given in the main text as NW.
19. Samuel Phillips, *Guide to the Crystal Palace and Park* (London: Crystal Palace Library and Bradbury and Evans, 1854), p. 15.
20. Phillips, p. 27.
21. Phillips, p. 11.
22. As Andrew Miller notes, the alignment between Crystal Palace and railway was already being established in 1851: 'As travelling on the railway reduces space and emphasizes time, so the Exhibition brought objects and people from across the world to a single point, where their rates of development could be measured and compared.' Andrew Miller, *Novels Behind Glass: Commodity Culture and Victorian Narrative* (Cambridge: Cambridge University Press, 1995), p. 55.
23. Phillips, p. 24.
24. Phillips, p. 24.
25. Phillips, p. 24.
26. Phillips, p. 149.
27. Rachel Bowlby's *Just Looking: Consumer Culture in Dreiser, Gissing and Zola* (Abingdon: Routledge, 1985) brings together Zola and Gissing, but Bowlby does not make this Louvre–Crystal Palace connection. Emma Liggins observes that Gissing denied any direct

influence from Zola in a letter of 1880, though the comparison was made by many reviews of his work in the 1880s. Emma Liggins, *George Gissing, the Working Woman, and Urban Culture* (Abingdon: Routledge, 2017 [2006]), p. 3.
28. Émile Zola, *L'Assommoir*, trans. by Margaret Mauldon (Oxford: Oxford University Press, 1995), p. 76.
29. *L'Assommoir*, p. 79.
30. See for instance Thomas Richards, *The Commodity Culture of Victorian England: Advertising and Spectacle, 1851–1914* (London: Verso, 1991), pp. 119–67; Peter Hoffenberg, *An Empire on Display: English, Indian, and Australian Exhibitions from the Crystal Palace to the Great War* (Berkeley and Los Angeles: University of California Press, 2001) and Wulf D. Hund, 'Advertising White Supremacy: Capitalism, Colonialism, and Commodity Racism', in *Colonial Advertising and Commodity Racism*, ed. by Wulf D. Hund, Michael Pickering and Anandi Ramamurthy (Zurich and Berlin: LIT Verlag, 2013), pp. 21–69.
31. See Roland Barthes, *Writing Degree Zero*, trans. by Annette Lavers and Colin Smith (London: Macmillan, 2012) and 'The Reality Effect', in *The Rustle of Language*, trans. by Richard Howard (Berkeley and Los Angeles: University of California Press, 1989), pp. 141–8; Peter Brooks, *Realist Vision* (New Haven: Yale University Press, 2005); Fredric Jameson, *Antinomies of Realism* (London and New York: Verso, 2013). Rancière is discussed below.
32. Barbara Leckie, *Open Houses: Poverty, the Novel, and the Architectural Idea in Nineteenth-Century Britain* (Philadelphia: University of Pennsylvania Press, 2018), p. 7.
33. Sigfried Giedion, *Building in France, Building in Iron, Building in Ferroconcrete*, trans. by J. Duncan Berry (Chicago: University of Chicago Press, 2014), p. 90, quoted in Leckie, p. 7.
34. Leckie, p. 7.
35. Leckie, p. 18.
36. Sharon Marcus, *Apartment Stories: City and Home in Nineteenth-Century Paris and London* (Berkeley, Los Angeles and London: University of California Press, 1999), p. 5.
37. Marcus, p. 38.
38. 'Coupe de maison', image by Karl Girardet, text by Dugald Stewart, *Magasin pittoresque* 15 (1847), 400. Quoted in Marcus, p. 37.
39. Sambudha Sen, *London, Radical Culture and the Making of the Dickensian Aesthetic* (Columbus: Ohio State University Press, 2012), p. 89.
40. Quoted in Leckie, p. 13.
41. *Arcades*, p. 406.
42. Stephen Eskilson, *The Age of Glass: A Cultural History of Glass in Modern and Contemporary Architecture* (London and New York: Bloomsbury, 2018), p. 27.

43. Eskilson, p. 27, p. 28.
44. Eskilson, pp. 43–4.
45. Eskilson, p. 48.
46. Douglas Murphy, *The Architecture of Failure* (Alresford: Zero Books, 2012), p. 2.
47. Murphy, p. 2.
48. *Arcades*, p. 13.
49. For more on this topic, see Jan Piggott, *Palace of the People: The Crystal Palace at Sydenham 1854–1936* (London: Hurst and Company, 2004).
50. Murphy, p. 27, p. 30, p. 32.
51. Murphy, p. 35.
52. Nikolai Chernychevsky, *A Vital Question; or, What Is to Be Done?*, trans. by Nathan Dole and S. S. Skidelsky (New York: Crowell and Co., 1886), p. 378.
53. Chernychevsky, p. 378.
54. Chernychevsky, p. 382, p. 383.
55. Marshall Berman, *All That Is Solid Melts into Air: The Experience of Modernity* (London: Verso, 2010), p. 243.
56. Fyodor Dostoevsky, *Notes from Underground/The Double*, trans. by Jessie Coulson (Harmondsworth: Penguin, 1972), p. 42.
57. Dostoevsky, p. 42.
58. Dostoevsky, p. 43.
59. See Mikhail Bakhtin, *Problems of Dostoevsky's Poetics*, ed. and trans. by Caryl Emerson (Minneapolis: University of Minnesota Press, 1984).
60. Berman, p. 245.
61. Charles Dickens, *Bleak House* (Oxford: Oxford University Press, 1999), Ch. 22, p. 330. Michael Allen proposes Fox Court in Holborn as Dickens's inspiration in 'Locating Tom-All-Alone's', *Dickens Quarterly*, 29.1 (2012), 32–49.
62. Williams, p. 221.
63. Joseph Conrad, *Heart of Darkness*, in *The Norton Anthology of English Literature*, 9th edn, vol. F, *The Twentieth Century and After*, ed. by Stephen Greenblatt (New York and London: Norton, 2012), pp. 1951–2010 (p. 1955). On this theme, see for instance John Marriott, *The Other Empire: Metropolis, India and Progress in the Colonial Imagination* (Manchester: Manchester University Press, 2003).
64. *Arcades*, p. 93. I discuss this quotation in the context of threshold experiences in '"When I went to Lunnon town sirs": Transformation and the Threshold in the Dickensian City', *Dickens Quarterly*, 29.4 (2012), 336–49 (p. 344).
65. The term runs throughout Rancière's work, but see in particular *Aisthesis: Scenes from the Aesthetic Regime of Art*, trans. by Zakir Paul (London and New York: Verso, 2013) and *The Politics of Aesthetics: The Distribution of the Sensible*, ed. and trans. by Gabriel Rockhill (London and New York: Bloomsbury, 2004), pp. 18–19,

where the aesthetic regime is defined as 'the regime that strictly identifies art in the singular and frees it from any specific rule, from any hierarchy of the arts, subject matter and genres'.
66. *Politics of Aesthetics*, p. 18.
67. *Aisthesis*, p. 51.
68. *Aisthesis*, p. 58.
69. *Aisthesis*, p. 59.
70. *Aisthesis*, p. 62.
71. Jacques Rancière, *Mute Speech*, trans. by James Swenson (New York: Columbia University Press, 2011), p. 67.
72. *Mute Speech*, p. 67.
73. *Mute Speech*, p. 53, p. 54. Victor Hugo, *Notre Dame de Paris*, trans. by Alban Krailshelmer (Oxford: Oxford University Press, 1993), pp. 192–206.
74. *Mute Speech*, p. 115.
75. Gustave Flaubert to Louise Colet, 27 March 1853, in *The Letters of Gustave Flaubert 1830–1857*, ed. and trans. by Francis Steegmuller (Cambridge, MA: Belknap Press, 1979), p. 154. Quoted in a modified form in *Mute Speech*, p. 115.
76. *Aisthesis*, pp. xii–xiii. On the links between Ruskin and modernism see Giles Whiteley, *The Aesthetics of Space in Nineteenth-Century British Literature, 1843–1907* (Edinburgh: Edinburgh University Press, 2020).
77. Michel de Certeau, *The Practice of Everyday Life*, trans. by Steven Rendall (Berkeley and Los Angeles: University of California Press, 1984), pp. 91–110.
78. David Pike, *Subterranean Cities: The World Beneath Paris and London, 1800–1945* (Ithaca, NY: Cornell University Press, 2005), p. 12.
79. Haewon Hwang, *London's Underground Spaces: Representing the Victorian City, 1840–1915* (Edinburgh: Edinburgh University Press, 2013), p. 9.
80. Briggs, p. 53. Deborah Nord offers a slightly different form of this opposition when she identifies 'two dominant perceptual and literary modes of evoking the nineteenth-century city: the panoramic view and the sudden, instructive encounter with a solitary figure'. Deborah Epstein Nord, *Walking the Victorian Streets: Women, Representation, and the City* (Ithaca, NY: Cornell University Press, 1995), p. 21.
81. Certeau, p. 107, p. 106.
82. Gaston Bachelard, *The Poetics of Space*, trans. by Maria Jolas (Boston: Beacon Press, 1994), p. 6.
83. Bachelard, p. 19, p. 18, p. 19.
84. Lefebvre's other two categories in his famous trialectics of space are 'spatial practice', or space as it is experienced and perceived, and 'representational spaces', or space as a field of contested ideas and values. Henri Lefebvre, *The Production of Space*, trans. by Donald Nicholson-Smith (Oxford: Blackwell, 1991), p. 33.

85. Certeau, p. 110; quoting Wassily Kandinsky, *Du spirituel dans l'art* (Paris: Denoël, 1969), p. 57.
86. For the classic text on the *dérive* see Guy Debord, 'Theory of the Dérive', in *Situationist International Anthology*, ed. and trans. by Ken Knabb, revised and expanded edition (Berkeley, CA: Bureau of Public Secrets, 2006), pp. 62–6.
87. Sen, p. 87.
88. Tanya Agathacleous, *Urban Realism and the Cosmopolitan Imagination in the Nineteenth Century: Visible City, Invisible World* (Cambridge: Cambridge University Press, 2011), p. xvii.
89. Certeau, p. 108.
90. Graham MacPhee, *The Architecture of the Visible: Technology and Urban Visual Culture* (London: Continuum, 2002), p. 10.
91. Jonathan Potter, *Discourses of Vision in Nineteenth-Century Britain: Seeing, Thinking, Writing* (Palgrave: Cham, 2018), p. 10.
92. Berman, p. 146.
93. 'Exchange with Theodor W. Adorno on the Essay "Paris, the Capital of the Nineteenth Century"', in Walter Benjamin, *Selected Writings, Volume 3, 1935–1938*, ed. by Howard Eiland and Michael Jennings (Cambridge, MA: Belknap Press, 2002), p. 54. The quotation is from Michelet, 'Avenir! Avenir!' and appears at Benjamin, *Arcades*, p. 150.
94. *Selected Writings, Volume 3*, p. 55.
95. See *The Painter of Modern Life*, p. 12.
96. *Arcades*, p. 14.
97. Benjamin is speaking of Baudelaire and has Freud in mind. Walter Benjamin, 'On Some Motifs in Baudelaire', in *The Writer of Modern Life*, ed. by Michael Jennings (Cambridge, MA: Belknap Press, 2006), pp. 170–212 (p. 177).
98. Irving Wohlfarth, '"Construction Has the Role of the Subconscious": Phantasmagorias of the Master Builder (with Constant Reference to Giedion, Weber, Nietzsche, Ibsen, and Benjamin)', in *Nietzsche and the Architecture of Our Minds*, ed. by Alexandre Koskka and Irving Wohlfarth (Los Angeles: Getty Research Institute, 1999), pp. 141–98 (p. 185).
99. Wohlfarth, p. 185.
100. Walter Benjamin, *Selected Writings, Volume 4: 1938–1940*, ed. by Howard Eiland and Michael Jennings (Cambridge, MA: Belknap Press, 2003), p. 389.
101. Kaufmann nuances this picture, positioning Brecht as the key materialist influence on Benjamin, with Adorno somewhat sympathetic to theology. See David Kaufmann, 'Beyond Use, Within Reason: Adorno, Benjamin and the Question of Theology', *New German Critique*, 83 (2001), 151–73. On the extensive correspondence between Adorno and Scholem, see Asaf Angermann, 'Adorno and Scholem:

The Heretical Redemption of Metaphysics', in *A Companion to Adorno*, ed. by Peter Gordon, Espen Hammer and Max Pensky (Hoboken, NJ: Wiley Blackwell, 2020), pp. 531–48.
102. *Selected Writings, Vol. 4*, p. 396.
103. Walter Benjamin, *Selected Writings, Volume 2, Part 2, 1931–1934*, ed. by Michael Jennings, Howard Eiland and Gary Smith (Cambridge, MA: Belknap Press, 1999), p. 673.
104. *Arcades*, p. 463.
105. *Arcades*, p. 463.
106. *Arcades*, p. 88.
107. Patricia McKee, *Reading Constellations: Urban Modernity in Victorian Fiction* (Oxford: Oxford University Press, 2014), p. 3.
108. Philippe Hamon, *Expositions: Literature and Architecture in Nineteenth-Century France*, trans. by Katia Sainson-Frank and Lisa Maguire (Berkeley and Los Angles: University of California Press, 1992), p. 5, p. 6.
109. Hamon, p. 8.
110. Nicole Reynolds, *Building Romanticism: Literature and Architecture in Nineteenth-Century Britain* (Ann Arbor: University of Michigan Press, 2010), p. 3.
111. David Spurr, *Architecture and Modern Literature* (Ann Arbor: University of Michigan Press, 2012), p. x.
112. Spurr, p. 6. On Gothic architecture and literature, see also Tom Duggett, *Gothic Romanticism: Architecture, Politics and Literary Form* (New York: Palgrave, 2010).
113. Klaske Havik, *Urban Literacy: Reading and Writing Architecture* (Rotterdam: nai0I0, 2014), p. 21, p. 23, p. 29.
114. Elias Constantopoulos, 'Preface: On Reading Architecture', in *Reading Architecture: Literary Imagination and Architectural Experience*, ed. by Angeliki Sioli and Yoonchun Jung (New York and London: Routledge, 2018), pp. xix–xxi (p. xx).
115. Sarah Edwards and Jonathan Charley, eds, *Writing the Modern City: Literature, Architecture, Modernity* (Abingdon: Routledge, 2012). Klaske Havik et al., eds, *Writingplace: Investigations in Architecture and Literature* (Rotterdam: nai010, 2016). Jonathan Charley, ed., *The Routledge Companion on Architecture, Literature and the City*, (London: Routledge, 2018).
116. Jonathan Charley, 'Introduction: Narrative Construction and Constructing Narratives', in *Routledge Companion*, pp. 1–6 (p. 2).
117. See Walter Benjamin, 'Paris, the Capital of the Nineteenth Century' [1935], in *Arcades*, pp. 3–13. Horowitz contends that London 'was closer to fulfilled modernity than Paris or any other nineteenth-century metropolis'. Evan Horowitz, 'London: Capital of the Nineteenth Century', *New Literary History*, 41.1 (2010), 111–28 (p. 116). Steve Dillon uses 'London, Capital of the Nineteenth Century' as a

subtitle in 'Victorian Interior', *Modern Language Quarterly*, 62.2 (2001), 83–115 (p. 83). See also the special journal issue 'Paris and London, Capitals of the Nineteenth Century', ed. by Dana Arnold, Tore Rem and Helle Waahlberg, *Synergies Royaume-Uni et Irlande*, 3 (2010). Janet Wolff, 'Manchester, Capital of the Nineteenth Century', *Journal of Classical Sociology*, 13.1 (2013), 69–86.

I: Writers and Cities

Chapter 1

The Hidden City: James Kay, Friedrich Engels and *Mary Barton*'s Cellars

This chapter focuses on the structural role played by invisible architecture in Manchester, the 'shock-city' of the 1830s and 40s, in the writing of James Kay (1804–77; Kay-Shuttleworth from 1842), Friedrich Engels (1820–95) and Elizabeth Gaskell (1810–65).[1] In different ways, these writers each position hidden, underground and unconscious spaces, in particular the cellar-dwelling, as both structurally necessary and disruptive to the industrial capitalist system which generates such spaces. This arrangement is the result of a spatial and social repression that seeks to preserve the existing form of capitalist relations of production, but in doing so throws up spaces whose invisibility to dominant forms of power provides an opportunity for emergent or residual forms of thought and praxis to subsist within the city, albeit in tenuous and marginal ways.[2] As I will show, such invisibility is a risk. It provides limited opportunities for self-definition to some working-class characters in *Mary Barton* (1848), such as Alice Wilson, but leads to absolute degradation for others, such as the Davenport family.

I approach visibility and invisibility in these texts as two sides of what Henri Lefebvre calls the 'double illusion' by which space conceals its socially produced nature. This double illusion consists of 'the illusion of transparency' on one hand and 'the illusion of opacity, or "realistic" illusion' on the other.[3] In the illusion of transparency, visibility is foremost and space appears to be an open realm of free activity, in the same way as free-market capitalism appears to allow individual freedom. In the realistic illusion, invisibility takes precedence, so that objects encountered in space function as material blocks of ideology, appearing to have a 'natural' reality that conceals their origins. In this second illusion, contingent structures are given a cloak of permanence, obviousness and self-sufficiency. In *Mary Barton*, we might think of the attitude taken towards a desperately hungry Jem Wilson by the Carson family's servants, who 'would have willingly given him meat and bread in abundance; but they were like the rest of us, and not feeling hunger themselves, forgot it was possible another might'.[4] The relative plenty that surrounds these servants makes scarcity unthinkable. These two illusions are not separate or self-sufficient, but rather 'each illusion embodies and nourishes the other. The shifting back and forth between the two, and the flickering or oscillatory effect that it produces, are thus just as important as either of the illusions considered in isolation'.[5] As a whole, this system can be characterised as (in)visible architecture, since it puts visibility and invisibility to work together as components of a self-regenerating and self-concealing process. (In)visible architecture in this sense is an ideology machine, which reproduces the social and spatial conditions of production and consumption, and at the same time makes those conditions appear natural and self-sustaining.

While the main goal of this chapter is to explore Manchester's invisible and underground spaces, it is worth noting that, in line with Lefebvre's argument, Manchester in the 1830s and 40s was shocking not only for its invisibility but also for its excessive visibility. According to Deborah Nord, the central problem posed by Manchester was the threat of female 'exposure': the risk of 'being looked at on the street and assessed as an object of interest', a danger always associated with prostitution, which the crowded streets of industrial Manchester seemed to promote.[6] This apparent contradiction by which visibility and invisibility both become excessive is, as I will go on to show, characteristic of the functioning of invisible architecture as it operates in the texts considered here.

James Kay: Unreserved Exposure

Before turning to Gaskell's Manchester, I want to consider the relationship between the spatial organisation of the city and its class divisions in two major social science texts of the 1830s and 40s, with rather different politics: James Kay's pamphlet *The Moral and Physical Condition of the Working Classes Employed in the*

Cotton Manufacture in Manchester (1832) and Friedrich Engels's *The Condition of the Working Class in England* (1845). As Mary Poovey notes, Kay's research was highly influential, leading to the foundation in 1833 of the Manchester Statistical Society, the first of its kind, and in turn the inspiration for the Statistical Society of London in 1834. The Manchester Statistical Society played a key role in shaping the direction of social reform in Britain in the years that followed, by promoting the use of statistics and other social-scientific tools to analyse poverty and other social problems.[7] Engels's work, meanwhile, was an avowedly leftist rather than liberal project, and would become one of the major influences on Marx's theory of capitalism as it developed in the 1840s and 50s.[8]

From the start, Kay's language indicates that his main purpose is to open up the lives of the working classes to view. In the 'Advertisement' which opens the first edition, Kay cites 'the importance of minutely investigating the state of the working classes', referring to 'the evils here unreservedly exposed'.[9] This drive towards 'unreserved exposure' suggests a need to work against a constitutional closure or resistance at work in the city: a mode of investigation, according to Mary Poovey, that is indebted to the anatomical investigations of eighteenth-century medicine, which opened up the human (as opposed to social) body to scientific view for the first time.[10] It is a desire comparable to that which motivates the narrator in *Dombey and Son*, who calls for 'a good spirit who would take the house-tops off [. . .] and show a Christian people what dark shapes issue from amidst their homes', to be discussed in Chapter 2, though Dickens writes in a literary and ethico-religious rather than social-scientific register.[11]

In Kay's pamphlet, the role of the 'good spirit' is to be fulfilled by a new organisation based on the Provident Society of Liverpool, which includes 'a great many of the most influential inhabitants' of that city.[12] Kay describes the methodology of this thoroughly bourgeois society:

> The town is divided into numerous districts, the inspection and care of which is committed to one or two members of the association. They visit the people in their houses – sympathise with their distresses, and minister to the wants of the necessitous; but above all, they acquire, by their charity, the right of enquiring into their arrangements – of instructing them in domestic economy – of recommending sobriety, cleanliness, forethought and method.[13]

Visiting and sympathy are both aligned with exposure, and explicitly formulated as a means of social control, in which working-class people are first investigated and then imbued with the middle-class virtues of 'sobriety, cleanliness, forethought and method'. Implicitly, this desire is driven by an anxiety that arises from the invisibility, unknowability and unrepresentability of the city and its working classes, problems which Kay's division of the city into discrete areas ('numerous districts') and abstraction into statistical tables of data are supposed to address. Martin Hewitt has recently argued that 'Foucauldian impulses [. . .] were not the primary mode of social knowledge formation' when it came to visiting practices in Victorian Manchester, but if this was the case in practice it is certainly not true of Kay's conception of the city, as Hewitt recognises.[14] Hewitt points out also that Kay's analysis is quite specific to the 1830s, after which the statistical movement he inspired began to shift towards single-issue campaigns, such as sanitary reform, through the founding of bodies like the Manchester and Salford Sanitary Association in 1853. Such movements, though, continue to display 'sustained efforts to uncover the precise details of the social conditions they sought to reform'.[15]

The process of social mapping Kay proposes has been described by Poovey, drawing on Lefebvre (and to some extent Foucault), as the 'production of abstract space'.[16] Abstract space can be understood as a form of representation that is socially productive rather than passive, where rationalisation and quantification become the means to comprehend and master what is unseen in modern society, including the urban poor. Abstraction is employed to bring what is socially and spatially concealed into visibility, though at the cost of reducing and homogenising it. Poovey describes this process with reference to an 1838 study by Kay into the workhouse poor: 'In Kay's plan, the problem of the poor's invisibility was solved by the application of accounting: written records made virtue visible as they rendered labor quantifiable and diligence a matter for certification.'[17] The development of this framework of visibility, bureaucracy and quantification reached its apex, Poovey suggests, in Edwin Chadwick's *Sanitary Report* of 1842.[18]

Kay's concern with visibility, and the underlying class anxieties that attend it, comes to the fore when he describes the thoughts of a typical visitor to Manchester. This implicitly middle-class and explicitly male visitor is cast as a spectator who adopts an all-encompassing gaze. This gaze is, however, disrupted in the second part of the following passage by the presence of the working classes:

> Visiting Manchester, the metropolis of the commercial system, a stranger regards with wonder the ingenuity and comprehensive capacity, which,

in the short space of half a century, have here established the staple manufacture of this kingdom. He beholds with astonishment the establishments of its merchants – monuments of fertile genius and successful design: – the masses of capital which have been accumulated by those who crowd upon its mart, and the restless but sagacious spirit which has made every part of the known world the scene of their enterprize. The sudden creation of the mighty system of commercial organization which covers this country, and stretches its arms to the most distant seas, attests to the power and the dignity of man. Commerce, it appears to such a spectator, here gathers in her storehouse the productions of every clime, that she may minister to the happiness of a favoured race.

When he turns from the great capitalists, he contemplates the fearful strength only of that multitude of the labouring population, which lies like a slumbering giant at their feet. He has heard of the turbulent riots of the people – of machine breaking – of the secret and sullen organization which has suddenly lit the torch of incendiarism, or well nigh uplifted the arm of rebellion in the land. He remembers that political desperadoes have ever loved to tempt this population to the hazards of the swindling game of revolution, and have scarcely failed. In the midst of so much opulence, however, he has disbelieved the cry of need.[19]

This is the picture of a city divided. The overwhelming excess of the first half of the passage ('monuments of fertile genius and successful design') draws on a predominantly visual register ('regards', 'beholds', 'spectator') while the second half employs an ambiguous mix of sensory and non-sensory perception ('contemplates', 'heard', 'remembers') as it considers the 'fearful strength' of the working classes. The shift is from visibility to invisibility, or at least to visibility's unsettlement and confusion. This movement culminates in the final sentence, where the 'opulence' of commerce (the visible) is revealed to carry an ideological force sufficient to overwhelm the 'cry of need' of the poor (the invisible). The poor, neither seen nor believed, are concealed behind the wealth their labour has produced. This is, in effect, the same process by which for Marx the fetish form of the commodity conceals the real conditions of its production behind its phantasmagoric appeal.[20]

This passage shows that it is the specific form taken by capitalist production in Manchester – one both produced and reflected by the divided form of the city, and reproduced in the passage itself – that makes the poor literally and metaphorically invisible. The invisibility Kay wants to overcome through 'unreserved exposure' is only the other side of the bourgeois system of commerce which stimulates wonder in the imagined visitor. The 'sudden creation' of this system seems magical, but only because its basis in mass labour has been systematically repressed. The totalising ideology of this system, which 'stretches its arms to the most distant seas', is like that of Dickens's Mr Dombey, according to whom 'the earth was made for Dombey and Son to trade in, and the sun and moon were made to give them light' (DS 1.2). By colonising space and time, the House of Dombey and Son acts as the 'favoured race' of Kay's description, reduced absurdly but appropriately to a single bourgeois family: appropriately, because Kay's defence of capital is also a defence of the ideals of the middle-class Victorian family ('sobriety, cleanliness, forethought and method') that he wants to promote in the working classes.

The passage reveals that in order to maintain part of the invisible architecture of the industrial city (the part associated with commerce) while reforming the part which is problematic (the part associated with the working classes), Kay has to ignore or conceal the structural interdependence of these two terms. The result is the repeated claim in the pamphlet that 'the evils affecting [the lower orders] result *from foreign and accidental causes*', rather than any kind of systemic crisis.[21] Having diagnosed the situation in this way, Kay can respond by setting up an alternative form of abstract invisible architecture, reclassifying the city into districts numbered from 1 to 14, each of which is an expression of the aggregated population it contains, information about which is displayed in a series of numerical charts.[22] Even within the terms of this system, however, full visibility is impossible: 'It is [...] to be lamented, that even these numerical results fail to exhibit a perfect picture of the ills which are suffered by the poor.'[23] Kay expresses concern, too, about the invisibility of the poor's sexual behaviour, described as 'a licentiousness capable of corrupting the whole body of society, like an insidious disease, which eludes observation'.[24] For Thomas Carlyle, a fierce opponent of political economy, these are fundamental problems of statistical abstraction: 'Tables are like cobwebs, like the sieve of the Danaides; beautifully reticulated, orderly to look upon, but which will hold no conclusion. Tables are abstractions, and the object a most concrete one, so difficult to read the essence of.'[25] As Carlyle suggests, even with perfect data sets Kay's method could never bring about absolute visibility, because its object – the city and its people – resists systematisation. More than this though, Kay's revelations are predicated on the continued invisibility of the structural connection between the successes of commerce and the miseries of the poor. One sign of this absent link is Kay's displacement of the unresolvable causes of Manchester's social problems onto the most foreign and abject of its citizens: the Irish. Irish immigrants, Kay writes in a representative passage, present a 'contagious example of ignorance and a barbarous disregard of forethought and economy'.[26] As Amy Martin shows, Carlyle, and even to some extent Engels, also position the Irish as scapegoats in this way.[27]

Friedrich Engels: The Spatial Unconscious

If Kay's construction of abstract space offers a middle-class response to the invisibility of Manchester's poor, then Friedrich Engels, who responds to Kay's text among others, provides a reading of Manchester which seeks to deconstruct rather than ameliorate the status quo.[28] For Engels, the architecture of the city consigns the poor to the place of death, waste and abjection, not accidentally as in Kay, but through the logic of capitalism itself. Engels's description of Manchester's spatial layout goes to the heart of this logic:

> The town itself is peculiarly built, so that a person may live in it for years, and go in and out daily without coming into contact with a working people's quarter or even with workers, that is, so long as he confines himself to his business or to pleasure walks. This arises chiefly from the fact, that by unconscious tacit agreement, as well as with outspoken conscious determination, the working people's quarters are sharply separated from the sections of the city reserved for the middle class; or, if this does not succeed, they are concealed with the cloak of charity.[29]

Concealment of the working classes, Engels argues, is fundamental to the city's constitution. Charity, which implicitly assigns poverty to what Kay calls 'foreign and accidental causes', plays its part in this concealment. Particularly important is Engels's recognition of the partly 'unconscious' manner in which Manchester is spatially constituted. Following up on this hint, a psychoanalytic reading can recognise that the exclusion of the working classes is analogous to the psychical process of repression, where sources of anxiety are concealed in order to facilitate the smooth functioning of the conscious mind, here represented by the smooth operations of commerce. For Freud, *'the essence of repression lies simply in turning something away, and keeping it at a distance, from the conscious'*, an operation which 'demands a persistent expenditure of force'.[30] The workers are not absent, nor are they unnecessary, but they are made invisible by the persistently reproduced appearance of a background of homogeneous, abstract space. Abstract space, Lefebvre argues, is identical to the abstract Cartesian thought of Western philosophy. Such thought separates consciousness from the material conditions of the body, then repositions this artificial split as normative.[31] In this sense, abstraction and repression are coextensive processes, in which body and unconscious material respectively are excluded from representation. The repression in Engels's topography of Manchester can be explicated through Lefebvre's triad, or trialectics, of space, consisting of 'spatial practice', 'representational spaces' and 'spaces of representation'. The spatial practice of Manchester (daily material reality, perceived space) excludes workers from the city's primary representational spaces ('space as directly *lived* through its associated images and symbols'), while the city's representations of space ('conceptualized space, the space of scientists, planners, urbanists, technocratic subdividers and social engineers') either exclude the working classes or, as in Kay's pamphlet, include them only in an abstracted and reified form.[32]

For Engels, the link between the architecture of Manchester and the exclusion of the working class is important. Whereas in Kay the evils affecting the working classes are 'foreign' and 'accidental', for Engels these evils are fundamental to the spatial constitution of the city. They may appear accidental, but in fact serve the interests of the bourgeoisie. He observes that

> the thoroughfares leading from the Exchange in all directions out of the city are lined, on both sides, with an almost unbroken series of shops, and are so kept in the hands of the middle and lower bourgeoisie [. . .] True, these shops bear some relation to the districts which lie behind them [. . .] but they suffice to conceal from the eyes of the wealthy men and women of strong stomachs and weak nerves the misery and grime which form the complement to their wealth.[33]

The dialectical connection between wealth and misery is here rendered invisible by the facade of commerce, which as in Kay functions like a fetishised commodity, concealing the conditions of its own production. Engels later expands on this idea:

> anyone who knows Manchester can infer the adjoining districts, from the appearance of the thoroughfare, but one is seldom in a position to catch from the street a glimpse of the real labouring districts. I know very well that this hypocritical plan is more or less common to all great cities; I know, too, that the retail dealers are forced by the nature of their business to take possession of the great highways; I know that there are more good buildings than bad ones upon such streets everywhere,

and that the value of land is greater near them than in remoter districts; but at the same time I have never seen so systematic a shutting out of the working classes from the thoroughfares, so tender a concealment of everything that might affront the eye and the nerves of the bourgeoisie, as in Manchester. And yet, in other respects, Manchester is less built according to a plan, after official regulations, is more an outgrowth of accident, than any other city; and when I consider in this connection the eager assurances of the middle class, that the working class is doing famously, I cannot help feeling that the liberal manufacturers, the bigwigs of Manchester, are not so innocent after all, in the matter of this sensitive method of construction.[34]

Both passages make Manchester a spatialised form of the Freudian unconscious. For Freud, 'an unconscious conception is one of which we are not aware, but the existence of which we are nevertheless ready to admit on account of other proofs or signs'.[35] It is suggestive that Engels points to the 'eye' and the 'nerves' of the bourgeoisie as the senses affronted by the working classes. The reference to affronted eyes suggests that the city may be producing a form of Walter Benjamin's 'optical unconscious', in which elements of the visual field cannot be seen: a form of invisibility that film explodes.[36] The reference to nerves anticipates Freud's claim, concerning the pleasure principle, that the psychic apparatus of the mind seeks to suppress and avoid sources of nervous stimulation, especially pain.[37] In Engels, Freud's psychical system has been realised spatially, with Manchester's architecture protecting the representative of the system of consciousness (the bourgeoisie) from potentially disruptive sources of stimulation (the workers).

It is also notable that Engels returns to the puzzling fact that while Manchester is organised in a way which perfectly suits the bourgeoisie, it is predominantly 'an outgrowth of accident'. Whereas Kay is willing to accept this, Engels suspects an underlying intentionality in the 'bigwigs of Manchester' who are chiefly responsible for the city's construction. Engels's apparent dissatisfaction with the details of his diagnosis, detectable in 'I cannot help feeling . . .', which suggests an absent causal link, implies that he does not have the theoretical tools to reconcile accident and intentionality.[38] Later theories of ideology, such as Althusser's, provide an answer to this problem, allowing us to see that the bourgeoisie has not only concealed the working class, but also concealed from themselves their culpability for this act. Alternatively, a psychoanalytic understanding of repression, which recognises that unconscious drives underlie conscious thought, allows for the city to be organised 'unintentionally' without this being either random or accidental.

Another way to read Engels's description of Manchester is through Dostoevsky's *Notes from Underground* (1864), whose protagonist is characterised by *ressentiment* and self-division, and speaks of 'having the misfortune to live in St Petersburg, the most abstract [отвлеченном] and intentional [умышленные] city in the whole round world'.[39] The underground man follows this up with the remark 'towns can be either intentional or unintentional [неумышленные]'.[40] Abstraction for the underground man, as for Lefebvre, is associated with thought and opposed to action; he remarks that 'to think too much is a disease, a real, actual disease'.[41] An abstract and intentional city is therefore not only one organised by Western rationality, but one crippled by thought. The underground man reiterates this view when he states that for the purposes of ordinary human life, 'It would be quite enough [. . .] to have the consciousness of all our so-called men of action and public figures'.[42] Such a consciousness, which privileges action over thought, becomes untenable in the intentional city. An intentional city simultaneously privileges thought and renders it excessive; such a city is planned and bureaucratic, like St Petersburg, designed by Peter the Great as an ideal European capital.[43] An unintentional city, by contrast, would be unplanned, perhaps shaped instead by principles of *laissez-faire*, like Manchester.[44] It would not be coherently thought-out or conceptualised, but would privilege action. Mr Thornton, Gaskell's archetypal Manchester employer of *North and South*, is thus appropriately called a 'man of action'.[45] Manchester is unintentional also because its structure, which excludes the working classes, is unavailable to the thought of those within it, though it is actively lived every day. This is perhaps why it takes Engels, an outsider, to diagnose its condition. If Kay's project of abstraction aims to retroactively make the city intentional, dividing it into a series of discrete and comprehensible areas, then Engels, by contrast, finds in Manchester signs of the unconscious intentionality which drives capitalism. In order to explore this unconscious intentionality in more detail, I turn now to one of its most important spatial symptoms: the cellar-dwelling.

Cellar-Dwelling

The cellar-dwelling is an invention of the nineteenth century. Though the word 'cellar' is medieval, the terms 'cellar-dwelling' and 'cellar-dweller' are first recorded by the OED in 1837 and 1844 respectively, meaning Engels was dealing with a new concept when he wrote of Manchester in 1844 that 'cellar dwellings are general here; wherever it is in any way possible, these subterranean dens are constructed, and a very considerable portion of the population dwells in them'.[46] They are spaces that render the working classes unseen to the middle-class gaze, with the result that the working classes become associated with whatever is hidden, unknown and invisible. Such dwellings should be regarded as the spatial dimension of a social repression, and it is in this manner that they are central to both *Mary Barton* and Dickens's short story 'George Silverman's Explanation' (1868).

Gaskell's detailed depiction of working-class spaces and their inhabitants was unusual for the time, and has often been the most highly praised aspect of *Mary Barton*. Kathleen Tillotson, employing a phrase from Disraeli's *Sybil* (1845), comments that 'the denizens of the "other nation" [the poor] are neither harrowing victims nor heroic martyrs; they are shown in their natural human dignity'.[47] Similarly, for Raymond Williams, 'the really impressive thing about the book is the intensity of the effort to record, in its own terms, the feel of everyday life in the working-class homes'.[48] Part of this evocation of working-class life comes from an awareness of the significance of cellars and garrets, which are associated with the lowest form of poverty, as in this passage from chapter 8, which addresses the reader directly, apparently in Gaskell's own voice:

> It is so impossible to describe, or even faintly to picture, the state of distress which prevailed in the town at that time [1839–41], that I will not attempt it. [. . .] And when I hear, as I have heard, of the sufferings and privations of the poor [. . .] of parents sitting in their clothes by the fireside during the whole night for seven weeks together, in order that their only bed and bedding might be reserved for the use of their large family [. . .] – of others being compelled to fast for days together, uncheered by any hope of better fortune, living, moreover, or rather starving, in a crowded garret, or damp cellar [. . .] – can I wonder that many of them, in such times of misery and destitution, spoke and acted with ferocious precipitation? (MB 83)

The narrator refers to the Chartist agitation of the years around 1840 when she talks of acts of 'ferocious precipitation', suggesting that the cellar formed a major part of the marginal and excluded position which generated this unrest. This is indirectly the case in her own narrative, since John Barton, the main figure of working-class violence, is motivated by witnessing the terrible living conditions of others. To live in a cellar, Gaskell suggests, is to risk entering a condition which it is impossible 'even faintly to picture': a condition of unrepresentability exacerbated by the location of cellars and garrets at the extreme edges of the house. Gaskell draws on established tropes here, echoing Dickens, for instance, on the Rookery in London: 'The filthy and miserable appearance of this part of London can hardly be imagined by those (and there are many such) who have not witnessed it.'[49] Poised at the top or bottom of a building, often concealed from other inhabitants, cellars and garrets are barely rooms at all, neither inside nor out. Such a position is appropriate for a repressed space. The psychoanalytic unconscious, too, is impossible to describe, and can only be talked about through the moments when it erupts into consciousness, such as jokes and dreams.[50] Although the unconscious is more inaccessible than cellars and garrets, which can be physically entered, Gaskell's narrator nonetheless indicates a failure of communication that goes beyond the physical, since those who visit such spaces (as she has done) can viscerally comprehend them, but any language that seeks to transmit this knowledge seems doomed to failure. Just as the psychoanalytic unconscious is detected only through its symptoms, this architectural unconscious is recognised by the wider nation only when it erupts into violence.

In the context of Gaskell's Manchester, riots and Chartism are eruptions which signify the presence of this repressed architectural unconscious. Thomas Carlyle's *Chartism* (1840) seems to recognise this in its opening pages:

> The distracted incoherent embodiment of Chartism, whereby in late months it took shape and became visible, this has been put down; or rather has fallen down and gone asunder by gravitation and law of nature: but the living essence of Chartism has not been put down.[51]

For Carlyle, the 'living essence' of Chartism remains after the failure of 1839, when the People's Charter was rejected by Parliament, though it is now unseen. This, he contends, is because it is hidden rather than abolished – the descriptions 'put down', 'fallen down' and 'gone asunder by gravitation' imply going underground. Taken alongside Gaskell and Engels's texts, Carlyle's statement implies that Chartism has fallen back into a social and spatial unconscious that is strongly associated with cellar-dwelling. At the same time, the form of Chartism that briefly emerged into social consciousness cannot be considered entirely authentic, since it was only a 'distracted incoherent embodiment' of a more powerful unseen force, which remains under the surface.

Gaston Bachelard's poetics of space is one theoretical account that aligns repression with underground space, though he opposes 'the rationality of the roof' to 'the irrationality of the cellar'. Whereas roof and attic have a 'solid geometry' that is logical and comprehensible, the cellar is different:

> As for the cellar, we shall no doubt find uses for it. It will be rationalized and its conveniences enumerated. But it is first and foremost the *dark entity* of the house, the one that partakes of subterranean forces. When we dream there, we are in harmony with the irrationality of the depths.[52]

For Bachelard, the cellar reverberates within the human subject as an unconscious dream-space, where 'the impassioned inhabitant digs and re-digs, making its very depth active'.[53] Although for Bachelard this unconscious is primarily intimate and personal, rather than disturbing as for Gaskell, the cellar (though not here the garret) is again its primary locus, as a spatial correlative of all that is primal and oneiric.

It is no coincidence that one of Dickens's characters most subject to repression, George Silverman, is first encountered in a cellar. Silverman features in Dickens's late short story of 1868, 'George Silverman's Explanation', which begins, after two abortive first chapters reflecting on the difficulty of beginning 'to explain my explanation', with Silverman describing his early life:

> My parents were in a miserable condition of life, and my infant home was a cellar in Preston. I recollect the sound of father's Lancashire clogs on the street pavement above, as being different in my young hearing from the sound of all other clogs; and I recollect, that, when mother came down the cellar-steps, I used tremblingly to speculate on her feet having a good or an ill-tempered look, – on her knees, – on her waist, – until finally her face came into view, and settled the question. From this it will be seen that I was timid, and that the cellar-steps were steep, and that the doorway was very low.[54]

The range of Silverman's world is bounded by the four walls of this cellar, where he is often locked up 'for a day or two at a time' while his parents look for work. Driven by hunger, thirst and lack of understanding, he appears uncaring when his parents die, and is condemned as a 'worldly little devil' (GS 380), a phrase first used by his mother that haunts him throughout the text. It is the business of his life and his 'explanation' to prove or disprove his right to this name. As well as being called 'worldly', Silverman is presented with his own dangerous infectiousness: 'you are going', he is told upon removal from the cellar, 'to a healthy farm-house to be purified' (GS 383), and is advised that 'you had better not say much – in fact, you had better be very careful not to say anything' (GS 383). These injunctions – seeing oneself as devilish, being infectious, not saying anything – form the outlines of Silverman's character, to the extent that he later brings together the girl he loves, and who loves him, with another man, out of a belief in his own inferiority.

The tragedy of the story is that Silverman never really leaves his cellar. Once physically removed from it, he rebuilds it internally as a form of repression. He is now both inside and outside the cellar, both the little boy and the parents who lock him in. The story dramatises Bachelard's observation that fear becomes exaggerated in the cellar, so that 'the cellar [. . .] becomes buried madness, walled-in tragedy'.[55] Unrepresentability is at the heart of this tragedy, as it is in Gaskell, Engels and Kay's readings of Manchester. It is indicated in the difficulty Silverman faces in beginning his explanation: he hopes to show his true self in writing, as he could not do in life, but writing fails him too. Repression and the cellar-dwelling come together here as the components of an invisible architecture which is at once spatial and psychological.

Cellars and Surplus Population

In order for cellars to operate effectively as sites of psychical and social repression, they must be conceptually available for dwelling. The cultural change which allows this to take place is the development of a form of capitalism that relies on reserve-labour, as traced by Marx in *Capital* Volume 1, chapter 25, section 3, 'Progressive Production of a Relative Surplus-Population or Industrial Reserve Army'. Marx argues that the increasing accumulation of capital leads to a relative fall in the proportion of capital directed to labour-power (i.e. the workers). This accumulation is due to the increased concentration of capital, so that the process is reflexive, and to improvements in the technological basis of production, both of which lead to increased productivity. According to Marx, it is capitalistic accumulation itself that constantly produces, and produces in direct ratio of its own energy and extent, a relatively redundant population of labourers, i.e. a population of greater extent than suffices for the average needs of the self-expansion of capital, and therefore a surplus-population.[56]

The accumulation of capital is correlated with the accumulation of workers, as a pool of labour upon which capitalism can draw as required. This surplus population must be stored, just as capital or commodities are stored, and this takes place in the hidden and marginal spaces of the city, above all attics and cellars, spaces formerly reserved for goods, in a reifying process in which people take the place of commodities. The relationship between capitalist accumulation and surplus population thus formed is a dialectical one:

> if a surplus labouring population is a necessary product of accumulation or of the development of wealth on a capitalist basis, this surplus-population becomes, conversely, the lever of capitalistic accumulation, nay, a condition of existence of the capitalist mode of production.[57]

The accumulation of capital generates an accumulation of population, with which it is in tension, but upon which it relies. In an *Aufhebung* movement, this tension between capital and labour is cancelled and sublimated at the level of the capitalist mode of production as a whole, though this does not mean that conditions on the ground are by any means resolved.

The submerged dialectical connection between the wealthiest and most excluded sections of the population helps explain Gaskell's reference in *Mary Barton* to *Frankenstein*, as a metaphor for the urban working classes:

> The actions of the uneducated seem to me typified in those of Frankenstein, that monster of many human qualities, ungifted with a soul, a knowledge of the difference between good and evil.
>
> The people rise up to life; they irritate us, they terrify us, and we become their enemies. Then, in the sorrowful moment of our triumphant power, their eyes gaze on us with mute reproach. Why have we made them what they are; a powerful monster, yet without the inner means for peace and happiness? (MB 165)[58]

Kay, who sees population growth as an 'accidental' cause of misery rather than an inevitable outcome of capitalism, gestures towards

Frankenstein's monster when he describes the labourers as a 'slumbering giant' at the feet of the capitalists.[59] An entry in Benjamin's *Arcades Project* from 1839 instead associates the monster with the machines, and the workers with his creator Victor: 'the machines have behaved like Frankenstein's monster [. . .], who, after acquiring life, employed it only in persecuting the man who had given it to him'.[60] Marshall Berman takes another route, comparing Marx's bourgeoisie with Victor Frankenstein and Goethe's Faust.[61] Gaskell's passage, though, is revealing in its confusion of Victor Frankenstein and his creation. This mistake should remind us that in Mary Shelley's novel, Victor and the monster are bound together as doubles and opposites of each other, just as for Marx the bourgeoisie and the working class, or capital and surplus-population, are under capitalism.[62] Speaking to Walton, Shelley's primary narrator, Victor describes his existential connection with the monster: 'I must pursue and destroy the being to whom I gave existence; then my lot on earth will be fulfilled and I may die.'[63] Similarly for Marx and Engels, if the bourgeoisie were to destroy the proletariat it would also destroy itself, since neither class can survive in its current form without the other. What is truly monstrous in the working class, then, is that it gives rise to a Benjaminian dialectical image – a moment in which two opposing and separate images turn into one another and the world is seen allegorically – in which the bourgeoisie sees not only the working classes but also itself as monstrous. As in Gaskell, where the monster has no knowledge of 'the difference between good and evil', in this dialectical image there is, impossibly, no difference between workers and bourgeoisie: the workers are monsters because the monstrous capitalists have made them so. This indicates one more reason why surplus workers must be concealed in cellars: in case they present to the bourgeoisie an unbearable reflection of themselves.

Mary Barton's Cellars I: Preservation of Tradition

Mary Barton includes two notable cellar-dwellings, with different symbolic roles. Taken together, they map out a particular orientation towards the spatial and class structure of Manchester, which finds hope in community cohesion and the preservation of the past, whilst fearing urban alienation and the loss of identity. The first is inhabited by Alice Wilson, who is Mr Wilson's sister and Jem's aunt, and the second by the Davenport family, after the family breadwinner Ben Davenport is put out of work by the factory-owning Carson family.

Alice Wilson, a poor washerwoman, is part of an older generation of characters, also represented by Job Legh, who provide a link to the pre-industrial past through their association with the countryside and rural traditions, depicted as under threat from the growth of the industrial city. This role becomes most clear in Alice's final illness, when she imagines herself as a child, singing romanticised songs 'such as are sung in country churches half draperied over with ivy, and where the running brook, or the murmuring wind among the trees makes fit accompaniment to the chorus of human voices uttering praise and thanksgiving to their God' (MB 260–1). The novel's first reference to Alice, by Mr Wilson, gives her place of residence: 'our Alice lives in the cellar under No. 14, in Barber Street' (MB 12). Shirley Foster notes that Barber Street had been replaced by London Road train station by the time Gaskell was writing in the late 1840s.[64] In fact, the first station built on this site was Store Street Station in 1842, not long after the novel closes in approximately 1840. By this point Alice has died, following her mental regression (MB 327), while the mode of life she represents, defined by close engagement with local community and resistance to the alienating city, has been symbolically replaced by the modern, industrial values of the railway, associated with the bewildering experience of Mary's journey to Liverpool (MB 273).

According to John Parkinson-Bailey, Store Street Station was initially built for the Manchester and Birmingham Railway, a company taken over in 1846 by the newly formed London and North Western Railway, which also took control of the Liverpool and Manchester Railway, London and Birmingham Railway, and Great Junction Railway. Store Street, now renamed London Road Station, became part of the new company, later becoming Manchester Piccadilly Station.[65] From 1846 the London and North Western Railway also controlled the London and Birmingham Railway, building work for which creates the upheaval of Staggs's Gardens in *Dombey and Son*, a novel whose serial publication concluded in 1848, the year *Mary Barton* was published.[66] But whereas *Mary Barton* implicitly positions Alice's death and the construction of the railways as the end of a way of life, in *Dombey and Son* the construction of the railway is part of an ongoing instability within the city, as the next chapter will show.

In the first half of Gaskell's novel, however, Alice's cellar-home is a space for the maintenance of rural knowledge, as an early passage makes clear:

> Alice Wilson had but just come in. She had been out all day in the fields, gathering wild herbs for drinks and medicine, for in addition to her

> invaluable qualities as a sick nurse and her worldly occupations as a washerwoman, she added a considerable knowledge of hedge and field simples; and on fine days, when no more profitable occupation offered itself, she used to ramble off into the lanes and meadows as far as her legs could carry her. This evening she had returned loaded with nettles, and her first object was to light a candle and see to hang them up in bunches in every available place in her cellar room. It was the perfection of cleanliness; in one corner stood the modest-looking bed, with a check curtain at the head, the whitewashed wall filling up the place where the corresponding one should have been. The floor was bricked, and scrupulously clean, although so damp that it seemed as if the last washing would never dry up. (MB 16)

Alice's traditional knowledge of herbs is an 'addition' to her 'worldly occupations'. More specifically, it is a knowledge located below the 'worldly' (the same word used to describe George Silverman), in the cellar. It is a form of underground knowledge, outside the visual field of the conscious city, preserved by certain members of the working classes. This preservation is symbolised by the bunches of herbs which hang 'in every available place', redefining the cellar's role as a store for commodities to make it a location for the storage and protection of rural culture. It is an example of what Lefebvre calls 'appropriated space', described by Isobel Armstrong as 'the space of limited *freedom within the capitalist project*'.[67] The narrator continues:

> As the cellar window looked into an area in the street, down which boys might throw stones, it was protected by an outside shutter, and was oddly festooned with all manner of hedge-row, ditch and field plants, which we are accustomed to call valueless, but which have a powerful effect either for good or for evil, and are consequently much used among the poor. (MB 16)

Just as the shutter is a protection from the stones of the boys, the plants which festoon the window are a protection from the filth and degradation of the city.[68] Alice's knowledge and traditions act as a symbolic barrier to safeguard rural and communitarian values against the corrupting influence of Manchester. Elaine Freedgood critically notes that there is a certain 'coziness' in Alice's cellar, as it attempts to mitigate the 'homogenization and degradation of the new laboring class'.[69] At the same time, though, because Alice's underground knowledge is not only topographically but also socially hidden – a knowledge which 'we', the middle classes, 'are accustomed to call valueless' – it is invisible and even threatening, carrying what Freedgood calls a 'potential volatility'.[70]

Gaskell's depiction of Alice's hidden knowledge aligns with Engels's claim that 'The workers speak other dialects, have other thoughts and ideals, other customs and moral principles, a different religion and other politics than those of the bourgeoisie.'[71] This in turn recalls Egremont in *Sybil*:

> I was told [. . .] that an impassable gulf divided the Rich from the Poor; I was told that the Privileged and the People formed Two Nations, governed by different laws, influenced by different manners, with no thoughts or sympathies in common; with an innate inability of mutual comprehension.[72]

Despite her subordinate position, Alice has access to a form of knowledge beyond that available to either the rich or the narrator. Such underground knowledge, like repression in Freud, demands a persistent expenditure of force to maintain it. In Alice's case this consists of regular trips to the country to replenish the cellar's stock of plants and herbs, which are always slowly decaying.

This picture of Alice aligns her with what Diane Purkiss, following Mary Daly, calls 'the myth of the Burning Times'.[73] According to this feminist myth, the unfairly persecuted witch

> lived alone, in her own house surrounded by her garden, in which she grew all manner of herbs and other healing plants. [. . .] The woman was a healer and a midwife; she had practical knowledge taught her by her mother, and mystical knowledge derived from her closeness to nature, or from a half-submerged pagan religion. She helped women give birth, and she had healing hands; she used her knowledge of herbs and her common sense to help the sick.[74]

Purkiss criticises this myth as ahistorical, and as portraying women as 'nothing but the helpless victims of patriarchy', though she acknowledges its important role in forging an alternative form of history within feminism.[75] Relevant to *Mary Barton* is the way it 'offer[s] nostalgic pleasure to anxious urban residents', but Purkiss warns that 'precisely because the fantasy depends on an opposition between the modern urban world and the countryside of the past, it cannot serve as a blueprint for action'.[76] Such inaction is evident in Alice's relationship with the urban environment around her, which she passively resists but cannot change.

In preserving the culture of the countryside, Alice's cellar is associated with the old farmhouse in Green Heys Fields in the opening chapter, which has a 'little garden surrounding it [. . .] crowded with a medley of old-fashioned herbs and flowers, planted long ago, when the garden was the only druggist's shop within reach' (MB 6). Brigid Lowe takes this as an example of Gaskell's 'miscellaneous aesthetic', which prefers mixture and idiosyncrasy to homogeneity.[77] The implication is that 'long ago', or far away in the case of Mary's later removal to the colonies, might be the only place where rural working-class knowledge can be effectively preserved from the degrading effect of the city. Certainly, Alice's use of the cellar as a site of preservation is no permanent solution. Commenting on Alice's delirium, the narrator states: 'God had sent her a veiled blessing: she was once more in the scenes of her childhood' (MB 210), among 'the golden hills of heaven' (MB 33) mentioned earlier. This regression acts as a religious elevation, moving Alice away from the underground towards a more divine form of invisibility. The way of life Alice represents is spiritually preserved by this process, but at the cost of placing it behind a barrier more powerful than her cellar window: that between life and death. This preservation through separation parallels the emigration of Mary, Jem and Mrs Wilson to Canada at the end of the novel, where they live in 'a long low wooden house, with room enough and to spare' (MB 378). This retreat from the city is emphasised by the house's rural surroundings, consisting of a 'garden around the dwelling' and an 'orchard' stretching beyond (MB 378). For Raymond Williams, the novel's conclusion represents 'a cancelling of the actual difficulties and the removal of the persons pitied to the uncompromised New World'.[78]

In the end Alice Wilson's cellar fails as a site of preservation because it operates by passively resisting and denying the city rather than acknowledging and facing it, though such a confrontation would also risk annihilation or colonisation by middle-class agencies, such as those proposed by Kay. As a space outside the gaze and consciousness of the wider city, her cellar takes up an oppositional position which renders it marginal, precarious and, unlike the contents of the Freudian unconscious that it partly parallels, ultimately subject to destruction by the same historical forces which have created it, as exemplified by the railway.[79]

Mary Barton's Cellars II: Misery and Degeneration

In stark contrast to Alice's cellar is the cellar where Joseph Barton and Mr Wilson find the Davenport family in chapter 6, after Ben Davenport has been put out of work following the fire at the Carsons' factory

(MB 37–55). The Carsons have delayed the rebuilding of their mill, despite being 'well insured' for the damage, for reasons of political economy, to ensure that 'the weekly drain of wages given for labour, useless in the present state of the market, was stopped' (MB 56). This decision, which fails to count the human cost of delay, echoes Engels's comment that the English bourgeois 'cannot comprehend that he holds any other relation to the operatives than that of purchase and sale; he sees in them not human beings, but hands, as he constantly calls them to their faces'.[80] As a result, the Davenport family have 'sunk lower and lower, and pawned off thing after thing, and [. . .] they now lived in a cellar in Berry Street, off Store Street' (MB 57). This is the street that gave its name to Store Street Station, so the Davenports are very close to Alice's cellar in Barber Street. Isaac Slater's 1848 map of Manchester (Figure 1.1) shows that Berry Street was still in existence when the novel was published, now very close to the new train station.[81]

The filth Alice resists by keeping her home spotlessly clean is inescapable in this second cellar, where 'household slops of *every* description' are thrown into the street's overflowing gutters and a 'foul area' forms the entranceway (MB 58). It recalls Engels's description of the lowest and worst parts of Manchester, including on the south bank of the river Irk:

> In one of these courts there stands directly at the entrance, at the end of the covered passage, a privy without a door, so dirty that the inhabitants can pass into and out of the court only by passing through foul pools of stagnant urine and excrement.[82]

Urine and excrement form a threshold to the court, marking those who pass through it as themselves waste, rejected by the social body. Similarly, the entrance to the Davenports' cellar is reached by crossing a series of thresholds: first a set of steps which take visitors so low that 'a person standing would have his head about one foot below the level of the street', before 'you went down one step even from the foul area into the cellar in which a family of human beings lived' (MB 58). This gradual descent from street, to court, to cellar parallels the moral and spiritual descent of the Davenport family. It takes the visitors into a lower and more primal world than the main streets, from which the cellar is hidden, into a room where the windowpanes are 'broken and stuffed with rags' (MB 58). As Christoph Lindner points out, the well-lit shops above do not generate consumer fantasies, unlike in Thackeray or Trollope, but instead represent 'a strangely alien world systematically denied to John Barton and the novel's

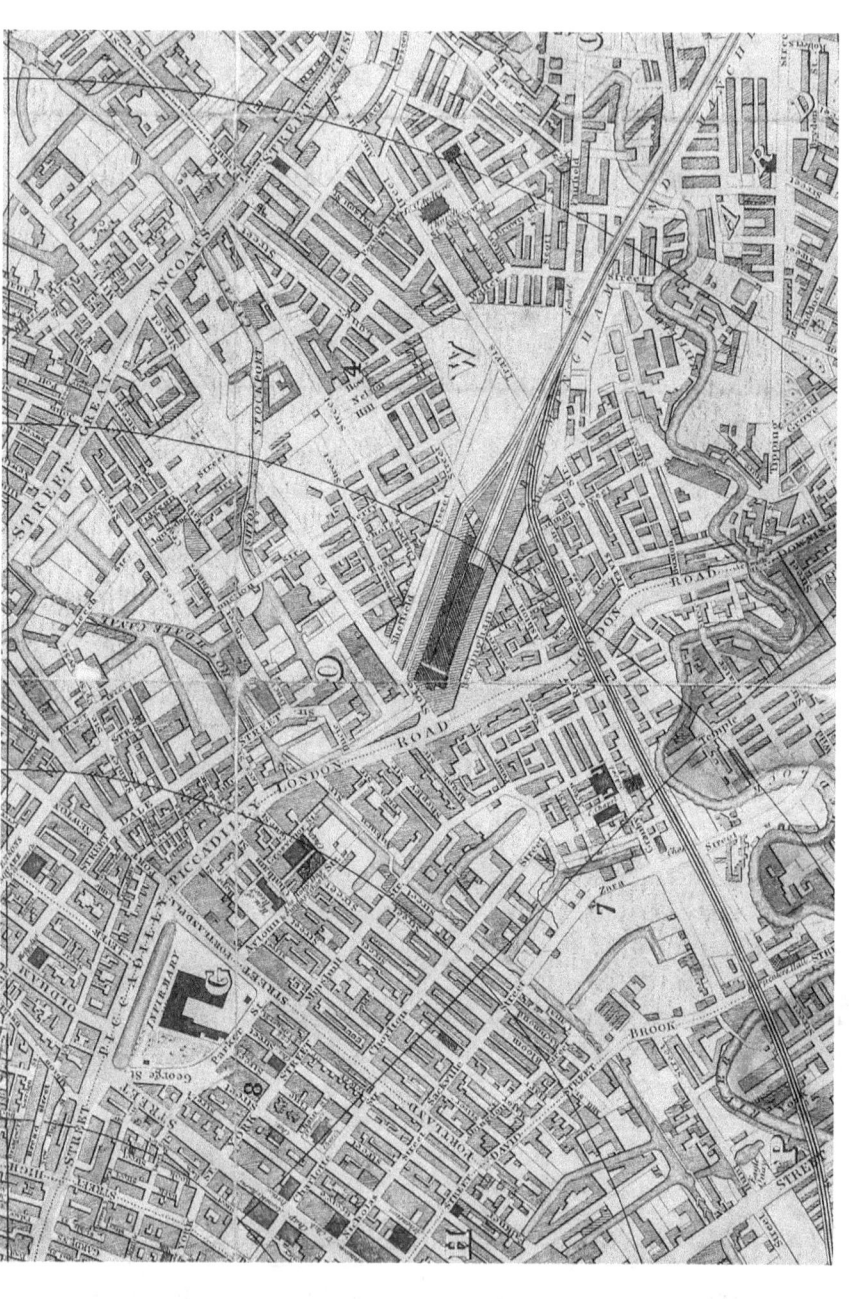

Figure 1.1 Detail from *A Plan of Manchester and Salford with Vicinities* (1848), Isaac Slater. Manchester Libraries, Information and Archives.

wider working community'.[83] Down below, by contrast, the smashed windows represent the family's social invisibility (no-one can see in or out) and their vulnerability (the broken panes offer no material protection). Unlike Alice Wilson's home, where the herbs in the window signify rural knowledge and traditions, here the smashed and blocked-up window registers an absolute absence of culture. There is no way this cellar can hold any alternative form of culture or praxis; it can only make its inhabitants appear pre- or sub-human.

The Davenports' cellar is an inversion of the Parisian arcades described by Walter Benjamin, those being commodified dream worlds from which matter and weather are thoroughly expelled.[84] In the cellar, the children roll on the floor like animals, and the 'stagnant, filthy moisture of the street' oozes through the bricks, while Ben Davenport lies on straw 'so damp and mouldy, no dog would have chosen it in preference to flags' (MB 60). Yet such hellish primality also strangely parallels the arcades which constitute its opposite. Benajmin writes:

> One knew of places in ancient Greece where the way led down into the underworld. Our waking existence likewise is a land which, at certain hidden points, leads down into the underworld – a land full of inconspicuous places from which dreams arise. All day long, suspecting nothing, we pass them by, but no sooner has sleep come than we are eagerly groping our way back to lose ourselves in the dark corridors. By day, the labyrinth of urban dwellings resembles consciousness; the arcades (which are galleries leading into the city's past) issue unremarked onto the streets. At night, however, under the tenebrous mass of the houses, their denser darkness protrudes like a threat, and the nocturnal pedestrian hurries past – unless, that is, we have emboldened him to turn into the narrow lane.[85]

Like the cellars of Manchester, the arcades of Paris are corridors into the unconscious, though the latter ambiguously attract while the former repel. For both Dickens and Freud, these two drives are not separate but intimately connected; Forster recorded Dickens's 'profound attraction of repulsion to St. Giles's', a poverty-stricken area of London which stimulated his imagination: '"Good Heaven!" he would exclaim, "what wild visions of prodigies of wickedness, want, and beggary arose in my mind out of that place!"'[86] Despite their differences, in Benjamin's Paris as in Dickens's London and Gaskell's Manchester the city is the site of an interplay of conscious and unconscious, out of which a new urban topography begins to arise. For Benjamin, the main threshold between conscious and unconscious is the transition between day and night, the point when emphasis passes from the city's dwellings, which 'resemble consciousness', to the arcades, which protrude 'like a threat'. In this shift, the repressed material of the architectural unconscious rises into view.

For Bachelard, the darkness of night is associated with the cellar: 'In the attic, the day's experiences can always efface the fears of night. In the cellar, darkness prevails both day and night, and even when we are carrying a lighted candle, we see shadows dancing on the dark walls.'[87] It is significant that *Mary Barton*'s most violent event, the murder of Harry Carson, takes place in the evening, causing the Carson family to stay up all night (MB 206). This murder is the moment when the repressed danger of the working class destructively emerges, pulling the Carson family into the night, which throughout the novel is the time of the workers. In a temporal corollary to the cellar, the night offers another kind of margin in which working-class subjects can act outside the purview of the bourgeoisie. Many other important events in the novel take place at night, particularly those associated with death and illness. Alice Wilson, for instance, sits up through the night to look after ill children (MB 12), and when Mary's mother dies, the 'cries of agony [. . .] resounded in the little court in the stillness of the night' (MB 19). Mr Wilson and John Barton stay overnight to look after the Davenports (MB 61), and Mary helps Alice through the 'long night' that follows the death of the Wilson twins (MB 77). At times, night itself has a spatial element, becoming accentuated in the city, as when the Wilsons and the Bartons return from Green Heys Fields, the narrator remarking that 'although the evening seemed yet early when they were in the open fields – among the pent-up houses, night with its mists and its darkness, had already begun to fall' (MB 13). The city, it seems, produces its own unnatural night.

If Alice's herbs are an attempt to ward off the shocks of the city, the bourgeois home of the Carson family fulfils a similar role: its 'comfortable, elegant, well-lighted drawing-room' (MB 196) insulates the family from the underground, nighttime world of the workers. For Benjamin, such insulation is the key characteristic of bourgeois furnishings:

> Ever since the time of Louis Philippe, the bourgeois has shown a tendency to compensate for the absence of any trace of private life in the big city. He tries to do this within the four walls of his apartment [. . .] Indefatigably, he takes the impression of a host of objects; for his slippers and his watches, his blankets and his umbrellas, he devises coverlets and

cases. He has a marked preference for velour and plush, which preserve the imprint of all contact.[88]

Furnishings preserve traces, as the city does not. They resist the death of self that the anonymity of the city, especially in its nighttime character, threatens. It seems natural, then, that the furnished interior is the family's first recourse when what has been repressed, the fact of working-class subjugation, forcibly enters their home. On hearing of Harry Carson's murder,

> One sister sat down on an ottoman, and covered her face, to try and realise it. That was Sophy. Helen threw herself on the sofa, and burying her head in the pillows, tried to stifle the screams and moans which shook her frame. (MB 199)

Harry's sisters submerge themselves in the furniture, impressing their own traces upon the interior from which death was supposed to be banished. By contrast, Mary Barton, on hearing the news that Jem, who she loves, may be tried and hanged,

> threw herself on the ground, yes, on the hard flags she threw her soft limbs down; and the comb fell out of her hair, and those bright tresses swept the dusty floor, while she pillowed and hid her face on her arms. (MB 223)

Mary has no soft furnishings in which to hide; her grief can only direct itself back onto her own body as she hides her face in her arms. There is no capacity here for the interior to absorb grief. The only dream world Mary can escape into is the literal one, when 'Heaven blessed her unaware, and she sank from remembering, to wandering, unconnected thought, and thence to sleep' (MB 225). If Mary's escape into sleep and 'the happy times of long ago' (MB 225) is a working-class equivalent to the bourgeois domestic interior, so is Alice's holy delirium, which inverts and parallels the preserving effect of the Carson family's furnishings. Though Mary and Alice do not have the benefit of the material wealth of the Carson girls, they too deploy forms of insulation that are at once symptoms of and forms of resistance to the city's alienating modernity.

The dream represented by the bourgeois interior, though alienating, is at least comforting. The alienation of the Davenports' cellar is different. Instead of taking the family away from death, it drives them towards it, installing it as a constant presence in their lives, most evidently in what is called the 'back apartment'. Mr Wilson opens the door to this apartment 'for an instant', revealing that

> it led into a back cellar, with a grating instead of a window, down which dropped the moisture from pigsties, and worse abominations. It was not paved; the floor was one mass of bad smelling mud. It had never been used, for there was not an article of furniture in it; nor could a human being, much less a pig, have lived there many days. Yet the 'back apartment' made a difference in the rent. The Davenports paid threepence more for having two rooms. (MB 62)

This primal space below the underground, where life is absolutely unsustainable, submerges its inhabitants in mud, like the lowest row of buildings on the banks of the river Irk, which 'stands so low that the lowest floor is uninhabitable, and therefore without windows and doors'.[89] The apartment represents both excrement ('the moisture from pigsties') and death ('nor could a human being [. . .] have lived there many days'). One way of reading this deathlike room is as showing directly what official architecture relies on but seeks to conceal: the presence of death. For Hegel, the function of the tomb, which stands at the origin of art and architecture, is to simultaneously preserve (by marking) and deny (by replacing) death.[90] In opening up the death and filth which tombs conceal, the back cellar puts in question the city as a site of art and culture, representing a regression to the primal beginnings of both architecture and humanity.

Benjamin, quoting Marx, puts such regression alongside alienation as characteristic of the working-class cellar:

> We have already said . . . that humanity is regressing to the state of cave dweller, and so on – but it is regressing in an estranged, malignant form. The savage in his cave . . . feels . . . at home there . . . But the basement apartment of the poor man is a hostile dwelling, 'an alien, restraining power, which gives itself up to him only insofar as he gives up to it his blood and sweat'. Such a dwelling can never feel like home, a place where he might at last exclaim, 'Here I am at home!' Instead, the poor man finds himself in someone else's home . . . someone who daily lies in wait for him and throws him out if he does not pay his rent. He is also aware of the contrast in quality between his dwelling and a human dwelling – a residence in that other world, the heaven of wealth.[91]

This passage modifies Bachelard's romanticised understanding of the primal home as the locus of an originary comfort and intimacy.

The archetypal primal home for Bachelard is the hermit's hut, which is a 'center of concentrated solitude', while for Marx and Benjamin the working-class home is the perversion of such a dwelling; unlike the cave of the 'savage' it turns against its inhabitants, embodying the owner who 'throws him out if he does not pay his rent', a representative of the entire capital-owning class.[92] The Davenports' cellar takes this alienation to its ultimate conclusion by dissolving human identity itself. Gaskell here attacks the view that unemployed workers are a necessary excess, a position associated with political economy and liberal politics. Surplus workers are instead shown to be a shamefully excluded and degraded invisible presence in the industrial city.

In this chapter, the unconscious has been associated with the underground and the night, understood respectively as forms of spatial and temporal repression which render the working classes socially and culturally invisible in industrial Manchester. This connection between the architectural unconscious and invisibility returns in the following chapter, where the railway of *Dombey and Son* and the river of *Our Mutual Friend* are read as ambiguous structures of repression and revelation. My emphasis in what follows, though, is on the dynamic instability of the city and its architecture, so that in turning from Gaskell to Dickens our focus shifts from concealment to mobility.

Notes

1. Briggs, p. 51.
2. On emergent, dominant and residual forms see Raymond Williams, *Marxism and Literature* (Oxford: Oxford University Press, 1977), pp. 121–7.
3. Lefebvre, p. 27.
4. Elizabeth Gaskell, *Mary Barton* (Oxford: Oxford University Press, 2006), pp. 65–6. Further references in main text.
5. Lefebvre, p. 30.
6. Nord, p. 144. Sue Zemka addresses a similar topic in 'Brief Encounters: Urban Street Scenes in Gaskell's Manchester', *ELH*, 76.3 (2009), 793–819.
7. Poovey, Mary, *Making a Social Body: British Cultural Formation, 1830–1864* (Chicago: University of Chicago Press, 1995), p. 57.
8. On the relationship to Marx see for instance Tristram Hunt, 'Introduction' to *The Condition of the Working Class in England*, pp. 1–31 (p. 23).
9. James Phillips Kay, *The Moral and Physical Condition of the Working Classes Employed in the Cotton Manufacture in Manchester* (London: James Ridgeway, 1832 [1st edn]), p. 1.

10. Poovey, pp. 73–97.
11. Charles Dickens, *Dombey and Son* (Oxford: Oxford University Press, 2001), p. 685. Further references in main text.
12. Kay, p. 63.
13. Kay, p. 63. This work is comparable to that of the Bible Societies described in Poovey, pp. 42–54.
14. Martin Hewitt, *Making Social Knowledge in the Victorian City: The Visiting Mode in Manchester, 1832–1914* (Abingdon: Routledge, 2020), p. 2.
15. Hewitt, p. 4.
16. Poovey, pp. 25–54.
17. Poovey, p. 36.
18. On the *Report*, see Poovey, pp. 98–114, pp. 115–31. On Chadwick in relation to the problem of waste, see Catherine Gallagher, *The Body Economic: Life, Death, and Sensation in Political Economy and the Victorian Novel* (Princeton: Princeton University Press, 2006), pp. 86–117.
19. Kay, pp. 46–7.
20. See Karl Marx, *Capital*, ed. by David McLellan (Oxford: Oxford University Press, 1995), pp. 42–50.
21. Kay, p. 47, and see also p. 1.
22. Kay, p. 16 onwards.
23. Kay, p. 18.
24. Kay, p. 38.
25. Thomas Carlyle, *Chartism* (London: James Fraser, 1840), p. 9.
26. Kay, p. 7. See also Poovey, pp. 55–72.
27. Amy Martin, 'Blood Transfusions: Constructions of Irish Racial Difference, the English Working Class, and Revolutionary Possibility in the Work of Carlyle and Engels', *Victorian Literature and Culture*, 32.1 (2004), 83–102.
28. See Friedrich Engels, *The Condition of the Working Class in England* (London: Penguin, 2009), pp. 100–2. The deconstructive nature of Engels's argument is evident when he states: 'I always preferred to present proof from *Liberal* sources in order to defeat the liberal bourgeoisie by casting their own words in their teeth.' Engels, p. 36.
29. Engels, p. 85.
30. Sigmund Freud, 'Repression', in *The Standard Edition, Volume XIV (1914–1916)*, ed. by James Strachey (London: Vintage, 2001), pp. 141–58 (p. 147, p. 151).
31. Lefebvre, pp. 1–7.
32. Lefebvre, pp. 38–9.
33. Engels, p. 86.
34. Engels, p. 87.
35. Sigmund Freud, 'A Note on the Unconscious in Psycho-Analysis', in *The Standard Edition, Volume XII (1911–1913)*, ed. by James Strachey (London: Vintage, 2001), pp. 257–66 (p. 260).

36. Walter Benjamin, *The Work of Art in the Age of Its Technological Reproducibility and Other Writings on Media*, ed. by Michael Jennings, Brigid Doherty and Thomas Levin (Cambridge, MA: Belknap Press, 2008), p. 37.
37. See for instance the opening sections of 'Beyond the Pleasure Principle', in *The Standard Edition, Volume XVIII (1920–1922)*, ed. by James Strachey (London: Vintage, 2001), pp. 3–66.
38. On the links between modern conceptions of accident and the development of the Victorian city see Paul Fyfe, *By Accident or Design: Writing the Victorian Metropolis* (Oxford: Oxford University Press, 2015). For the American context see Jason Puskar, *Accident Society: Fiction, Collectivity, and the Production of Chance* (Palo Alto: Stanford University Press, 2012).
39. For a classic reading of the underground man, see Michael Bernstein, *Bitter Carnival: Ressentiment and the Abject Hero* (Princeton: Princeton University Press, 1992), pp. 87–120. For a development of Bernstein's argument, see Alina Wyman, 'The Specter of Freedom: *Ressentiment* and Dostoevskij's *Notes from Underground*', *Studies in East European Thought*, 59.1–2 (2007), 119–40. On *ressentiment*, see Friedrich Nietzsche, *The Genealogy of Morals*, trans. by Douglas Smith (Oxford: Oxford University Press, 1996 [1887]).
40. Dostoevsky, p. 17.
41. Dostoevsky, p. 18.
42. Dostoevsky, p. 17, p. 18.
43. On the city's history, see Bruce Lincoln, *Sunlight at Midnight: St Petersburg and the Rise of Modern Russia* (New York: Basic Books, 2000).
44. On *Mary Barton* as a literary response to *laissez-faire* capitalism in England, see Louis Cazamian, *The Social Novel in England 1830–1850*, trans. by Martin Fido (London: Routledge and Kegan, 1973 [1903]), pp. 214–26.
45. Elizabeth Gaskell, *North and South* (Oxford: Oxford University Press, 1998), p. 276. Further references in main text.
46. *OED*, cellar, n.1. *OED Online*, Oxford University Press, <www.oed.com/view/Entry/29473>. Accessed 10 May 2023. Engels, p. 83.
47. Kathleen Tillotson, *Novels of the Eighteen-Forties* (London: Clarendon Press, 1954), p. 203.
48. Raymond Williams, *Culture and Society: 1780–1950* (London: Chatto and Windus, 1967), p. 87.
49. Charles Dickens, *Sketches by Boz* (London: Penguin, 1995), p. 217.
50. As in Freud's *The Interpretation of Dreams* (1900) and *The Psychopathology of Everyday Life* (1901).
51. *Chartism*, p. 2.
52. Bachelard, p. 18.
53. Bachelard, p. 18.

54. Charles Dickens, *Selected Short Fiction* (London: Penguin, 1976), pp. 379–407 (pp. 379–80). Further references in main text.
55. Bachelard, p. 20.
56. *Capital*, p. 351.
57. *Capital*, p. 352.
58. For a reading of *Frankenstein* as a class allegory, see Franco Moretti, 'Dialectic of Fear', in *Signs Taken for Wonders*, trans. by David Forgacs (London: Verso, 2005), pp. 83–108.
59. Kay, p. 47.
60. *Arcades*, pp. 705–6.
61. Berman, pp. 101–2.
62. On *Frankenstein*, subjectivity and doubleness, see Paul Sherwin, '*Frankenstein*: Creation as Catastrophe', *PMLA*, 96.5 (1981), 883–903 and Eleanor Salotto, '*Frankenstein* and Dis(re)membered Identity', *Journal of Narrative Technique*, 24.3 (1994), 190–211.
63. Mary Shelley, *Frankenstein* (London: Norton, 2012 [1818]), p. 153.
64. Shirley Foster in *Mary Barton*, p. 417n.
65. John J. Parkinson-Bailey, *Manchester: An Architectural History* (Manchester: Manchester University Press, 2000), pp. 50–1.
66. See Jeremy Tambling, *Going Astray: Dickens and London* (London: Pearson, 2009), pp. 103–20, especially p. 104.
67. Isobel Armstrong, 'Theories of Space and the Nineteenth-Century Novel', *19: Interdisciplinary Studies in the Long Nineteenth Century*, 17 (2013), 1–21 (p. 18). See Lefebvre, pp. 164–8.
68. Elaine Freedgood considers the symbolism of checked curtains in *Mary Barton* in *The Ideas in Things: Fugitive Meaning in the Victorian Novel* (Chicago: University of Chicago Press, 2006), pp. 55–80.
69. Freedgood, p. 60.
70. Freedgood, p. 60.
71. Engels, p. 150.
72. Benjamin Disraeli, *Sybil* (Oxford: Oxford University Press, 1998), p. 245.
73. Diane Purkiss, *The Witch in History: Early Modern and Twentieth-Century Representations* (London: Routledge, 1996), p. 7.
74. Purkiss, p. 7.
75. Purkiss, p. 17.
76. Purkiss, p. 21.
77. Brigid Lowe, 'Elizabeth Gaskell', in *The Cambridge Companion to English Novelists*, ed. by Adrian Poole (Cambridge: Cambridge University Press, 2009), pp. 193–209 (p. 196).
78. *Culture and Society*, p. 91.
79. On these issues, see Jill Matus, *Shock, Memory and the Unconscious in Victorian Fiction* (Cambridge: Cambridge University Press, 2009), especially pp. 21–2.
80. Engels, p. 276.

81. Isaac Slater, *A Plan of Manchester and Salford, with Their Vicinities, Embracing Every Improvement, From Actual Survey* (1848), Manchester City Council archive, <https://luna.manchester.ac.uk/luna/servlet/s/opi239>. Accessed 7 December 2022.
82. Engels, pp. 88–9.
83. Christoph Lindner, *Fictions of Commodity Culture: From the Victorian to the Postmodern* (Aldershot: Ashgate, 2003), p. 21.
84. See, for example, *Arcades*, pp. 101–19.
85. *Arcades*, p. 84.
86. John Forster, *The Life of Charles Dickens* (Oxford: Benediction Classics, 2011 [1872–4]), p. 12.
87. Bachelard, p. 19.
88. 'Paris, Capital of the Nineteenth Century' [1939], in *Arcades*, pp. 14–26 (p. 20).
89. Engels, p. 89.
90. See Denis Hollier, *Against Architecture: The Writings of Georges Bataille*, trans. by Betsy Wing (Cambridge, MA: MIT Press, 1989), pp. 3–6.
91. Karl Marx, *Der historische Materialismus*, ed. by Siegfried Landshut and Jacob Peter Mayer (Leipzig: Kröner, 1932), vol. 1, p. 325, quoted in *Arcades*, pp. 223–4. On this passage, see also Vidler, p. 5.
92. Bachelard, p. 32.

Chapter 2

The Unstable City: Rivers, Railways and Houses in *Dombey and Son* and *Our Mutual Friend*

In chapter 5 of *Dombey and Son*, Paul Dombey is christened in a 'chill and earthy' (DS 5.61) church that seems to anticipate his own untimely demise. Dickens quotes Hamlet's words to Polonius, 'into my grave?' (DS 5.61; *Hamlet* II.ii), in relation to it. In the manuscript version of the novel an addition appears, in John Forster's hand, describing the font as a 'rigid marble basin which seemed to have been playing a churchyard game at cup and ball with its matter-of-fact pedestal, and to have been just at that moment caught on the top of it'.[1] This note, whose status is uncertain, is not included in most editions of the novel from the original 1846 serialisation onwards.[2] Yet it usefully points to a peculiarity of architecture in Dickens, that no matter how 'rigid' or 'matter-of-fact' it seems, it is nearly always infused with movement, even playfulness. The solid, practical font is imagined as being on the verge of instability, poised at the momentary midpoint of a repeated movement up and down, part of a child's game; a *fort-da* movement perhaps.[3] This instability extends to the text itself, since it is unclear to what extent the description properly belongs to the novel, or to Dickens.

I take this paratextual addition as exemplifying the way architecture in Dickens is always infiltrated by its opposite, by anti-architecture.[4] It is my argument in this chapter that we should read Dickens as expressing a new understanding of architecture that is dynamic, based on movement rather than stability, and therefore appropriate to the modern city. Focusing on *Dombey and Son* and *Our Mutual Friend*, I read the railway and the river as forms of anti-architecture which both connect and divide urban space, and in doing so undo the conventional role of architecture as securing and stabilising the environments we inhabit. This anti-architectural tendency extends to the uncanny domestic houses of these two novels, so that what architecture does, and is, and its role within literature, are all called into question.

I read railway and river as lines of connectivity, or conduits, which have the capacity to break apart as well as connect city space, fracturing or transforming old forms of urbanism even as they create new ones. While the first is symbolic of nineteenth-century modernity, the second seems comparatively archaic, even primordial; yet each expresses a way of imagining the modern city that is typical of Dickens. The railway encompasses the creative destruction of the modern city, its capacity to produce new forms of technologised vision amidst scenes of spectacular ruination. It is associated both with what is unseeable, including death, and with transparency, by opening up the landscape to view. The river, meanwhile, encompasses a form of subjectivity in which the city-dweller is confronted by an urban landscape that seems to determine their identity, threatening to undo Enlightenment concepts of the rational, discrete individual. This disruptive capacity of the river takes shape in a play of surface which both resists comprehension and demands to be read.

In reading railway and river together, and tracing their relationship with domestic architecture, specifically the Dombey family home in *Dombey and Son* and the house of the Hexams in *Our Mutual Friend*, this chapter seeks to demonstrate that Dickens's houses parallel the shifting and unreliable behaviour of railway and river, including their play of visibility and invisibility. My readings also propose that in Dickens's sensorium modernity is not symbolised simply by the construction of new buildings or conduits – such as the railway – but by their dialectical connection with old ones – such as the river. Dickens thus produces conceptually a state which Baron Haussmann produced physically on the streets of Paris, as described by Fritz Stahl, quoted in the *Arcades Project*: 'the old city and the new are not left standing opposite each other, as is the case everywhere else, but are drawn together into one'.[5] Railway, river and uncanny houses, like Haussmann's boulevards, cut through time as well as space, bringing together the old city and the new. They collapse past, present and future, turning the city into a spatio-temporal palimpsest where ancient and modern cross over one another, interrupting and intervening in the other's realities. This leads to an urban landscape which is at once exhilarating and radically dislocating.

Railways, Ruins and the Architectural Unconscious

Much criticism concerning *Dombey and Son* has explored the function and symbolic value of the railway, which initially appears in two passages (in chapters 6 and 15) describing the changes in 'Staggs's Gardens', where the London and Birmingham Railway (L&BR) is being constructed.[6] The L&BR existed from 1833–46, before being taken over by the London and North Western Railway (L&NWR). The line it established, which operated out of Euston Station in Camden Town from 1837, now forms part of the West Coast Main Line. The railway features at two other significant points: in chapter 20, when Dombey travels from London to Leamington, and in chapter 55, when Mr Carker is destroyed by a train. It is also relevant to the 'good spirit' passage in chapter 47, which develops questions of visibility and architectural penetration that the railway has raised. In all these cases the railway destabilises and breaks apart city space, yet also reframes it in a new way. In exploring this process, I aim to show that although the railway is accompanied by fragmentation and ruin, its primary role is to reveal the ruin which already exists within the city. As part of this reading, I suggest that the railway illustrates the proposition, adapted from Sigfried Giedion, that engineering is the architectural unconscious of the nineteenth century.

One critic who discusses the railway is Kathleen Tillotson, for whom it is a 'ruthless' force associated with 'the fascination of the new as well as the horror of the strange'; it is 'destructive, ruthless, an "impetuous monster"', providing 'no suggestion of hope, of social progress'.[7] For Steven Marcus, by contrast, the railway is part of the novel's concern with change, as 'the great symbol of social transformation' which 'destroyed traditional notions of space and time'.[8] Frenk and Steveker take it as paradigmatic of Dickens's interest in change of all kinds – social, political, visual and linguistic.[9] Movement and change are also central for Raymond Williams, who sees the railway as 'the exciting and the threatening consequence of a new mobility', making it symptomatic of the modern city.[10] Jeremy Tambling notes the railway's association with modernity too, arguing that it helps shape a Foucauldian society which 'is becoming Panoptical, regulated, even by accurate clock-time'. For Tambling this does not imply negativity, but rather indicates that the railway's characteristic power is 'monstration', or making visible.[11] Trey Philpotts has explored in detail the ambiguity of Dickens's attitude to the railway, which was more complex than Ruskin's claim that he was 'a leader of the steam-whistle party par excellence', arguing that railway construction brought into conflict two of Dickens's 'most cherished ideas': concern for the dispossession of the poor, and faith in civic and technological improvement.[12]

For Stephen Kern, the railway's transformation of space and time is symptomatic of 1880–1918, when 'the thrust of the age was to affirm the reality of private time against that of a single public time and to define its nature as heterogeneous, fluid, and reversible'.[13] If the railway represents this transformation, it is part of what Benjamin calls the 'fore-history' of this later period. The railway, in this case, it is not fully comprehensible at the moment of its emergence. As Benjamin puts it, within a historical object,

> All the forces and interests of history enter on a reduced scale. It is owing to this monadological structure that the historical object finds represented in its interior its own fore-history and after-history. (Thus, for example, the fore-history of Baudelaire, as educed by current scholarship, resides in allegory; his after-history, in Jugendstil.)[14]

According to Benjamin, the interior and exterior of the historical object cannot be separated; its past and future exist within it in microcosm, forming what Benjamin calls a 'monad'. If the railway is a historical object in this sense, it should not be read as part of a historical continuum, but as an image which 'attain[s] to legibility only at a particular time'.[15] It must be approached like the poet Charles Baudelaire in Benjamin's example, who can only be understood if he is placed alongside – or 'constellated with' – seventeenth-century allegory and late nineteenth-century Jugendstil, both of which he nonetheless already contains within himself. The emergent railway, likewise, will only become legible when what precedes and follows it (such as the stagecoach, which is present in Carker's journey in chapter 55, and the world of modern travel, present in chapter 15) are recognised as parts of its own interior structure.

While most critics have found the railway to be an important part of the text, Ian Carter observes that '*Dombey* contains only four brief railway passages', which, despite their 'complex structure of feeling', are not sufficient to make it 'a railway novel'.[16] This should remind us that, as with any aspect of the novel, the railway should not be given sole analytical precedence, but related to the other spaces and structures which surround it. One way to do so is to view it as a component of the city's architecture. Yet if, as Denis Hollier suggests, 'society entrusts its desire to endure to architecture', the railway is a form of architecture that undoes any such permanence, as the ruinous transformation of Staggs's Gardens in chapter 6 indicates:

> Everywhere were bridges that led nowhere; thoroughfares that were wholly impassable; Babel towers of chimneys, wanting half their height; temporary wooden houses and enclosures, in the most unlikely situations; carcases of ragged tenements, and fragments of unfinished walls and arches, and piles of scaffolding, and wildernesses of bricks, and giant forms of cranes, and tripods straddling above nothing. There were a hundred thousand shapes and substances of incompleteness, wildly mingled out of their places, upside down, burrowing in the earth, aspiring in the air, mouldering in the water, and unintelligible as any dream. (DS 6.68)[17]

This scene of confusion shows that the construction of the railway is also its deconstruction, in Derrida's sense, referring to the tower of Babel, of 'an unfinished edifice whose half-completed structures are visible, letting one guess at the scaffolding behind them'.[18] This captures one of the key characteristics of the ruin: that it is an inverse image of construction which reveals a building's 'scaffolding', and hence its earliest beginnings. Philippe Hamon takes this temporal confusion in the opposite direction, finding that ruins can have a prophetic quality, so that 'the Romantic ruin somehow anticipated modern architecture', since both expose internal structure.[19] More generally, the ruin always refers to the future as well as the past because it shows what every building will one day become. This concept is captured in Gustave Doré's 1872 engraving of Thomas Macaulay's New Zealander, an imagined future visitor to the ruins of London first described in a review of 1840 (Figure 2.1). Blanchard Jerrold, co-author with Doré of *London: A Pilgrimage*, accompanies this image with a quotation from Edgar Allen Poe's 1845 poem 'To Helen', suggesting that the New Zealander contemplates something matching 'The glory that was Greece – / The grandeur that was Rome', drawing on readers' presumed familiarity with classical ruined landscapes by painters such as Giovanni Paolo Panini (1691–1765).[20] For Benjamin, the nineteenth-century city, especially Paris, evoked the spectre of ancient Greece, as in a passage I have already quoted: 'One knew of places in ancient Greece where the way led down into the underworld. Our waking existence likewise is a land which, at certain hidden points, leads down into the underworld.' He later suggests that the Parisian arcades recall the 'temple of Aesculapius', the Greek god of medicine and healing.[21]

The Unstable City 73

Figure 2.1 *The New Zealander* (1872), Gustave Doré. Yale Center for British Art.

The Staggs's Gardens passage makes direct reference to ancient ruins with the phrase 'Babel towers', suggesting that progress here is also the return to a primeval or biblical past. Later, in chapter 20, Dombey's train journey again demonstrates that the railway can produce a movement towards past as well as future when entering a tunnel is described as 'plunging down into the earth' (DS 20.298), as if towards the underworld, at which point, 'amidst the darkness and whirlwind the motion seems reversed, and to tend furiously backward' (DS 20.298). As Gillian Piggott notes, such spatio-temporal disorientation is also found in 'A Flight', an 1851 *Household Words* railway story which asks, 'why it is that when I shut my eyes in a tunnel I begin to feel as if I were going at an Express pace the other way?'[22] For Piggott, this is part of 'Dickens's urban sublime', an aesthetic mode which registers what Benjamin calls *Erlebnis* (experience that is momentary or ephemeral, and hence typical of modernity), as opposed to *Erfahrung* (experience as continuous and unified).[23] Moreover, as Alf Steebert points out, steam and rail in this story do not follow the contours of the land, but cut through them, as the railway construction cuts through Staggs's Gardens, 'in effect virtualizing the landscape outside the railway carriage'.[24] The outside is virtualised because it does not impinge on the sensations of the passenger other than visually, becoming a series of paratactic impressions, like the 'wildly mingled' shapes of Staggs's Gardens, rather than a continuum of experience, as in this passage: 'A double-barrelled Station! Now a wood, now a bridge, now a landscape, now a cutting, now a – Bang! a single-barrelled Station – there was a cricket-match somewhere with two white tents, and then four flying cows, then turnips.'[25] The landscape is broken into its constituent parts, no longer existing as a continuous whole.

In being as 'unintelligible as any dream', Staggs's Gardens is associated with the dreamlike stasis of the house where Florence Dombey dwells as a fairy-tale princess in chapter 23, which becomes more 'solitary and deserted' (DS 23.337) than any 'magic dwelling-place in magic story' (DS 23.337). Despite the activity in Staggs's Gardens, it exists in a suspended state, with bridges hanging in the air, leading nowhere. The 'giant forms of cranes' which fill the area recall the region surrounding Todgers's guest house in *Martin Chuzzlewit* (1844), where 'vast bags and packs of goods, upward or downward bound, were for ever dangling between heaven and earth from lofty cranes'.[26] These cranes combine mobility and immobility, their goods 'bound' towards ground or sky, yet seeming 'for ever dangling', neither up nor down. For Freud, such doubleness is characteristic of dreams, which have undergone 'condensation', meaning that a 'very great number of associations' can be produced for 'each individual element of the content of a dream'.[27] These associations are hard to untangle, since dreams 'show a particular preference for combining contraries into a unity or for representing them as one and the same thing'.[28] Perhaps this is the source of the railway construction's dreamlike unintelligibility: in seeking to condense together 'contraries' such as suspension and movement it creates a contradictory state that resists interpretation. This clarifies the monadic status of the railway in Benjamin's sense, since its contradictory constituents point towards both the past (Babel and the classical underworld) and the future (floating glass and iron architecture, like the department store or the Crystal Palace of 1851). This explains why the local neighbourhood is 'shy to own the Railroad' (DS 6.68): because it is unable to read the signs of its own future in the chaos that has descended upon it.

Benjamin directly links dreams and industrial construction in 'Paris, the Capital of the Nineteenth Century', his 1935 *exposé* to the *Arcades*. After discussing the period's use of iron, he introduces a line from Michelet: 'each epoch dreams the one to follow'.[29] The confusion of Staggs's Gardens is such a dream of a new epoch, which only emerges fully in chapter 15 when the area around Euston has become a 'Railway world' (DS 15.233), complete with 'railway hotels, coffee-houses, lodging-houses, boarding-houses; railway plans, maps, views, wrappers, bottles, sandwich-boxes, and time tables' (DS 15.233). Benjamin draws on Sigfried Giedion's argument that all genuinely new developments in nineteenth-century architecture occurred not in official architecture, like the Royal Exchange or East India House, both of which are near Mr Dombey's offices (DS 6.36), but in 'humbler structures' motivated by practical purposes, where 'industry unconsciously creates new powers of expression and new possibilities of experience'.[30] This split is evident in the period's new division between architects (who focus on artistic facades) and engineers (who focus on interior structure), formalised by the founding of the Royal Institute of British Architects in 1834.[31] Industrial construction is thus for Giedion 'the subconscious of architecture', or, to put it in psychoanalytic terminology, the architectural unconscious.'[32]

In *Dombey and Son*, the railway is a sign of this architectural unconscious. It brings death and ruin, which are elsewhere repressed (albeit not always successfully), to the surface. In doing so, it shares something with the river in *Our Mutual Friend*, discussed below. Michael Klotz suggests that the Victorian railway produces a 'tension between the way property functions outside and within the home', its movement of goods opposing the 'perception of the Victorian home as a safe and private space': a perception that ultimately relies on the goods which the railways have moved.[33] More than just bringing out the mobility inherent within domestic goods as Klotz argues, however, the train in Dickens also brings out the death and ruin which the domestic interior seeks to cover over. This is evident in Mr Dombey's train journey in chapter 20, where the train appears as 'the triumphant monster, Death' (DS 20.298), reflecting Dombey's growing resentment and thoughts of mortality following the death of his son, Paul. This phrase, repeated several times with minor variations, is associated with the train's unstoppable movement as it cuts through, and cuts open, the landscape:

> Away, and still away, onward and onward ever: glimpses of cottage-homes, of houses, mansions, rich estates, of husbandry and handicraft, of people, of old roads and paths that look deserted, small, and insignificant as they are left behind. (DS 20.298)

As in 'A Flight', the train gives only fragmentary 'glimpses' of its surroundings, yet these glimpses connect disparate parts of society, bringing together 'cottage-homes' and 'mansions'. The train's movement stitches together town and countryside, overcoming what Raymond Williams calls the

> ideological separation between the processes of rural exploitation, which have been, in effect, dissolved into landscape, and the register of that exploitation, in the law courts, the money markets, the political power and the conspicuous expenditure of the city.[34]

Yet the train also carries its passengers through the countryside, allowing the suppression of this link between exploitation and capital once again. This new repression is aided by the anaesthetising qualities of the train's soft furnishings; Klotz notes that railway carriages, particularly in first class, replicated bourgeois homes, as in Augustus Egg's painting *The Travelling Companions* (1862), where two middle-class women sit in a comfortable train carriage, one reading a novel while the other sleeps.[35] Neither looks out at the landscape, from which they are both separated and protected.

In chapter 20 of *Dombey and Son*, Dombey does look out of the window, but misinterprets what he sees. The train has entered an area of industrial poverty, which must be in the Midlands, since the train is for Leamington Spa:

> There are dark pools of water, muddy lanes, and miserable habitations far below. There are jagged walls and falling houses close at hand, and through the battered roofs and broken windows, wretched rooms are seen, where want and fever hide themselves in many wretched shapes, while smoke, and crowded gables, and distorted chimneys, and deformity of brick and mortar penning up deformity of mind and body, choke the murky distance. (DS 20.299)

The train breaks through architecture here, revealing the death and lack within. But this revelation is met by the refusal or inability of Dombey, a representative of the dominant classes, to confront the 'want' on which his own edifice of wealth is built: 'As Mr. Dombey looks out of his carriage window, it is never in his thoughts that the monster who has brought him there has let the light of day in upon these things: not made or caused them' (DS 20.299). All Dombey sees is a 'ruinous and dreary' (DS 20.299) scene, rendering the view little more than an externalisation of his own state of mind. He has no conception of space as a social product, since for him it exists purely to serve the firm, becoming an index of the firm's troubles, and his own. He comprehends the ruin outside as a monstrous, but virtual, excess that confronts him, rather than part of a system in which he is financially and morally invested. So pervasive is this pattern of thought that the narrator repeats Dombey's error, distinguishing the railway from the social system which has 'made or caused' this poverty, and so failing to acknowledge that, as a product of capitalist speculation, the train too is implicated in the ruin it reveals.

As Klotz observes, this scene puts Dombey in the position represented in 'Over London by Rail', another engraving by Gustave Doré (Figure 2.2).[36] In this well-known image, a train passes over a viaduct in the background, while a long row of terraced houses and yards fills the rest of the scene. The perspective from the train provides a panoptical view, yet this remains limited, since the passengers have only an instant to take in the scene as the train speeds past, and are unable to see inside the buildings. The train points the way towards total visibility and connectivity, but does not bring it about. As critics have noted, though, Dombey's train journey foreshadows chapter 47, where total visibility does become possible, at least within the pages of the novel. Here, the narrator ponders 'what Nature is, and how men work to change her, and whether, in the enforced distortions so produced, it is not natural to be unnatural' (DS 47.683). This leads to a desire to reveal the 'moral pestilence' (DS 47.684) of the city:

> Oh for a good spirit who would take the house-tops off, with a more potent and benignant hand than the lame demon in the tale [Asmodeus], and show a Christian people what dark shapes issue from amidst their homes, to swell the retinue of the Destroying Angel as he moves forth among them! For only one night's view of the pale phantoms rising from the scenes of our too-long neglect; and from the thick and sullen air where Vice and Fever propagate together, raining the tremendous social retributions which are ever pouring down, and ever coming thicker!

Bright and blest the morning that should rise on such a night: for men, delayed no more by stumbling-blocks of their own making, which are but specks of dust upon the path between them and eternity, would then apply themselves, like creatures of one common origin, owing one duty to the Father of one family, and tending to one common end, to make the world a better place! (DS 47.685)

As Raymond Williams observes, the 'potent and benignant hand' is 'the hand of the novelist; it is Dickens seeing himself'.[37] In this case, Dickens wishes not only to reveal the suffering of the poor, but to emphasise their connection with his implicitly middle-class readership. As Klotz, Mancini and Tambling all point out, this is also the perspective of the train.[38] If the good spirit is both novelist and train, the passage evokes two spatial modes simultaneously: the 'mental space' where the novelist constructs his world, and the 'physical space' of a train moving through the landscape, both of which work to make the invisible visible. This is an act which breaks through the apparent autonomy of separate social spheres, destabilising society, but with the ultimate aim of producing greater social unity.

Figure 2.2 *Over London by Rail* (1872), Gustave Doré. Yale Center for British Art.

The final appearance of the train follows Dombey's ex-manager Mr Carker's flight from Dijon, during which Carker experiences 'a fevered vision of things past and present all confounded together; of his life and journey blended into one' (DS 55.817). Again the train is linked to temporal confusion, this time even before it has appeared. Carker first travels by carriage, but just as Dombey carried 'monotony with him, through the rushing landscape' (DS 20.297) in chapter 20, so Carker has 'a vision of change upon change, and still the same monotony of bells and wheels, and horses' feet, and no rest' (DS 55.817). As Isobel Armstrong observes, space is divided up in this journey, but 'the more the spatial division, the more monotonous and undifferentiated the journey seems to Carker'.[39] For Armstrong, this is 'peculiarly modern space, empty meaningless space', a corollary to Benjamin's concept of empty homogeneous time.[40] This combination of monotony and change recalls Staggs's Gardens, which was simultaneously frozen and in motion in chapter 6. For Carker, the confusion of time and space is accompanied by the 'flight of Death' (DS 55.811), leading Tambling to suggest that 'repetition precedes the event [of Carker's death], which it brings on'.[41] Moreover, the railway turns Carker's own planned revenge against him: the 'red eyes' (DS 55.823) of the monstrous train that bears him down as he flees from Dombey recall the 'red eye' of the monster which sits at the heart of the firm in chapter 13 (DS 13.182), and which represents Carker. But whereas that eye was submerged and mysterious, these eyes openly announce the coming of ruin. The train has turned the House of Dombey inside out, bringing the death which was hidden at its centre to the fore.

If Carker, who betrayed and undermined Dombey's firm and family before leaving for France, represents death, lack and ruin within the house, then his obliteration by the train makes this visible. When he is smashed into 'mutilated fragments' (DS 55.823), Carker is 'opened up' in a violent parallel to the train's opening up of architecture during Dombey's journey. Carker's death takes place in front of Dombey, who is confronted with the disturbing image of 'something covered, that lay heavy and still, upon a board' (DS 55.823). This covering recalls the journals used as wrappings after the death of Fanny, Dombey's first wife, which displayed 'fragmentary accounts of deaths and dreadful murders' (DS 3.24). It indicates how architecture, especially railway architecture, operates in this text: seeking to contain or conceal death, but also bringing it to the surface. Though Dombey may not realise it, the covered corpse of Carker represents the internal structure of both his family and his business, which the train, with the force of the architectural unconscious, has thrust into the open.

The River, the Clue and the Gaze

It has long been recognised that *Our Mutual Friend* is 'primarily about change, and not only change as transition, but change as transformation as well', but J. Hillis Miller argues that Dickens's Thames is more radical than this; it confounds 'the rationalities of cognitive mapping', serving as a 'realm of otherness' or 'underwater locus of metamorphosis' which is resolutely non-topographical.[42] Tambling develops a similar idea, arguing that the river evokes the Derridean concept of 'life death', a 'reminder that every concept contains its other', making it a profoundly dialectical object, and a form of the Freudian unconscious, which, like dreams, and, I have argued, Dickens's railway, cannot express 'the alternative "either-or" [. . .] in any way whatever'.[43] My reading here builds on such interpretations, citing Freud and Lacan to argue that the river is both a highly uncanny urban conduit and a structure with two sides, one of which is unseeable and unrepresentable, and the other a site of signification that simultaneously demands and resists interpretation. As with the railway, I focus on how Dickens deploys visuality as an index to reading the river, especially in the novel's opening scene, which establishes the role the river will play throughout.

At the start of chapter 1, Gaffer Hexam, a boatman and scavenger, is out on the Thames at night with his daughter Lizzie, looking for something in the river. The text tells us that 'there was no clue what he looked for, but he looked for something, with a most intent and searching gaze' (OMF 1.1.1). Hexam's gaze, directed towards the river, has no defined object, though it will become clear he is looking for human bodies. Initially, however, the gaze gives 'no clue' about its purpose, yet is itself in search of a clue, in the form of disturbances in the water: 'Wheresoever the strong tide met with an impediment, [Hexam's] gaze paused for an instant' (OMF 1.1.2). This gaze that searches for clues while itself remaining inscrutable replicates the gaze of the detective, like the inspector who appears in chapter 3 and spends the night looking for Hexam in chapter 13, or of the criminal, which Hexam is later accused of being by Rogue Riderhood (OMF 1.12.150). It also suggests the gaze of the physiognomist, seeking to draw out a human logic from the blankness of the river, or the architect, seeking to impose a structural order onto the dark and indeterminate river. It is a gaze that hopes to uncover what is concealed, or bring to light what should have been left submerged, this being one of Freud's definitions of the uncanny, following Schelling.[44]

This opening echoes across the novel, the first instance where the visual field is defined by obscurity rather than clarity, and where a non-human structure serves as an index for the human. Another example is Mr Venus's shop, where 'nothing is resolvable into anything distinct, save the candle itself [. . .] and two preserved frogs' (OMF 1.7.77), and where Silas Wegg seeks to buy back his missing leg bone. In both cases something secret, and deathly, seems to be hidden in the city. As the opening continues, something is drawn out of the river: money, apparently taken from the pockets of a dead man, making Lizzie shiver and turn 'deadly faint' (OMF 1.1.3). For Lizzie, this money should not have returned to the surface. It recalls the money used to pay Charon, the ferryman of Hades in Greek mythology, from whom Gaffer symbolically steals, and whose character he partly takes on.

For Freud, the feeling of untimely re-emergence is typical of the uncanny. He associates this with the return of the repressed, such that 'an uncanny experience occurs either when infantile complexes which have been repressed are once more revived by some impression, or when primitive beliefs which have been surmounted seem once more to be confirmed'.[45] An archetypal example is the feeling that emerges in relation to 'death and dead bodies, to the return of the dead, and to spirits and ghosts'.[46] To the extent that *Our Mutual Friend* is concerned with the return of the dead, then, it is a novel about the place of the uncanny and the archaic in modern life. Patricia McKee reads such concerns in the opening passage by aligning Gaffer and Lizzie with Benjamin's figure of the ragpicker, so that the two 'work among remnants of the dreamscape of a capitalist culture', placing the dominant visual form of the panoramic spectacle in question and instead producing a 'colportage effect', in which fragments, refuse, residues and stains are brought to light not as a unified narrative, but as 'leftovers from a past that now appears incomplete and interrupted'.[47]

Another way to put this is that the river plays the role of the unconscious, if this is understood as the site of social and historical as well as individual repression. This comes out most clearly in a passage from which I have already quoted:

> Wheresoever the strong tide met with an impediment, his gaze paused for an instant. At every mooring-chain and rope, at every stationary boat or barge that split the current into a broad-arrowhead, at the offsets from the piers of Southwark Bridge, at the paddles of the river steamboats as they beat the filthy water, at the floating logs of timber lashed together lying off certain wharves, his shining eyes darted a hungry look. (OMF 1.1.2)

Hexam searches the river not for a body, but for the trace of a body, in the form of an 'impediment', which functions as a fracture or gap in the surface of the river. He looks for places where boats 'split the current' as evidence of what lies beneath. Lacan's Seminar XI is helpful here. Lacan insists on the distinction between the Romantic unconscious – 'the locus of the divinities of night' – and the Freudian one, which is 'at all points homologous with what occurs at the level of the subject'.[48] He draws attentions to what allows Freud to identify the unconscious as unconscious:

> In the dream, in parapraxis, in the flash of wit – what is it that strikes one first? It is the sense of impediment [*empêchement*] to be found in all of them.
> Impediment, failure, split. In a spoken or written sentence, something stumbles. Freud is attracted by these phenomena, and it is there that he seeks the unconscious.[49]

The *empêchement* or impediment is the sign which reveals the unconscious, though 'reveals' is perhaps the wrong word here, since the impediment can operate only as a clue, not as something which would lift the lid on the contents of the unconscious. It points towards, but does not undo, repression. Similarly, for Hexam, the impediment or split in the river only indicates the presence of the body, which takes on the role of repressed material, its return generating an uncanny effect.

The dead body is what should remain concealed (the uncanny), but also what the gazing subject desires, since it is from the bodies that Hexam gets his livelihood. Lizzie, however, views the river differently:

> [Hexam:] 'It's my belief you hate the sight of the very river.'
> 'I – I do not like it, father.'
> 'As if it wasn't your living! As if it wasn't meat and drink to you!' (OMF 1.1.3)[50]

While Lizzie hates the sight of the river, for her father it is the site (and sight) of desire. It conceals, but also bears witness to, the object for which Hexam's 'shining eyes darted a hungry look': the dead body, which can no longer feel or return desire. The closest Hexam can come to consummation is to plunge his arms into the water of the river – presumably into the pockets of a drowned body – and the actions he performs on the money he retrieves: 'He chinked it once, and he blew upon it once, and he spat upon it once [. . .] before he put it in his pocket' (OMF 1.1.3).

The play of vision goes further though. It is not only between Gaffer Hexam and the river, or Lizzie and the river, but between Lizzie and Hexam. While Gaffer observes the river, Lizzie observes him: 'She watched his face as earnestly as he watched the river. But, in the intensity of her look there was a touch of dread or horror' (OMF 1.1.1). There are at least two kinds of clue, then: the surface of the river and the surface of the face. Lizzie reacts to the slightest alteration in her father's face, as when he suddenly steers towards the Surrey shore, and 'always watching his face, the girl instantly answered to the action in her sculling' (OMF 1.1.2). Lizzie's response to the river is mediated and determined through her father; it is not so much the river she hates as her father's attitude towards it. Gaffer, meanwhile, reads Lizzie's facial reactions: when she shivers upon seeing a stain in the boat, he asks 'what ails you?', being 'immediately aware of it, though so intent on the advancing waters' (OMF 1.1.2). Like fear of the uncanny for Freud, Lizzie's dislike is not rational: 'What hurt can it do you?' Hexam asks, Lizzie replying, 'None, none. But I cannot bear it' (OMF 1.1.3). The river is harmless, and Lizzie knows it is harmless (though there is irony here, as it will later kill Rogue Riderhood and Bradley Headstone), but it is nonetheless intolerable. Her repetition of 'none' effectively carries a double meaning, like the word *Heimlich* itself, or the language of dreams, forming a kind of double negative which means both no and yes. More generally, the opposing attitudes of Lizzie and Hexam here represent the two sides of the uncanny, and of the subject's relationship to repressed material; for Hexam, the river is *Heimlich*, familiar and desirable, whereas for Lizzie it is *Unheimlich*, repulsive and disturbing, though only through her father's reaction – through the *Heimlich*. In this sense, the river produces a 'profound attraction of repulsion', as St Giles's did for Dickens.[51] Here, though, these contrasting affective states are split between two different figures, who nonetheless remain intimately bound together by family ties.

After the body is recovered from the water, it might seem that the secret of the river is recovered, that its uncanny state has been defused by knowability. Yet the positions of Hexam and Lizzie remain unreconciled, so that still neither attitude to the river can be accepted as definitive. Lizzie refuses to sit next to the body (OMF 1.1.3), while Gaffer seems to foreclose on the possibility of it being anything other than a source of money. The final sentence of the chapter registers this continuing duality by commenting on the corpse, now towed behind the boat: 'A neophyte might have fancied that the ripples passing over it were dreadfully like faint changes of expression on a sightless face; but Gaffer was no neophyte and had no fancies' (OMF 1.1.5). Though Gaffer rejects the body's signifying potential, for the narrator, and presumably Lizzie, it continues to generate ambiguous signs. Except that now face and river have combined into a single, indecipherable clue, as the corpse seems to turn its own 'sightless' gaze onto the living, through the ripples of the Thames.

Lizzie's sense of the river as intolerable is extended to the poverty-stricken masses who live along its banks. As becomes clear during Mortimer Lightwood and Eugene Wrayburn's journey across London to see John Harmon's body in chapter 3, the poor threaten the 'respectable' city, by seeming at once living and dead, human and inhuman, and thus potentially diseased and contagious:

> The wheels rolled on, and rolled down by the Monument and by the Tower, and by the Docks; down by Ratcliffe, and by Rotherhithe; down by where the accumulated scum of humanity seemed to be washed from higher ground, like so much moral sewage, and to be pausing until its own weight forced it over the bank and sunk it in the river. In and out among vessels that seemed to have got ashore, and houses that seemed to have got afloat – among bowsprits staring into windows, and windows staring into ships – the wheels rolled on, until they stopped at a dark corner, river-washed and otherwise not washed at all, where the boy alighted and opened the door. (OMF 1.3.20–1)

The people of Limehouse Hole are 'moral sewage', a term which cuts two ways: they are both a source of moral contagion, and a product of the social morality of the affluent (and effluent) middle classes. Moral sewage comes from the social body, but might also return to infect it. This passage harks back to the 'good spirit' passage of *Dombey and Son*, where the term 'moral pestilence' (DS 47.684) is used, though the metaphor there is of gases and vapours rather than water, making it more obviously miasmic. The sentiment, though, remains the same: the middle classes have cut themselves off from the poor, but remain tied to them by the conduits that run through Dickens's city.

Mortimer and Wrayburn's journey cuts across London from West to East, starting at the Veneerings' house in 'Stucconia' (OMF 1.10.117), usually taken to be Tyburnia in Bayswater.[52] Franco Moretti suggests that in this journey we see Dickens's 'stroke of genius', which is to 'see the city as a whole, a single system'.[53] Like

Balzac, says Moretti, Dickens finds a third way between the upper-class silver-fork and lower-class Newgate novels of the 1820s and 30s, uncovering the hidden connections between these two social orders which the earlier genres had obscured. This distinguishes Dickens from a writer such as Thackeray, who as Sen notes, wrote from the position of a political and aristocratic insider, confining his fictions to one social group.[54] Dickens, by contrast, ties the city together even as he cuts it apart, so that the same river which disrupts the unity of the modern city also becomes a conduit or line of connection between classes, even if, as in the passage above, this is often more threatening than comforting.

The Lacanian Gaze of the River

So far I have ignored something important: the gaze of the river itself. Lacan argues that vision must be understood not only 'geometrally' – consisting of straight lines which connect the object to the viewer – but also in terms of what he calls the 'point of light'.[55] Thinking geometrally is a logocentric approach associated with the realist perspective developed during the Renaissance in Western art, which puts the viewer in a position of primacy. To understand vision as vision, rather than just another form of space, says Lacan, we must instead consider the object we perceive as 'the point of irradiation, the play of light, fire, the source from which reflections pour forth'.[56]

A little story ('une petite apologue') Lacan tells to illustrate this point suggests its relevance to *Our Mutual Friend*:[57]

> One day, I was on a small boat, with a few people from a family of fishermen in a small port. At that time, [. . .] there were no trawlers. The fisherman went out in his frail craft at his own risk.[58] [A]n individual known as Petit-Jean [. . .] pointed out to me something floating on the surface of the waves. It was a small can, a sardine can. [. . .] It glittered in the sun. And Petit-Jean said to me – You see that can? Do you see it? Well, it doesn't see you!
>
> [. . .] If what Petit-Jean said to me [. . .] had any meaning, it was because in a sense it was looking at me, all the same. It was looking at me at the level of the point of light, the point at which everything that looks at me is situated.[59]

The light emanating from the can, or any other object, 'grasps me, solicits me at every moment, and makes of the landscape something other than landscape, something other than what I have called the picture'.⁶⁰ Rather than just presenting a flat image, the point of light adds depth to the visual field and decentres the subject, who is constituted by this point of light, which Lacan calls the gaze, before they see: 'What determines me, at the most profound level, in the visible, is the gaze that is outside.'⁶¹ This idea is illustrated by Holbein's painting *The Ambassadors* (1533), whose anamorphic skull is a 'singular object floating in the foreground, which is there to be looked at, in order to catch, I would almost say, *to catch in its trap*, the observer'.⁶²

Similarly, when Lizzie attentively 'eyes' Gaffer's face,

> it happened now, that a slant of light from the setting sun glanced into the bottom of the boat, and, touching a rotten stain there which bore some resemblance to the outline of a muffled human form, coloured it as though with diluted blood. This caught the girl's eye, and she shivered. (OMF 1.1.2)

This 'slant of light', like Holbein's slanting skull, undoes geometral perspective. The 'stain' it highlights catches Lizzie's eye, functioning as a Lacanian gaze in putting the source of vision outside the self, as the verb 'glanced' also subtly does. The stain, which McKee reads as a Benjaminian dialectical image, implies the presence of something which cannot be directly seen, perhaps bodies in the river, since it recalls a 'human form', though this remains uncertain as it is 'muffled', only 'resembling' an 'outline'.⁶³ For Lacan, the 'stain' is identified with the gaze, eluding the Cartesian subject who believes themselves in control of vision:

> the function of the stain and of the gaze is both that which governs the gaze most secretly and that which always escapes from the grasp of that form of vision what is satisfied with itself in imagining itself as consciousness.⁶⁴

Lacan's use of the term 'floating' (*flottant*) to describe both skull and sardine can also indicates that vision escapes fixity and control, as does the surface of the Thames.

The stain has aspects of Benjamin's 'optical unconscious', which inheres undetected in the visual field, as revealed by photography and cinema:

> Whereas it is a commonplace that, for example, we have some idea what is involved in the act of walking (if only in general terms), we have no

idea at all what takes place during the split second when a person actually takes a step. [. . .] This is where the camera comes into play, with all its resources for swooping and rising, disrupting and isolating, stretching or compressing a sequence, enlarging or reducing a subject.[65]

The slant of light, like a focusing camera, brings the stain into view for Lizzie in a new way, revealing something unknown within the visual field, which was nonetheless there the whole time. This combination of unseen and seen, familiar and unfamiliar, suggests there is an uncanniness to the optical unconscious. As the authors of *Benjamin's Arcades: An UnGuided Tour* observe, this unconscious differs from Freud's:

> For Benjamin, the unconscious is simply a place which 'exists' and can be revealed or can reveal hitherto unknown things, a far cry from Freud's unconscious which is accessible only through its traces. Benjamin operates within a visual model in which there is an order of the seen or not-seen, an order simply brought to light by virtue of photography.[66]

For Freud, as for Lacan, the visual can only indicate the presence of the unconscious, not reveal it. The optical unconscious, by contrast, is revealed by the gaze of the camera, though it also promotes distraction, where conscious knowledge is replaced by 'habits', which 'even the distracted person can form'.[67] Photography does not simply bring the unseen to light, it actively reshapes perception; slow motion, for instance, in disclosing aspects of movement that 'do not appear as the retarding of natural movements but have a curious gliding, floating character of their own', multiplies rather than reduces the unknown.[68] Despite the usefulness of Benjamin's concept, Lacan's reorientation of the gaze onto the landscape as a form of stain remains, I would suggest, most productive for reading Dickens here, through the emphasis it places on the active insistence of the unconscious within the field of vision.

Lacan's concept of the stain is more complex than indicated so far. It is also the place of the subject, since 'if I am anything in the picture [produced by the point of light], it is always in the form of the screen, which I earlier called the stain, the spot'.[69] The subject attempts to coincide with the gaze, and to find a place in the 'picture' (both of which are outside), by means of 'mimicry': 'It is not a question of harmonizing with the background but, against a mottled background, of becoming mottled.'[70] Following this logic, the 'muffled human form' whose presence Lizzie infers is also her perception of herself; this is the self as stain, determined by something which exceeds us, and which we cannot comprehend: the unconscious, or the Other, or the real, all of which the river evokes. As Lacan puts it: 'To imitate [. . .] is, for the subject, to be inserted in a function whose exercise grasps us.'[71] The alignment of Lizzie and the stain I am arguing for is supported by the text, since her position coincides with the bodies pulled out of the river. As Hexam tells her: 'The very fire that warmed you when you were a babby, was picked out of the river alongside the coal barges. The very basket that you slept in, the tide washed ashore' (OMF 1.1.3). Before she was conscious of herself, the river already determined Lizzie's identity, providing the means to warm and comfort her, surrounding and 'grasping' her in an instance of Lacanian imitation.

Gaffer's statement that Lizzie hates 'the sight of the very river' can thus be turned around: it is rather the river's sight of her that she hates. It has formed the role she wishes to escape, revealing that her fate is not in her own hands but externally determined. Lizzie's relationship with Eugene Wrayburn, whom she loves uncontrollably, against her will, is another instance of this determination from outside. Yet her openness to the gaze of the river is also what later allows her to identify Eugene's drowning body: 'An untrained sight would never have seen by the moonlight what she saw at the length of a few strokes astern. She saw the drowning figure rise to the surface, slightly struggle, and as if by instinct turn over on its back to float' (OMF 4.6.700). Like the camera in Benjamin's optical unconscious, Lizzie sees the minute signs normal eyes would miss, and through the apparatus of the novel this personal vision becomes collective, in a process Benjamin associates with cinema, where 'the individual perceptions of the psychotic or dreamer can be appropriated by collective perception'.[72]

The gaze from outside, Lacan argues, is also the object of desire: '*The* objet a *in the field of the visible is the gaze.*'[73] This idea becomes clearer if we recognise that the gaze emanates not just from the stain, but also from the money which Gaffer retrieves and the bodies it represents. The concept of money as gaze is evoked by Dickens in more beneficent terms in *The Old Curiosity Shop* (1841), where a workman gives Nell 'two old, battered, smoke-encrusted penny pieces', the narrator commenting: 'Who knows but they shone as brightly in the eyes of angels, as golden gifts that have been chronicled on tombs?'[74] Adorno interprets this incident, in an essay Benjamin quotes, as signifying that 'the possibility of transition and dialectical rescue was inherent in this world of things, this lost, rejected world'.⁷⁵ While Benjamin and Adorno focus on the transformative power of the commodity, this moment also hints that money itself gazes at the (be)holder, like the eyes of angels, or of death, since it suggests 'tombs'. Money, as this example indicates, always refers to something other than itself: the commodities it might purchase, or the services it might procure. In this way, as Marx shows, it expresses infinite possibilities, possessing 'the *property* of being able to buy everything and appropriate all objects'.⁷⁶ Psychoanalytically speaking, it is not money itself which is the *objet a*, but this something else, which could be anything else, to which it refers. In this way, commodity capitalism, and the detritus it leaves behind, exaggerates and disperses the gaze, generating an endless series of objects from which the gaze might emanate, each of which is capable of representing the desire of the other, and so of both fixing the subject (or affixing them, like a pinned butterfly, or like the preserved frogs in Venus's shop) and promising them redemption.

Writing of the gaze of the painter, which seems to impose itself in every painting, Lacan claims 'there was always a gaze behind'.⁷⁷ Nell's pennies represent this pre-existing gaze, as does the stain Lizzie sees. In both cases there is a sense that death is the ground of subjectivity, that the gaze behind works beyond the pleasure principle, in the sphere of the death drive. But though the gaze grasps us, it is also what is always missed, which is why it is closely associated with desire as lack. One of Lacan's formulations recognises this: 'In our relation to things [. . .] by the way of vision [. . .] something slips, passes, is transmitted, from stage to stage, and is always to some degree eluded in it – this is what we call the gaze.'⁷⁸ The gaze, then, always escapes us, acting as a secret within vision that the viewing subject desires but cannot master.

As this chapter so far has shown, by generating instability and reshaping vision the railway and the river evoke a spatial and architectural unconscious which, like the Davenports' cellar in *Mary Barton*, brings into view a deathliness that is usually socially and psychically repressed. In this way, they act as forms of anti-architecture. This anti-architectural character is not confined to railway and river, however, but also seeps into the more apparently ordinary buildings of *Dombey and Son* and *Our Mutual Friend*, including the Dombey family home and the house of the Hexams. As the following two sections will show, both are examples of architecture that is in movement, shifting in and out of visibility and use, marked by traces of a past which continues to reverberate in the present, and which at times ambiguously anticipates the future. The bourgeois house of the

Dombey family provides an instance of the concealed erupting into sudden visibility, echoing the railway, while the deprived, working-class home of the Hexam family is the setting for a complex play of visibility and invisibility, echoing the river. Yet neither of these parallels is straightforward or clear-cut, so that reading the two houses in parallel allows us to see the shared uncanniness of these domestic spaces, and to recognise them as sites of invisible architecture where the hidden, visible and transparent refuse to stay in their places.

Uncanny Houses I: The House of Dombey

As has often been recognised, in *Dombey and Son* the word 'house' means both the firm and the family home.[79] While my focus here is on the domestic house, whose architectural form 'teems with mobilities' in David Ellison's phrase, the issues of vulnerability and instability that I explore cut across both houses.[80] I begin with chapter 3, where an oft-cited passage describes the withdrawal of life from the family home, following the death of Fanny, mother of Florence and Paul:

> mysterious shapes were made of tables and chairs, heaped together in the middle of rooms and covered over with great winding sheets. Bell-handles, window-blinds, and looking-glasses, being papered up in journals, daily and weekly, obtruded fragmentary accounts of deaths and dreadful murders. Every chandelier or lustre, muffled in Holland, looked like a monstrous tear depending from the ceiling's eye. Odours, as from vaults and damp places, came out of the chimneys. The dead and buried lady was awful in a picture-frame of ghastly bandages. (DS 3.24)

The house is wrapped up, as if like Fanny it too were a corpse. Everything is obscured and incomplete, from the 'mysterious shapes' of the furniture to the 'fragmentary accounts' of death on the newspaper. Dombey's home here anticipates Mr Thornton's house in Gaskell's *North and South*, where the furniture is covered in dust-sheets to protect it from the dust produced by the city of Milton-Northern, 'bagged up with as much care as if the house was to be overwhelmed with lava, and discovered a thousand years hence' (NS 112). In both cases the safety of the domestic interior is at stake, yet Ellison notes the 'futility of Dombey's efforts to secure domestic space by wrapping it up', suggesting that the 'architectural apertures' which remain visible in Hablot Browne's accompanying illustration undermine his attempts.[81] For Wolfreys, the passage shows the house as unhomely and uncanny, dominated by traces of death which cannot be expunged, while Surridge suggests that in a house drained of female care, the real fear is that 'the dreadful crimes of the daily and weekly newspapers will [. . .] come to rest in the middle-class home'.[82]

Importantly, the house is not fully but only partially dead. The frame of Fanny's picture is obscured in 'ghastly bandages', giving the sense that she is somehow still alive, albeit in a wounded state, perhaps persisting in the odours that emerge from the chimney. The 'eye' in the ceiling seems to cry a single tear, suggesting the house too still lives, and is in mourning. Elfenbein contrasts this 'frozen' state of mourning with the 'full-scale mourning' that follows Paul's death.[83] Indeed, the house is not entirely shut up, since Dombey reserves certain apartments for his own use, including a sitting room, library and conservatory (DS 3.24). These reserved rooms maintain a form of withdrawn life, making a parallel with the subaquatic operations of the firm, whose clerks are 'as much abstracted in appearance, from the world without, as if they were assembled at the bottom of the sea' (DS 13.182). Like Dombey's clerks, the house has become monstrous, as the 'monstrous tear[s]' of the muffled chandeliers indicate, making it also like the train later in the novel, which is 'a type of the triumphant monster, Death' (DS 20.298).

It is hard to tell whether death is central here or on the borders, creating what Derrida calls a parergonal structure:

> The *parergon* inscribes something which comes as an extra, *exterior* to the proper field [of reason, philosophy etc.] [. . .] but whose transcendent exteriority comes to play, abut onto, brush against, rub, press against the limit itself and intervene in the inside only to the extent that the inside is lacking. It is lacking *in* something and it is lacking *from itself*.[84]

What is properly exterior to the home (such as death) is also a kind of internal lack. A confusion of interior and exterior, replicating the function of the train, is indeed evident in Dombey's house, which is 'as blank a house inside as outside' (DS 3.24). This confusion is at work in Fanny's picture, whose frame is wrapped in 'ghastly bandages', indicating a change in the status of the picture's subject even as the painting itself remains the same. The horror which attaches to this picture is hard to pin down: is it the sitter's death or the 'bandages' which make it 'awful'? Do the newspapers used as wrappings represent the external imposition of death, or that death is somehow inside these objects, so that they must now be hidden from view? Is the horror in the centre or on the margins? There is no clear answer, except to acknowledge that the uncertainty of this interplay of the homely and parergonal creates a house where death is both present and absent, and present in its absence, without ever being stable or locatable.

The next major transformation of the house follows the death of Paul, which destroys the fragile future potential of both home and firm. At this point the domestic house falls almost completely into ruin, with only Florence and a few servants remaining. It withdraws from the public world, like a 'magic dwelling-place in magic story' (DS 23.337), guarded by a monster that, like Carker, threatens with its gaze: a 'glowering visage, with its lips parted wickedly, that surveyed all comers from above the archway of the door' (DS 23.337). To enter the house is to be separated from the world of the city, since 'noise ceased to be, within the shadow of the roof' (DS 23.337). The 'blankness' which already typified the mansion now deepens into absence, as it has 'slowly become a dark gap in the long monotonous street' (DS 23.339). The house is here most explicitly an instance of invisible architecture, an abyss in the street. It has a peculiar parallel in the gaps that open up in the language of Mrs Skewton, Edith's mother, following her stroke later in the novel. Mrs Skewton begins to leave certain syllables unsaid, so that their presence is only implied as a haunting possibility, in phrases such as 'Sterious wretch, who's he?'; 'it's most trodinary thing'; and 'little repose – and all that sort of thing – is what I quire' (DS 40.603). A similar ghostly interplay of presence and absence is at work in Dombey's mansion, which gains a reputation as a 'haunted house' (DS 23.341), with Florence the ghost who haunts it. As if to emphasise this connection between architecture and language, the latter disappears completely from the house following Dombey's collapse, at which point the house stands 'frowning like a dark mute on the street' (DS 60.892).

The affinity between these two kinds of 'gap' is indirectly suggested by Major Bagstock, who remarks to Dombey of Mrs Skewton that 'a fair friend of ours has removed to Queer Street' (DS 40.605). This flippant comment, if taken seriously, in the way Freud took jokes seriously, as signs left by the unconscious, makes language a kind of street, and Queer Street broken or fractured language. Language then becomes spatially located outside the self, as a place to which one might remove. These dual gaps in language and architecture correspond to the double gap left in the name and structure of the firm by Paul's death, so that the domestic house registers the shifts in the firm's fortunes in the way dreams register the unconscious thoughts of the sleeper for Freud: in a condensed and displaced form.[85]

Benjamin rearticulates this relationship in Marxist terms, writing that 'the superstructure is the expression of the infrastructure. The economic conditions under which society exists are expressed in the superstructure – precisely as, with the sleeper, an overfull stomach finds not its reflection but its expression in the content of dreams'.[86] The house, in its 'sleeping' or 'enchanted' state, expresses the vicissitudes of the firm in a partial and ambiguous way, without directly reflecting them. Among these vicissitudes is the gradual hollowing out or decaying of the firm, which Carker has begun, but which is not yet visible. For this reason the company, like the house, only ever appears to be in stasis; it is in fact being slowly consumed from within.

Just as the potential for ruin always exists in architecture, the potential for reanimation always exists within the ruin, especially in the city. Dombey's 'wilderness of a home' (DS 23.339) is suddenly brought back to life in chapter 28, in anticipation of Dombey's second marriage. This scene, which recalls the upheaval of Staggs's Gardens at the coming of the railway, sees the house enveloped by a 'labyrinth of scaffolding raised all around the house, from the basement to the roof' (DS 28.426). These 'great alterations' (DS 28.427) aim to make the house a fashionable modern dwelling, partly through the lavish use of 'great rolls of ornamental paper' (DS 28.426). The narrator's term 'labyrinth' recalls the chaos of Staggs's Gardens in chapter 6 and reinforces the home's links to the company, which Carker has made into a 'great labyrinth of which only he has held the clue' (DS 53.790). It also makes the home an allegory of the city at large, since when Florence is lost in chapter 6 she is tricked by Good Mrs Brown into travelling 'through a labyrinth of narrow streets and lanes and alleys' (DS 6.79). As in chapter 3, there is no distinction during these renovations between interior and exterior: work goes on 'inside and outside alike' (DS 28.427), and the house is opened up to public view, with 'no furniture [. . .] to be seen through the gaping and broken windows in any of the rooms', which are instead full of workmen 'swarming from the kitchens to the garrets' (DS 28.427). This intermixing of interior and exterior is characteristic of the bourgeoisie in the nineteenth century, Benjamin argues:

> The domestic interior moves outside. It is as though the bourgeois were so sure of his prosperity that he is careless of façade and can exclaim: My house, no matter where you choose to cut into it, is façade. Such façades, especially, on the Berlin houses dating back to the middle of the previous century: an alcove does not jut out, but – as niche – tucks in. The street becomes room and the room becomes street.[87]

Such a mixing of inside and outside replicates the operation of the railway, which as shown above opens up the houses of the poor for Dombey like a monstrous other to the imagined good spirit.

The events of chapter 28 precipitate a radical reversal in the house's visibility. Once the building work has been completed,

> The dark blot on the street is gone. Mr. Dombey's mansion, if it be a gap among the other houses any longer, is only so because it is not to be vied with in its brightness, and haughtily casts them off. (DS 35.525)

The house has metamorphosed from dark ruin to magnificent 'brightness'. It now displays the 'haughtiness' which characterises Dombey, who has made, in Mrs Skewton's words, a 'perfect palace' (DS 35.529) of the building. As he tells her: 'It is handsome [. . .]. I directed that no expense should be spared; and all that money could do has been done, I believe' (DS 35.529). For Michal Ginsburg, 'the house now represents not so much Dombey's status as money's purchasing power', making it an architectural embodiment of capital, a conjunction which reaches new heights in Zola's *Au Bonheur des Dames*, as Chapter 3 will show.[88] Notably, the word 'handsome' is repeatedly used to describe Edith (DS 21.305, DS 21.315, DS 26.394 for instance), whom Dombey has also acquired through money. This link between money and 'handsomeness' is made explicit by a young man at the Major's club, who is willing to 'give a handsome sum to be able to rise and go away, but cannot do it' (DS 31.478). Mrs Skewton's response to Dombey's handsome outlay is to ask 'and what can it [money] not do, dear Dombey?' (DS 35.529), recalling Paul's earlier naïve but profound question, 'what's money after all?' (DS 8.99), and hence the fact that money cannot overcome death, including Paul's own death. Mrs Skewton inadvertently reveals that money cannot expunge death from the mansion, though it can buy parergonal ornamentation to cover it over. The 'ornamental paper' used to decorate the house, then, is not the opposite of the 'ghastly bandages' that wrap the frame of Fanny's picture, but their return in another form. Although the gap in the street has been covered up, the lack within the house is not expunged.

At this point, the domestic house has descended from bourgeois respectability to semi-ruin, before returning to glorious 'brightness'. In chapter 59 it reverses once more, into complete ruin. This time, the fall of one house follows the fall of the other, with Dombey's home stripped by builders and auctioneers just as the financial House is stripped by Carker. As the narrator comments, it is 'a great house still [...] but it is a ruin none the less, and the rats fly from it' (DS 59.871). Although the house previously elided inside and outside, in its final state of ruin the interior becomes fully exposed. Ornaments and furniture are sold off in a public auction (DS 59.876–7), so that there is 'not a secret place in the entire house' (DS 59.874). The opening up which began with the house's refurbishment is completed when 'two brokers invade the very fire-escape, and take a panoramic survey of the neighbourhood from the top of the house' (DS 59.876), adopting a view from above that replicates and parodies Dombey's original worldview from chapter 1, that 'the earth was made for Dombey and Son to trade in' (DS 1.2).

The house's sudden movement in chapter 59 from wholeness to ruin seems to replicate the final swing of a stock market in crisis, in which case Marx's comments on this topic also apply to Dombey: 'the contradictions inherent in the movement of capitalist society impress themselves upon the practical bourgeois most strikingly in the changes of the periodic cycle, [...] whose crowning point is the universal crisis'.[89] Marx's point is that reversal and crisis emerge from capitalism itself, rather than being parergonal disruptions of it, as they seem to be, so that they are finally inseparable from the processes of wealth creation they undo. This makes capitalism tragic in Benjamin's sense in *The Origin of German Tragic Drama*, where he writes that 'tragic existence acquires its task only because it is intrinsically subject to the limits of both linguistic and physical life which are set within it from its very beginning'.[90] In this reading, the house's descent into ruin, and more generally its instability, are not isolated or aberrational events, but expressions of the basic contradictions of capitalist society. The trajectory of the house thus makes visible in a symptomatic form the invisible architecture of capitalism itself.

Uncanny Houses 2: The House of the Hexams

If the house of Dombey brings the upheaval of railway architecture within the sphere of the domestic home, then in *Our Mutual Friend* the much less fashionable house of the Hexam family does something similar with the ambiguous surfaces of the river Thames. This home, which 'had the look of having once been a mill' (OMF 1.3.21), is sparsely furnished and in poor condition, with a 'look of decomposition' (OMF 1.3.21) in its roof, walls and floor. Starting from chapter 3 of the novel, which mirrors the opening scene, I show in this section that the home replicates the river in acting as both invisible architecture and anti-architecture, that which dissolves architectural thought.

Chapter 3 addresses the fire in the hearth, and specifically what Lizzie calls the 'hollow down by the flare' (OMF 1.3.29). As she tells her brother Charley, the 'dull glow' next to the coals 'comes like pictures to me' (OMF 1.3.28), making it a kind of phantasmagoria in which Lizzie sees images of the past and future. For Lizzie, who is illiterate, the hollow down by the flare is her 'library of books' (OMF 1.3.30). Not everyone can see what Lizzie sees, however: 'show us a picture', demands Charley, 'tell us where to look', to which she replies 'ah! It wants my eyes, Charley' (OMF 1.3.28). These pictures are highly subjective, a form of optical unconscious that is not accessible to all, implying a shift away from the fixed viewpoint of the camera obscura and towards the panorama, phantasmagoria and kaleidoscope, mobile visual technologies which spread rapidly in the early nineteenth century. This shift, argues Jonathan Crary, produced 'a freeing up of vision, a falling away of the rigid structures that had shaped it and constituted its objects'.[91] Such newly liberated (but also potentially exclusionary) forms of vision alter the subject's relationship to both space and time. Freud's imagined view of Rome in *Civilization and Its Discontents* (1930), used as a metaphor for the persistence of memory in the unconscious, provides an image of this shift:

> On the Piazza of the Pantheon we should find not only the Pantheon of today, as it was bequeathed to us by Hadrian, but, on the same site, the original edifice erected by Agrippa; indeed, the same piece of ground would be supporting the church of Santa Maria sopra Minerva and the ancient temple over which it was built. And the observer would perhaps only have to change the direction of his glance or his position in order to call up the one view or the other.[92]

In Freud's fantasy, what the observer sees of Rome is a function of their gaze, not an objective external reality, so that the view alters as the viewer changes their perspective. Multiple times and spaces are opened up to those able to adopt the right way of looking. Lizzie's fire is the same. She responds to Charley's request for knowledge of the future by relaying what she sees, which is also a projection of her internal thoughts and feelings: 'Well! There am I, continuing with father and holding to father, because father loves me and I love father' (OMF 1.3.29). Although Lizzie sees this 'as plain as plain can be' (OMF 1.3.30), Charley sees 'deuce-and-all in the hollow down by the flare' (OMF 1.3.29), forcing him to pay close attention to

Lizzie, just as Lizzie closely watched their father in the opening scene. Charley's schooling, which gives him knowledge that is rational and logical – 'that's gas, that is' he remarks of the fire (OMF 1.3.28) – prevents him from reading the hollow as Lizzie does. She, like Alice Wilson in *Mary Barton*, is privy to hidden knowledge that the educated cannot access. Such vision is blocked to Charley, who lacks both imagination and the ability to access the unconscious, making him a copy of Bradley Headstone, his schoolmaster, the novel's foremost figure of repression.

Although Lizzie's reading of the ambiguous surface of the fire replicates Gaffer's reading of the river, her attempts to produce a coherent narrative from it also oppose the fire to the cold, senseless river, from which Harmon finds it impossible to draw any narrative at all. The home is a place where thoughts, feelings and stories can be gathered and recombined, and the hearth, even one as compromised as this, is its symbolic centre. For the German architect Gottfried Semper (1803–79), the hearth was '*one of the four fundamental elements of architecture, along with the* earthwork, *the* roof *and the* screen wall'.[93] Herman Melville parodies this idea in the short story 'I and My Chimney' (1856), where the narrator's house is built around a chimney that he suspects, like the dust mounds of *Our Mutual Friend*, of harbouring a secret. Mr Scribe, a possibly deceptive 'master-mason', claims that 'there is architectural cause to conjecture that somewhere concealed in your chimney is a reserved space, hermetically closed, in short, a secret chamber, or rather closet'.[94] Yet this chimney always returns the searcher to where he started: 'it is like losing one's self in the woods; round and round the chimney you go, and if you arrive at all, it is just where you started, and so you begin again, and get nowhere'.[95] For Anthony Vidler, Melville's story anticipates Freud's essay on the uncanny, where Freud describes becoming lost in an Italian town, returning repeatedly to a 'quarter of whose character I could not long remain in doubt', where his presence begins to excite attention.[96] As Steve Pile points out, Freud not only returns to the same spot, but experiences the return of a repressed desire to have sex with the 'painted women' he sees around him.[97]

John Harmon experiences a similar psychological and architectural disorientation when trying to remember the circumstances of his presumed death, associated with the experience of passing through or under the river:

> He tried a new direction, but made nothing of it; walls, dark doorways, flights of stairs and rooms, were too abundant. And, like most people

so puzzled, he again and again described a circle, and found himself at the point from which he had begun. 'This is like what I have read in narratives of escape from prison', said he, 'where the little track of the fugitives in the night always seems to take the shape of the great round world, on which they wander; as if it were a secret law.' (OMF 2.13.365)

Harmon's desired object, like the picture in Lizzie's fire, is both outside and inside himself, at once a place that cannot be reached and a memory that cannot be recalled. Harmon can only circulate around this point, which is the point of his own feigned death, and which he has entombed within himself as the basis for his new identity. What Harmon lacks is a clue – 'I have no clue to the scene of my death' he remarks (OMF 2.13.366) – so that if Hexam looks for clues on the river, Harmon's failure to find a clue to what lies beneath it testifies to the erasure of memory, making the Thames a version of the mythical river Lethe:

> As to this hour, I cannot understand that side of the river where I recovered the shore, being the opposite side to that on which I was ensnared, I shall never understand it now. Even at this moment, while I leave the river behind me, going home, I cannot conceive that it rolls between me and that spot, or that the sea is where it is. (OMF 2.13.370)

Although the surface of the river might, at times, be read, its underside, which carried Harmon, resists all conscious thought.

The hearth in Lizzie's house gathers up these tensions; it is both an echo of the river which disrupts time, space and thought, and a site where the imaginative work of the domestic woman might, perhaps, be able to restore narrative cohesion. The fire signals this indeterminacy, being held only 'in a rusty brazier, not fitted to the hearth' (OMF 1.3.21). Like the fire, Lizzie's house and family are broken, held together only by her persistent expenditure of force. The moral function of the hearth, allegorising Lizzie, is ironically recognised by Eugene Wrayburn, who insists on having a kitchen in the apartment he will share with Mortimer, even if they never use it, claiming 'its moral influence is the important thing' (OMF 2.6.284). If in nineteenth-century Britain the virtuous woman was frequently seen as vital to the functional domestic interior, including by Dickens, then Wrayburn's desire for a kitchen reveals a need for feminine morality that underlies his overt sexual desire for Lizzie.[98]

The hollow down by the flare also recalls, once again, the chapter of *The Old Curiosity Shop* where Nell encounters the man who gives

Figure 2.3 *Watching the Furnace Fire*, Hablot Browne (Phiz). Michael John Goodman, Charles Dickens Illustrated Library.

her tarnished coins, whose job is to tend a furnace (Figure 2.3). 'It's like a book to me', he tells her:

> the only book I ever learned to read; and many an old story it tells me. It's music, for I should know its voice among a thousand, and there are other voices in its roar. It has its pictures too. You don't know how many strange faces and different scenes I trace in the red-hot coals. It's my memory, that fire, and shows me all my life.[99]

Fire is here associated with memory, unlike the river, which erases memory. Yet fire dislocates the subject, as the river does, separating the worker from his memory in order to enable its reincorporation as an external object, through viewing the pictures it produces. The fire thus seems to offer a sense of unified subjectivity, it 'shows me all my life', but paradoxically does so only by means of the split it generates between subject, gaze and memory.

In chapter 13, 'Tracking the Bird of Prey', the river and the hollow down by the flare come together. Wrayburn and Lightwood join a police inspector who hopes to arrest Hexam when he returns from a night spent on the river. Eugene's ulterior motive is to observe Lizzie, so while the inspector hides under a moored-up boat he 'turn[s] his eyes upon the building where, as he had been told, the lonely girl with the dark hair sat by the fire' (OMF 1.13.163), before moving to the window. Marcus Stone's illustration (Figure 2.4) puts the viewer in the position of Eugene, gazing at Lizzie as she watches the fire, making us complicit in his voyeuristic gaze. Alan Shelston compares Lizzie here to Florence in *Dombey and Son* and Louisa in *Hard Times* (1854), suggesting she has no notion of her future, which is represented by Eugene's hidden figure.[100] Lizzie has, however, already projected a version of her future, as described to Charley, making it more accurate to say that her future is a contested region. Stone's picture should be compared to a later illustration of Bella (Figure 2.5), who sits in the same pose, but watches a fireplace rather than a brazier, surrounded by rich furnishings and holding her baby, as Mr Boffin looks on. Bella is in possession of everything Lizzie lacks, emphasising the divergence in class and material comfort between these characters.

Figure 2.4 *Waiting for Father*, Marcus Stone. Michael John Goodman, Charles Dickens Illustrated Library.

The Unstable City 101

Figure 2.5 *Mr Boffin Does the Honours of the Nursery Door*, Marcus Stone. Michael John Goodman, Charles Dickens Illustrated Library.

Both like and unlike Boffin, Eugene sees Lizzie only by the light of the fire, into which she stares:

> She sat on the ground, looking at the brazier, with her face leaning on her hand. There was a kind of film or flicker on her face, which at first he took to be the fitful firelight; but on a second look, he saw that she was weeping. A sad and solitary spectacle, as shown him by the rising and the falling of the fire. (OMF 1.13.163)

An intricate network of gazes is established here. The inspector looks for Hexam, while Eugene looks at Lizzie, separated from her by the window, and she looks at the fire. In a Lacanian sense, the firelight also gazes at Lizzie, allowing Eugene to see the 'flicker' (or stain) on her cheek, but preventing her from seeing him, since by contrast he is in the dark. In Stone's illustration, the brazier itself seems to have eyes, which gaze out of the frame towards the viewer, emphasising that this play of looking also involves the inanimate. Whereas Lizzie previously translated pictures for Charley, here she becomes a picture herself, both for Eugene and the reader. Static and fixed where the fire is shifting, she is described in painterly terms, as a 'deep rich piece of color' (OMF 1.13.164). Eugene watches her as one looks at a painting in a gallery, 'long and steadily', whereas he only 'glance[s] slightly' (OMF 1.13.164) at the bills on the wall advertising drowned people. In Benjamin's terms, Eugene sees Lizzie 'auratically', and the bills transiently, as if they are frames in a film reel.[101] Such a gaze recalls Mr Carker in *Dombey and Son*, who 'looks with a musing smile at a picture' (DS 33.500) that resembles Edith, the second Mrs Dombey. Carker's paintings are 'mere shows of form and colour – and no more' (DS 33.499), indicating his desire to possess Edith not as a hallowed, auratic object but as a depersonalised commodity that will reflect back to him his own dominance. Eugene's desires are more ambiguous, but he seems to reveal the nature of his own gaze when he tells Mortimer 'best not make a show of her' (OMF 1.13.166), since this is, of course, what Eugene has been doing. However we read Eugene's intentions, it is clear that this domestic home offers no sort of protection for Lizzie but rather, like Dombey's house in the earlier novel, exposes its interior contents to view.

At the same time, invisibility as well as visibility is at work in this scene. The tableau places Eugene's gaze, and the implicitly male gaze of the presumed reader, in a privileged position, yet this gaze remains inhibited. While Eugene can see the trace, or clue, of tears on Lizzie's cheek, he cannot be sure what this indicates. He is in the same position as Hexam on the river, unable to penetrate beneath the surface he attempts to read. Moreover, the light which aids Eugene threatens to turn against him. Not only does the 'fitfulness' of the fire limit his ability to read Lizzie, as it had earlier resisted Charley, but the larger light of day – the 'gaze outside' in Lacan's terms – could at any moment pick him out. As the men continue to watch for Hexam, the inspector warns, 'it will be light at five [. . .] and then *we* shall be seen' (OMF 1.13.167). The field of vision, like the river, cannot be controlled, even when it seems to serve the desire of the male subject.

In these passages, seeing, perceiving and reading become unstable and mobile practices, exacerbated by the anti-architectural tendencies of Dickens's uncanny houses. It is characteristic of these buildings that they break down distinctions between interior and exterior, compromising the 'desire to endure' that Hollier ascribes to traditional architecture. In doing so, they repeat, while also altering and rearticulating, the temporal, spatial and psychological disruptions brought about by railway and river. Both railway and river, as well as the houses that peculiarly replicate them, simultaneously stitch the city together and unstitch the coordinates that make it comprehensible, blending the signs of progress with the return to a primeval, archaic past, which acts upon the city like an architectural unconscious. It is through this duality of past and future, known and unknown, *Heimlich* and *Unheimlich*, that these forms of invisible architecture contribute to Dickens's distinctively modern vision of urban space and subjectivity.

Notes

1. Charles Dickens, *Dombey and Son*, ed. by Alan Horsman (Oxford: Clarendon, 1974), p. 59 n. 2.
2. Charles Dickens, *Dealings with the Firm of Dombey and Son*, no. 2 (London: Bradbury and Evans, Nov. 1846), p. 41. It is also not included in the 1848, 1858, 1859 or 1867 editions, or the current Oxford World's Classics edition.
3. Freud, 'Beyond the Pleasure Principle', p. 15.
4. 'Anti-architecture' is associated with deconstruction in Nikos Salingaros, *Anti-Architecture and Deconstruction* (Solingen, Germany: Umbau-Verlag, 2004) and with Bataille in Hollier. For more on this topic see Ben Moore, 'Architecture', in *The Edinburgh Companion to Charles Dickens and the Arts*, ed. by Juliet John and Claire Wood (Edinburgh: Edinburgh University Press, forthcoming 2024).
5. *Arcades*, p. 148.
6. On the railway in this period see Wolfgang Schivelbusch, *The Railway Journey: The Industrialization of Time and Space in the Nineteenth Century* (Berkeley and Los Angeles: University of California Press, 1986) and Michael Freeman, *Railways and the Victorian Imagination* (New Haven: Yale University Press, 1999).
7. Tillotson, p. 200.
8. Steven Marcus, *Dickens: From Pickwick to Dombey* (London: Chatto and Windus, 1965), p. 306, p. 307.
9. Joachim Frenk and Lena Steveker, 'Introduction: Changing Dickens', in *Charles Dickens as an Agent of Change*, ed. by Joachim Frenk and Lena Steveker (Ithaca, NY: Cornell University Press, 2019), pp. xi–xx (pp. xiii–xv).
10. *The Country and the City*, p. 164.
11. Jeremy Tambling, *Dickens, Violence and the Modern State* (Houndmills: Macmillan, 1995), p. 60. Jacques Derrida uses the word 'monstration' in this way in 'The First Session', in *Acts of Literature*, ed. by Derek Attridge (London: Routledge, 1992), pp. 127–80 (p. 157).

12. John Ruskin, letter to Charles Eliot Norton, 19 June 1870, in *The Correspondence of John Ruskin and Charles Eliot Norton*, ed. by John Bradley and Ian Ousby (Cambridge: Cambridge University Press, 1987), p. 194. Trey Philpotts, 'Dickens, the Metropolis and the Railway: Displacement or Progress?', *Dickens Quarterly*, 31.4 (2014), 334–42 (p. 339). For another perspective on Dickens and the railway, see Daragh Downes, '"Excellent Monsters": The Railway Theme in Dickens's Novels', *English*, 61.235 (2012), 382–93. On Dickens's relation to urban construction and destruction, see Hofer-Robinson.
13. Stephen Kern, *The Culture of Time and Space 1880–1918* (Cambridge, MA: Harvard University Press, 1983), p. 34.
14. *Arcades*, p. 475.
15. *Arcades*, p. 462.
16. Ian Carter, '"The lost idea of a train": Looking for Britain's Railway Novel', *Journal of Transport History*, 21.2 (2000), 117–39 (p. 119).
17. Hollier, p. 49.
18. Jacques Derrida, 'Roundtable on Translation', trans. by Peggy Kamuf, in *The Ear of the Other: Otobiography, Transference, Translation*, ed. by Christie McDonald (New York: Schocken, 1985), pp. 91–162 (p. 102). See also Derrida, 'Des tours des Babel', trans. by Joseph Graham, in *Difference in Translation* (Ithaca, NY and London: Cornell University Press, 1985), pp. 165–207, which is a commentary on Benjamin's 'The Task of the Translator' (1923).
19. Hamon, p. 60.
20. 'The New Zealander', in Gustave Doré and Blanchard Jerrold, *London: A Pilgrimage* (London: Grant & Co., 1872), p. 190.
21. *Arcades*, p. 84, p. 410.
22. 'A Flight', in Dickens, *Selected Short Fiction*, pp. 142–51 (p. 144). Gillian Piggott, *Dickens and Benjamin: Moments of Revelation, Fragments of Modernity* (Farnham: Ashgate, 2012), p. 104.
23. Piggott, p. 105.
24. Alf Steebert, '"Steam of Consciousness": Technology and Sensation in Dickens' Railway Sketches', *Philament*, 14 (2009), 91–115 (p. 98).
25. 'A Flight', p. 145.
26. Charles Dickens, *Martin Chuzzlewit* (Oxford: Oxford University Press, 1984), p. 114.
27. Sigmund Freud, *The Interpretation of Dreams*, trans. by James Strachey (London: Penguin, 1976), p. 384.
28. *Interpretation of Dreams*, p. 429.
29. 'Paris, the Capital of the Nineteenth Century' [1935], in *Arcades*, p. 4.
30. Giedion, *Space, Time and Architecture*, p. 167.
31. RIBA was first established as the Institute of British Architects in London, gaining a Royal Charter in 1837.
32. *Space, Time and Architecture*, p. 183.
33. Michael Klotz, '*Dombey and Son* and the "Parlour on Wheels"', *Dickens Studies Annual*, 40 (2009), 61–79 (p. 66, p. 65).

34. *The Country and the City*, p. 46.
35. Klotz, p. 68.
36. Klotz, p. 75. *London: A Pilgrimage*, p. 120.
37. *The Country and the City*, p. 156.
38. Klotz, p. 75; Michelle Mancini, 'Demons on the Rooftops, Gypsies in the Streets: The "Secret Intelligence" of *Dombey and Son*', *Dickens Studies Annual*, 30 (2001), 113–40 (p. 116); *Going Astray*, p. 116. Mancini notes that Murray Baumgarten has also made this argument.
39. 'Theories of Space and the Nineteenth-Century Novel', p. 13.
40. 'Theories of Space and the Nineteenth-Century Novel', p. 13.
41. *Going Astray*, p. 116.
42. F. S. Schwarzbach, *Dickens and the City* (London: Athlone Press, 1979), p. 194. J. Hillis Miller, 'The Topography of Jealousy in *Our Mutual Friend*', in *Dickens Refigured: Bodies, Desires and Other Histories*, ed. by John Schad (Manchester: Manchester University Press, 1996), pp. 218–36 (p. 222).
43. *Going Astray*, p. 248. *Interpretation of Dreams*, p. 427. On the river in the novel see also Richard Lehan, *The City in Literature: An Intellectual and Cultural History* (Berkeley and Los Angles: University of California Press, 1998), pp. 45–7; *The Body Economic*, pp. 86–117; Michelle Allen, *Cleansing the City: Sanitary Geographies in Victorian London* (Athens: Ohio State University Press, 2008), pp. 86–114; and for a survey of the Thames in Dickens's writing, Luc Bouvard, 'The Thames Persistently Revisited: Dickens on the Edge of Water', *Études Anglaises: Revue du monde anglophone*, 65.1 (2012), 80–95.
44. Sigmund Freud, 'The Uncanny', in *The Standard Edition, Volume XVIII (1920–1922)*, ed. by James Strachey (London: Vintage, 2001), pp. 219–52 (p. 225).
45. 'The Uncanny', p. 249. Freud is in the end ambivalent about this definition; see Ben Moore, 'The Eyes of the Other: Mary Shelley's *Frankenstein* and the Uncanny', in *The Bloomsbury Handbook to Literature and Psychoanalysis*, ed. by Jeremy Tambling (London: Bloomsbury, 2023), pp. 35–48.
46. 'The Uncanny', p. 241.
47. McKee, p. 71, p. 72.
48. Jacques Lacan, *The Seminar of Jacques Lacan, Book XI: The Four Fundamental Principles of Psychoanalysis*, trans. by Alan Sheridan (London: Norton, 1981), p. 24.
49. *Seminar XI*, p. 25.
50. On this conversation and the dead body as a nexus of economic exchange, see *The Body Economic*, p. 93.
51. Forster, p. 12.
52. *Going Astray*, p. 240.
53. Franco Moretti, *Atlas of the European Novel 1800–1900* (London: Verso, 1998), p. 116. A map showing this journey appears on p. 115.

54. Sen, pp. 36–8.
55. *Seminar XI*, p. 94.
56. *Seminar XI*, p. 94.
57. Spivak glosses the term *apologue* as 'apology, excuse, but also something that is just a little off to the side of the *logos*', so that the standard English translation 'a little story' does not do it justice. Gayatri Chakravorty Spivak, *An Aesthetic Education in the Era of Globalization* (Cambridge, MA: Harvard University Press, 2012), p. 257.
58. Risk is also the condition of river scavengers such as Hexam and Rogue Riderhood, as becomes clear when Riderhood's boat is run down by a foreign steamer (OMF 3.2.440).
59. *Seminar XI*, p. 95.
60. *Seminar XI*, p. 96.
61. *Seminar XI*, p. 106.
62. *Seminar XI*, p. 92.
63. McKee, p. 73.
64. *Seminar XI*, p. 74.
65. *The Work of Art*, p. 37. On this concept in relation to modernism see Rosalind Krauss, *The Optical Unconscious* (Cambridge, MA: MIT Press, 1993).
66. Peter Buse et al., *Benjamin's Arcades: An UnGuided Tour* (Manchester: Manchester University Press, 2005), p. 162.
67. *The Work of Art*, p. 40.
68. Rudolf Arnheim, quoted in *The Work of Art*, p. 37.
69. *Seminar XI*, p. 97.
70. *Seminar XI*, p. 97, p. 99.
71. *Seminar XI*, p. 100.
72. *The Work of Art*, p. 38. On film and Dickens, see Grahame Smith, *Dickens and the Dream of Cinema* (Manchester: Manchester University Press, 2003).
73. *Seminar XI*, p. 105.
74. Charles Dickens, *The Old Curiosity Shop* (Oxford: Oxford University Press, 1998), p. 337.
75. Adorno, quoted in *Arcades*, p. 208.
76. Karl Marx, *Economic and Political Manuscripts*, in *Early Writings*, trans. by Rodney Livingstone and Gregor Benton (Harmondsworth: Penguin, 1975), pp. 279–400 (p. 375).
77. *Seminar XI*, p. 113.
78. *Seminar XI*, p. 73.
79. See for instance Raymond Williams, 'Introduction', in Charles Dickens, *Dombey and Son* (Harmondsworth: Penguin, 1970), p. 17; Tambling, *Dickens, Violence and the Modern State*, p. 57; John Butt and Kathleen Tillotson, *Dickens at Work* (Abingdon: Routledge, 2009 [1957]), p. 105; Andrew Elfenbein, 'Managing the House in *Dombey and Son*: Dickens and the Uses of Analogy', *Studies in Philology*,

92.3 (1995), 361–82; Julian Wolfreys, *Literature, in Theory: Tropes, Subjectivities, Responses and Responsibilities* (London: Continuum, 2010), p. 22; Ann Gaylin, *Eavesdropping in the Novel from Austen to Proust* (Cambridge: Cambridge University Press, 2002), p. 100; Lisa Surridge, *Bleak Houses: Marital Violence in Victorian Fiction* (Athens: Ohio University Press, 2005), pp. 54–5.
80. David Ellison, 'Mobile Homes, Fallen Furniture, and the Dickens Cure', *South Atlantic Quarterly*, 108.1 (2009), 87–114 (p. 92).
81. Ellison, p. 93. The illustration appears on p. 33 of the Oxford edition.
82. Wolfreys, p. 32. Surridge, p. 55.
83. Elfenbein, p. 62.
84. Jacques Derrida, *The Truth in Painting*, trans. by Geoff Bennington and Ian McLeod (London: University of Chicago Press, 1987), p. 56.
85. *Interpretation of Dreams*, pp. 381–419.
86. *Arcades*, p. 392.
87. *Arcades*, p. 406.
88. Michal Ginsburg, 'House and Home in *Dombey and Son*', *Dickens Studies Annual*, 36 (2005), 57–73 (p. 66).
89. *Capital*, p. 12.
90. Walter Benjamin, *The Origin of German Tragic Drama*, trans. by John Osborne (London: Verso, 1998), p. 114.
91. Jonathan Crary, *Techniques of the Observer: On Vision and Modernity in the Nineteenth Century* (Cambridge, MA: MIT Press, 1992), p. 24.
92. Sigmund Freud, *Civilization and Its Discontents*, in *The Standard Edition, Volume XXI (1927–1931)*, ed. by James Strachey (London: Vintage, 2001), pp. 57–146 (p. 70).
93. Quoted in Simon Unwin, *Analysing Architecture*, 2nd edn (London: Routledge, 2003), p. 89.
94. Herman Melville, 'I and My Chimney', in *Billy Budd, Sailor and Selected Tales* (Oxford: Oxford University Press, 1997), pp. 248–78 (p. 264, p. 268). For a reading of the chimney as a spiritual symbol for 'the heart of man', see Merton Sealts, 'Herman Melville's "I and My Chimney"', *American Literature*, 13.2 (1941), 142–54 (p. 145). For a reading that links architecture and writing in the text, see Katja Kanzler, 'Architecture, Writing, and Vulnerable Signification in Herman Melville's "I and My Chimney"', *Amerikastudien/American Studies*, 54.4 (2009), 583–601.
95. Melville, 'I and My Chimney', p. 262. Quoted in *Architectural Uncanny*, p. 43.
96. 'The Uncanny', p. 236.
97. Steve Pile, 'Sleepwalking in the Modern City: Walter Benjamin and Sigmund Freud in the World of Dreams', in *A Companion to the City*, ed. by Gary Bridge and Sophie Watson (Oxford: Blackwell, 2000), pp. 75–86 (p. 81). 'The Uncanny', p. 236.

98. See for instance Deborah Gorham, *The Victorian Girl and the Feminine Ideal* (London: Croom Helm, 1982).
99. *Old Curiosity Shop*, p. 335.
100. Alan Shelston, 'Nell, Alice and Lizzie: Three Sisters Amidst the Grotesque', in *Master Narratives: Tellers and Telling in the English Novel*, ed. by Richard Gravil (Aldershot: Ashgate, 2001), pp. 148–73 (p. 170).
101. See *The Work of Art*, p. 24.

Chapter 3

The Transparent City: Mansions, Montage and Commodity Architecture in *The Kill* and *The Ladies' Paradise*

This chapter addresses the invisibilities, openings and transparencies of city architecture in Émile Zola's Paris, focusing on *La Curée* (*The Kill*) from 1872 and *Au Bonheur des Dames* (*The Ladies' Paradise*) from 1883, the second and eleventh books in the twenty-novel *Rougon-Macquart* cycle (1871–93), which endeavoured to provide 'A Natural and Social History of a Family under the Second Empire'. The architecture which dominates these two novels – Haussmann's boulevards and their mansions in *La Curée*, the modern department store in *Au Bonheur des Dames* – comes closer to bringing about total visibility and connectedness than any of the city spaces I have considered so far. Yet even as they seem to achieve total openness in the city, these forms of architecture continue to repress and exclude other spaces and forms of life, especially working-class spaces. They do so not through darkness or obfuscation as in *Mary Barton*, but through the promotion of visibility to an absolute and overwhelming principle. This process involves a phantasmagorical blending of architecture and commodities, in which the commodity's mystifying and alienating character comes to be incorporated into the structure of the city. Glass and iron allow transparency to become heightened in these predominantly bourgeois spaces, but in such a way that new kinds of ideological enclosure are created, thereby taking to an extreme Lefebvre's illusion of transparency. This involves a confusion of interior and exterior which recalls what we saw in Dickens, but now operating less through processes of mobile ruination and restoration (though these are also present) than through the extension of the intoxicating logic of the commodity into a principle of architectural structure.

The multiplication of visibility and transparency brought about by these new forms of architecture is both described and enacted by Zola's use of literary montage, which anticipates cinema, as Sergei Eisenstein was the first to point out. For Eisenstein the *Rougon-Macquart* cycle was not only a single ecstatic whole built out of a series of montage effects (matching what Eisenstein sought to achieve in his films), but also 'poetic and musical', in the way Zola

> painstakingly selects from 'all possible ones' those particular details and those hours or moments and those very conditions of temperature and light that repeat emotionally the same psychological nuance with which Zola is trying to overwhelm the reader at a given moment.[1]

The key principle of naturalism is in this case not description, as for Lukács, but selection.[2] This is for Eisenstein a new kind of materialism, one which relies not on stylistic devices, but on 'stringing out such realistic, everyday (and mostly naturalistic) details that, by their nature, as signs of everyday reality, increase proportionally to the impression they produce'. A 'crescendo' is produced by building up material details towards a heightened emotional impression.[3] In my reading, this literary technique is also what characterises architecture in Zola. His buildings, especially those of bourgeois Paris, are formed by processes of visual, material and affective accumulation that mimic the capitalist accumulation which the society of the Second Empire (1852–70) is shown to fetishise.

Eisenstein himself understood Zola as an architectural novelist. The section of *Nonindifferent Nature* (a posthumous book collecting material written in 1939–47) from which I have been quoting is titled 'Twenty-Two Supporting Columns', alluding to the twenty novels of the *Rougon-Macquart* and the two novel cycles of Zola's later life, the *Three Cities* (1894–7) and *The Four Evangelists* (1899–1903).[4] According to Eisenstein, the 'well-constructed colonnade of Zola's ten pairs of novels became the solid support' of the filmmaker's own experiments in ecstatic montage.[5] Yet whereas the colonnade is a classical form, in the pages that follow I emphasise the very modern way that Zola's depictions of the boulevard and the department store deploy visual excess to create architectures that appear transparent and all-encompassing, while also, precisely through this appearance of totality, ideologically constraining what is available to be seen, thought and felt. One of the key figures upon which such architecture is secured is the sexualised, commodified and orientalised (but still racially white) woman of fashion.

In this chapter I build on the work of Jacques Rancière and Fredric Jameson, both descendants of Eisenstein in that they approach Zola as a writer of montage and visual excess, though both also directly or indirectly challenge features of Eisenstein's reading.[6] Rancière's *The Future of the Image*, for instance, argues for the inextricability of language and image in modern culture, through the concept of the 'sentence-image', which has a 'paratactic syntax' that 'might also be called montage', and which unsettles the relatively fixed hierarchies of order that came before it.[7] Rancière's form of montage is much less unified than Eisenstein's, since the former's central contention is that the aesthetic regime, exemplified by Zola among others, is radically non-hierarchical and non-totalising. Jameson, meanwhile, though not directly citing Eisenstein, deploys his terms in *The Antinomies of Realism* when describing the 'ecstatic dizziness' generated by the 'visual multiplicity of the things themselves and the sensations they press on the unforewarned observer' in the fish market in *Le Ventre de Paris* (1873), which he takes to stand for Zola's artistic practice as a whole.[8] Yet for Jameson this dizziness is only one side of Zola's writing, and of the practice of realism more generally. While such perceptual confusion points forwards to the impressionistic texts of modernism, the other side of Zola is a 'centrifugal movement of mastery and subsumption, of the ordering of raw nameless things into their proper genetic classifications', which looks back to earlier practices of narrative or *récit*, what Rancière calls the representational regime, a concept indebted to Foucault's work in *The Order of Things*.[9] In this interpretation, realism is not a unified genre but one in tension with itself, caught between two different modes of perception, narration and aesthetic organisation. Like Jameson, my reading finds a doubleness in Zola, but I argue that this doubleness should be read as the literary exploration of a particular form of invisible architecture, associated with Second-Empire Paris, in which transparency and the multiplication of the visual paradoxically produces new forms of concealment.

La Curée and Haussmann's Paris

La Curée, translated by Brian Nelson as *The Kill*, focuses on Aristide Saccard, a clerk turned wealthy land speculator, along with his second wife Renée and his effeminate, sexualised son Maxime, the latter two of whom embark on an affair during the course of the novel. The novel repeatedly uses forms of montage and visibility as techniques to represent, display or open up the city, but also to make it obscure in new ways. Through practices of de- and re-territorialisation, all the main characters become complicit in an attempt to erase the old city in favour of the new. This takes place through the construction of new boulevards and an accompanying projection of the dreamlike bourgeois interior onto the city. Ultimately, these processes replace one form of invisibility with another, exchanging the unseen for the unseeable.

In line with William J. Berg's suggestion that 'synecdoche of the part for the whole dominates Zola's novels', Zola's introduction indicates that *La Curée* was conceived as an allegory for the decadence of the Second Empire:[10]

> I wanted to show the premature exhaustion of a race which has lived too quickly and ends in the man-woman of rotten societies, the furious speculation of an epoch embodied in an unscrupulous temperament, the nervous breakdown of a woman whose circle of luxury and shame increases tenfold native appetites.[11]

Each of these 'three social monstrosities' (K 3) is embodied by one of the central characters: Maxime is the 'man-woman', a 'creature of indeterminate sex' who 'matched the follies and fashions of the age' (K 4.158); Saccard is the speculator who joins the 'blaze of unrestrained luxury' (K 2.49) that engulfs Paris; and Renée is the woman whose body is 'exhausted' and mind 'unhinged' (K 6.243) by her incestuous affair with Maxime. They form the cast of a specifically urban society. Richard Lehan notes that *La Curée* is the first *Rougon-Macquart* novel to 'establish the meaning of Paris as both the center of France and the center of Zola's narrative world', making Zola part of a broader trend in French literature observed by Philippe Hamon, in which, 'by the middle of the century, everything revolved around Paris as if around the sun, in the literal as well as figurative sense'.[12] Benjamin testifies to this tendency in the *Arcades Project*, where an 1855 quotation describes Paris as 'the capital of creation!'[13] The centripetal drive towards Paris was registered and accelerated by the World Exhibitions that took place in the city in the second half of the century, including under the Second Empire in 1855 and 1867. According to Sigfried Giedion, these events sought to contain 'all regions and indeed, retrospectively, all times'.[14] Yet despite this aspiration, the Exhibitions can only produce what Giedion calls a 'premature synthesis' – another version of what Zola calls 'premature exhaustion' – leading Benjamin to comment that 'these "premature syntheses" also bespeak a persistent endeavor to close up the space of existence and of development. To prevent the "airing out of the classes".'[15] To put this another way, the Exhibitions, like the bourgeois life depicted in *The Kill*, inhibit historical movement, denying the existence of genuinely different times and places, or of class conflict, instead insisting that everything can be encompassed by one single capitalist system, everything contained under one roof.

This centralising and synthesising drive of Paris was supported by the Haussmannisation of the city between 1853 and 1870, which forms the setting for the novel. At this time, new boulevards cut through the old city, promoting the movement of both soldiers and capital.[16] For P. M. Wetherill, 'Haussmann's factual architecture and Zola's non-metaphoric urban narrative are simultaneous and reciprocal products of the same mentality', so that *La Curée*'s architectural context is also the symbolic heart of the novel.[17] As Alison Walls notes, the boulevards helped make the new *grands magasins* possible, by facilitating deliveries, window displays and access for customers, so that *La Curée* prepares the ground for *Au Bonheur des Dames*.[18]

The scene that most strikingly depicts the new boulevards cutting through Paris is described retrospectively, having taken place on the Buttes Montmartre in 1854, before the death of Saccard's first wife, Angèle. This scene recalls the conclusion to Balzac's *Père Goriot* (1835), where Rastignac gazes out over Paris from the Père-Lachaise cemetery, challenging it with the words 'it's between the two of us now!', in a classic masculine adoption of the view from above, the position of Certeau's 'voyeur'.[19] Saccard, by contrast, does not challenge the city so much as explode it. By 1854, he has already amassed so much knowledge of the planned building work that 'he could have prophesied how the new neighbourhoods would look in 1870' (K 2.67). He projects the future city on top of the old, looking out over a Paris that is described through a series of telling metaphors:

> On this particular day they dined at the top of the hill, in a restaurant whose windows looked out over Paris, over the sea of houses with blue roofs, like surging billows that filled the horizon. [. . .] [B]eneath the pale sky the city lay listless in a soft and tender grey, pierced here and there by dark patches of foliage that resembled the broad leaves of water-lilies floating on a lake; the sun was setting behind a red cloud and, while the background was filled with a light haze, a shower of gold dust, of golden dew, fell on the right bank of the river, near the Madeleine and the Tuileries. It was like an enchanted corner in a city of the 'Arabian

Nights', with emerald trees, sapphire roofs, and ruby weathercocks. At one moment a ray of sunlight gliding from between two clouds was so resplendent that the houses seemed to catch fire and melt like an ingot of gold in a crucible.

'Oh! Look!' said Saccard, laughing like a child. 'It's raining twenty-franc pieces in Paris!' (K 2.68)

This passage is an exemplary instance of Eisensteinian ecstatic montage. It transforms Paris from a sea of houses into a lake, then an 'enchanted' oriental city, then finally melting gold, the whole series providing a continuously heightening sequence of juxtaposed but interrelated images. The first images (sea and lake) reimagine Paris as a sublime or picturesque landscape, an act of aesthetic reframing that recalls Baudelaire, Benjamin's 'lyric poet of high capitalism', and his use of pastoral techniques to describe the modern city. One unattributed quotation from the *Arcades* comments that 'in passing from all these Romantic poets to Baudelaire, we pass from a landscape of nature to a landscape of stone and flesh'.[20] Zola does something similar, turning Paris into a landscape, or rather the painterly image of a landscape, since the appearance of its greenery as 'water-lilies' anticipates Monet's series of impressionist water-lily paintings from the 1890s onwards.[21] The next move is into literature, fantasy and spectacle, as Paris becomes first a scene from the *Arabian Nights* (Zola would have known the first French translation of *The Thousand and One Nights*, by Antoine Galland in 1704–17), then a source of mythical wealth with coins falling from the sky, an image that recalls Zeus coming to Danaë as a shower of gold, adding an implicit sexual charge. The openness and expanse of the sea thus turns within a few lines into the enclosure of an oriental dream, a movement symptomatic of the wider novel and the bourgeois perspective it records, which at once registers the city's vastness and reduces and contains it, making the city aesthetically, if not topographically, comprehensible.

Saccard then shadows forth the city's coming destruction, remarking to Angèle, 'how stupid they are, those great cities! It has no idea that an army of picks will fall upon it one of these fine mornings' (K 2.68). He describes the cuts that will be made in a passage that metaphorically dissects Paris, imagined as a giant body, recalling Mary Poovey's argument that the opening of the city in the nineteenth century develops from the opening of the body in the eighteenth (see Chapter 2). As Saccard continues, it becomes clear that his dream of Paris's future is also its ruin, its opening up coinciding with a new domination by military and speculative capital:

'Look over there, near the Halles, they've cut Paris into four pieces.'

With his outstretched hand, open and sharp as a sabre, he indicated how the city was being divided into four parts.

'You mean the Rue de Rivoli and the new boulevard they're building?' asked his wife.

'Yes, the great transept of Paris, as they call it. [. . .] When the first network is finished the fun will begin. The second network will cut through the city in all directions to connect the suburbs with the first network. The rest will disappear in clouds of plaster. Look, just follow my hand. From the Boulevard du Temple to the Barrière du Trône, that's one cut; then on this side another, from the Madeleine to the Plaine Monceau; and a third cut this way, another that way, a cut there, one further on, cuts everywhere, Paris slashed with sabre cuts, its veins opened, providing a living for a hundred thousand navvies and bricklayers, traversed by splendid military roads which will bring the forts into the heart of the old neighbourhoods.'

Night was falling. His dry, feverish hand kept cutting through the air. Angèle shivered slightly as she watched this living knife, those iron fingers mercilessly slicing up the boundless mass of dark roofs. [. . .] [S]he fancied she could hear, beneath the gloom gathering in the hollows, distant cracking sounds, as if her husband's hand had really made the cuts he spoke of, splitting Paris from one end to the other [. . .]. The smallness of this hand, pitilessly attacking a giant prey, became quite disturbing; and as it effortlessly tore apart the entrails of the great city, it seemed to take on a steely glint in the blue twilight. (K 2.68–9)

The end of this passage invokes the novel's title, *la curée*, literally 'the part of an animal fed to the hounds that have run it to ground'.[22] Here it is Saccard who symbolically tears the city apart, echoing Baudelaire in 'Le Soleil', where he refers to his 'fantasque escrime' ('quaint swordsmanship'), as well as the false etymology Baudelaire gives for his name: 'my name is something terrible [. . .]. As a matter of fact, the *badelare* was a saber with a short, broad blade and a convex cutting edge, hooked at the tip'.[23] There is a difference between the two, though, since Baudelaire's poems tend to fence with the city as a kind of psychical defence or form of play, whereas Saccard goes in for the kill, brutally disembowelling it. Saccard's hand does not hold a sword but becomes it; his 'iron fingers' take on a 'steely glint', evoking the use of iron in the new ferrovitreous architecture of the city. If iron is the century's architectural unconscious, as I suggested in Chapter 2, then the 'steely glint' of Saccard's hand is an image of that unconscious erupting and turning upon the city with a destructive force. This makes it most like the railway in *Dombey and Son*, which similarly cuts across London, though less mercilessly than Saccard.

This new Paris under construction will become the scene of Maxime and Renée's love affair, during which the whole city is for them transformed into a luxurious domestic interior. We see this, for instance, in the couple's view of the Parc Monceau, visible from Saccard's townhouse:

> They enjoyed looking at this charming corner of the new Paris, this clean, pleasant bit of nature, these lawns like pieces of velvet, interspersed with flower-beds and shrubs, and bordered with magnificent white roses. Carriages passed by, as numerous as on the boulevards; the ladies on foot trailed their skirts languorously, as though they were walking across their drawing room carpets. (K 5.168)

The couple's subsequent journey through the boulevards is described in similar terms:

> They often drove through the city, going out of their way to pass along certain boulevards, which they loved with a personal affection. [. . .] They drove on, and it seemed to them that the carriage was rolling over carpets along the straight, endless roadway, which had been made solely to save them from the dark backstreets. Every boulevard became a corridor of their house. (K 5.168–9)

In both cases the lovers are separate from the views in which they luxuriate: first in a house and then in a carriage, making them at once outside and inside, safely enclosed even while they traverse the newly exposed spaces (or 'veins') of the city. They are in a similar position to Dombey in his train carriage, except that the interior is no longer a mobile retreat from the exterior world, but has projected itself outwards onto the city. Philippe Hamon reads this passage as an example of the 'exposition' character of Zola's writing, arguing that in nineteenth-century France, 'the dream of transparency goes hand in hand with the dream of transforming the world or the house into a collection, a museum, or a place at a universal exposition'.[24] For Hamon, the exposition world dominated French literature after 1850, developing out of the earlier Romantic fascination with ruins. Benjamin, who suggests that 'in the years 1850–1890, exhibitions take the place of museums', sees this world as the natural habitat of the flâneur.[25]

In such exteriors reinvented as interiors, as also in interiors imagined as exteriors, bourgeois space takes on the appearance of universal space. Although this may involve the appearance of order or social control, as in the description of the Parc Monceau quoted above, such blurring of the city's topography also highlights the 'porous boundaries between proper society and the demi-monde', as Masha Belenky observes with reference to this park.[26] Benjamin quotes a 1925 account of a British embassy ball held in 1839, which calls the event, paradoxically, 'a true masquerade of space'.[27] A masquerade is at once a ball, a performance, a mask, an act of falsity and imitation, and a 'motley or fantastic collection of things', and hence aligns with the 'colportage phenomenon of space' mentioned in the preceding entry of the *Arcades*, a concept Brigid Delany reads as a form of montage.[28] The author of 1925 goes on:

> The garden, covered by a pavilion, was turned into a *salon de conversation*. But what a salon! The gay flower beds, full of blooms, were huge *jardinières* which everyone came over to admire; the gravel on the walks was covered with fresh linen, out of consideration for all the white satin shoes; large sofas of lampas and damask replaced the wrought-iron benches; and on a round table there were books and albums. It was a pleasure to take the air in this immense boudoir.[29]

Street and garden are reinvented as enclosed spaces, where domestic space and city space are intertwined. Sharon Marcus emphasises this blurring in her reading of Zola's *Pot-Bouille* (1882), set in a petty-bourgeois Paris apartment block, framing it as a response to 'the critical tendency to oppose the city and the home, and hence assume that a novel about domestic interiors cannot be a novel about the city'.[30] Marcus, like Benjamin, posits that bourgeois home and city have become intimately connected from mid-century onwards, so that they are no longer opposed (as they are for the Carsons in *Mary Barton*, for instance), but instead form a new perceptual and architectural complex – although, as my reading of *Mary Barton* in Chapter 1 indicated, the reinvention of the cellar as a place for dwelling in the 1830s and 40s is already a blurring of urban and domestic space.

Benjamin comments of the embassy ball description that 'today, the watchword is not entanglement but transparency (Le Corbusier!)'.[31] This recalls Giedion's – and following him Leckie's – emphasis on 'interpenetration' as a connective principle of nineteenth-century architecture (see Introduction), since entanglement (*Verschränkung*) and interpenetration (*Durchdringung*) both refer to the mixing of disparate elements. Benjamin implies that there is a decisive shift from the nineteenth-century epoch of entanglement to modernist transparency. Yet it is also the case that in both Zola's novels and

Benjamin's own examples, bourgeois profusion or entanglement often enables forms of transparency rather than blocking them. Saccard sees the clean lines of future boulevards precisely through their contrast with the messiness of early 1850s Paris; the city opens itself out before Maxime and Renée even while they are cosseted and entangled by it; visitors to the garden ball 'take the air' even while standing under a pavilion. In all these cases transparency grows alongside, or under the cover of, the stifling weight of bourgeois commodification. Nowhere in the novel is this duality more apparent than Saccard's mansion and its accompanying glass hothouse, to which I now turn.

The Mansion and the Hothouse

The central domestic setting in *La Curée* is Saccard's mansion, built in the new but derivative Second Empire style. It is located in the Rue Monceau in the 17th arrondissement, just off the Boulevard Malesherbes, a street inaugurated under Haussmann in 1861. The mansion is based on the Hôtel Menier on the Parc Monceau, four drawings of which are included in Zola's notes for the novel.[32] Zola's version includes a 'pretty lodge vaguely suggestive of a little Greek temple' (K 1.15), a 'great glass awning' (K 1.5) over the steps on the street side, and a 'far more sumptuous' (K 1.15) facade on the park side, where

> The display of decoration was profuse. The house was hidden under its sculpture. Around the windows and along the cornices ran volutes of flowers and branches; there were balconies shaped like baskets full of blossoms, and supported by tall naked women with wide hips and jutting breasts; and here and there were faithful escutcheons, clusters of fruit, roses, every flower it is possible for stone or marble to represent. (K 1.16)

This arabesque design produces an overwhelming visual spectacle, which is both fantastical and meaningless, its evocation of classical images and natural fecundity serving only to indicate excess rather than generating a narrative or holding artistic merit. It is architecture divested of all quality, becoming pure quantity, a mere heap of capital. Unlike in some conceptions of the arabesque surface, which I discuss in Chapter 5, there is no potential here for the emergence of a transcendent absolute. The same is true of the goods in Mouret's department store in *The Ladies' Paradise*, as will be seen. The architecture of the mansion suggests a reversal of Eisenstein's reading of Zola, such that ecstatic accumulation signals not a developing potential for communist cinema but the profusion of capitalist consumption, which rather than opening up a path to social unity makes invisible whatever lies outside its own sphere.

Standing on the right-hand side of the Saccard's mansion is an 'enormous hothouse' (*une vaste serre* – the term connoting pressure and enclosure more strongly than in English) (K 1.16), which is 'a miniature version of the new Louvre, one of the most typical examples of the Napoleon III style, that opulent bastard of so many styles' (K 1.16–17). This makes it an example of what Nikolai Gogol condemns in an essay of 1835 as the domestication of monumental architecture, referring to its reproduction in 'little bridges and gates'.[33] The 'new Louvre' referred to is the extension built from 1852–7, which was connected to the Tuileries Palace, and subsequently burnt down during the Paris Commune in May 1871, an event depicted in Zola's *La Débâcle* (1892), so that the hothouse subtly foreshadows both the family's and the Second Empire's collapse. Its windows have 'sheets of glass so wide and clear that they seemed like the window-fronts of a big modern department store, arranged so as to display to the outside world the wealth within' (K 1.17). These turn the interior outwards upon the external world, so that the space of the city becomes colonised by bourgeois decadence, itself based on a fantasy of the tropical world, since the hothouse is heated to a 'suffocating' (K 4.157) temperature and contains 'palm trees and [. . .] tall Indian bamboos' (K 4.158) among its 'thick tangle of plants' (K 4.158).

Relevant here is Benjamin's reference to 'the dreamy and, if possible, oriental interior' of bourgeois Paris, given alongside a quotation from Gutzkow which evokes the *Arabian Nights*, as Saccard's view of Paris does. It serves as a commentary on *La Curée*:

> Everyone here dreams of instant fortune; everyone aims to have, at one stroke, what in peaceful and industrious times would cost a lifetime of effort. The creations of the poets are full of sudden metamorphoses in domestic existence; they all rave about marquises and princesses, about the prodigies of the *Thousand and One Nights*.[34]

Saccard's ascent from clerk to one of Paris's wealthiest men is just such a metamorphosis, and the hothouse embodies the dreamy and oriental interior which is its outcome, offering Maxime and Renée their most 'acrid form of intoxication' (K 4.157). To Eisenstein's other examples of Zola's heated environments, such as 'the little iron stove burning so hot it induces stupor in the small room in *The Human-Beast*', we can add the tropical plants ('vanilla plants [. . .] Indian berries [. . .] quisqualias' (K 4.159)) that fill this hothouse and intensify Maxime's sexual otherness.[35] It is in this setting especially that Maxime seems 'born and bred for perverted sexual pleasure [. . .] this creature of indeterminate sex' (K 4.158). The oriental fantasy also spreads outside, through the hothouse's visual transformation of the world outside it: 'Through the little panes of the hothouse they could catch glimpses of the Parc Monceau, clumps of trees with fine black outlines [. . .], even tints reminiscent of Japanese prints' (K 4.158). The park, which has already been presented as a domestic interior, here becomes a commodified Asiatic image, appearing like one of the items available in the Ladies' Paradise, the 'Chinese and Japanese curiosities [. . .] which the customers were eagerly snatching up'.[36] In both novels, the oriental is experienced in a highly mediated and refashioned form, with little connection to actual Asian life. Asia instead becomes the source of a fantastical and fetishised otherness that seems to offer an escape from the city while also, in fact, remaining within it: 'They were a thousand miles from Paris, from the easy life of the Bois and official receptions, in a corner of an Indian forest, of some monstrous temple of which the black marble sphinx became the deity' (K 4.160). This is enclosure and escape at once. It is no coincidence that this same novel which makes Paris the centre of the world also dissolves the city into sheer spectacle and fetishised desire, making the new Paris appear as an interior which is nothing but facade, defined by sexual and architectural excess. This dual process makes the lives of anyone outside a privileged bubble unreadable for those within it, unless in egotistical and commodified terms, as new sources of stimulation to relieve a state of boredom and ennui that is historically contingent, but which Zola also makes congenital.

This condition, in which the visual field becomes autonomous without leading to increased social awareness or connectivity, is what Guy Debord calls the spectacle. As Graham MacPhee observes, Debord extended the concept of reification developed by Georg Lukács to visual experience, making spectacle the condition of modern capitalism.[37] It gives an appearance of unity while in fact separating people from the real conditions of their social life:

> The spectacle appears at once as society itself, as a part of society and as a means of unification. As a part of society, it is that sector where all attention, all consciousness, converges. Being isolated – and precisely

for that reason – this sector is the locus of illusion and false consciousness; the unity it imposes is merely the official language of generalized separation.[38]

The spectacle is both an appearance of totality ('society itself') and a particular 'sector'. In it, a part of society separates from the whole only to turn back upon it as an illusory image of completeness. For Debord, this is an extension of the fetish character of the commodity, which has become absolutely hegemonic: 'The real consumer [. . .] becomes a consumer of illusion. The commodity is this illusion, which is in fact real, and the spectacle is its most general form.'[39] The subject's relationship is no longer with commodities, which at least have a material existence, but with the image of the commodity, or rather the commodity as image. Commodities, already the embodiment of alienated social labour, are now consumed as illusion, alienating them even from their own materiality, so making spectacle the alienation of an alienation. Though Debord sees spectacle as a twentieth-century development, in Saccard's mansion and the Paris of Maxime and Renée we can trace what Benjamin calls its fore-history.

A counterpoint to the hothouse, where Renée 'assumed the masculine role' (K 4.158) with Maxime, is her dressing room, which is explicitly figured as an architectural echo of her own highly feminised naked body. Evoking simultaneously *ancien régime* decadence (it is talked about like 'the Hall of Mirrors at Versailles' (K 4.151)), fantasies of the Orient and the Americas ('one was reminded of a large circular tent, a magical tent, pitched in a dream by some lovelorn Amazon' (K 4.151)), and a classical bower, or more precisely a neoclassical projection of eroticised classical life ('a laughing Cupid looking down and preparing his dart' (K 4.1152)), the room is a kind of frozen montage, a colportage of space that brings together indiscriminately the luxuries of all times and spaces ('two ottomans, some white satin stools [. . .] antique Bohemian crystal' (K 4.152)). Anticipating the great white sales of Mouret's department store, discussed below and in Chapter 6, this dressing room makes no distinction between architecture, furnishings, commodities and human bodies. The dominant impression is of pink, presented as an externalised form of Renée's body. Commenting that she often stays in her bath until midday, the narrator observes that

> The round tent was naked too. The pink bath, the pink slabs and basins, the muslin of the walls and ceiling, under which pink blood seemed to

course, had the curves of flesh, the curves of shoulders and breasts; and, according to the time of day, one would have imagined the snowy skin of a child or the warm skin of a woman. It was redolent of nudity. (K 4.152)

The sexualised, infantilised, white European but exoticised woman is the heart of this structure, which is architectural but also dissolves architecture, becoming a 'tent'. In *Le Ventre de Paris*, Zola has the painter Claude Lantier pronounce 'his most beautiful work to be the ephemeral arrangement of turkeys, sausages and black puddings in the Quenu *charcuterie*', but this is also a case where beauty becomes grotesque, symbolising 'the gluttony of Christmas Eve' and making the turkey 'obscene'.[40] In Renée's room, objects and bodies similarly become component parts of not just an artwork but an architectural structure which verges on the grotesque, and whose profusion of display hints at a connection with the World Exhibitions. Here we see Zola take on the role of Lantier, with literature the medium that allows him to transform built space into an aesthetic allegory. Yet although the layers of cloth, flesh and furnishing seem to take us deep into a fleshy interior, and hence into the body of Renée, presented as a decadent apogee of woman, as Nana is in Zola's novel of 1880, the text also denies us entry, or perhaps cannot find a way in. Peter Brooks makes the point that *Nana* cannot make good on its claim to 'say everything', because 'Zola's prime motors and machines in his novels are elaborately detailed, patiently described, but in their essence unsayable', especially when they involve female sexuality.[41] In a related way, what is described in *La Curée* is a series of exterior surfaces, which, like the commodity form in general, are both openly available and yet indifferent to the purchaser, narrator, viewer or reader. The room is like 'some precious jewel-case enlarged as if to display a woman's naked body instead of the brilliancy of a diamond' (K 4.152), but like the 'paraphernalia and toilet utensils' (K 4.152) laid out on a silver-inlaid table, all that seems possible is display and spectacle. We have absolute openness to view and absolute transparency, like a department-store window, but also absolute withdrawal. In this scene, the reified body of the woman stands in for and symbolically becomes a 'diamond', the ultimate example of a commodity measured by exchange value rather than use value. This institutes unfulfillable capitalist desire as the shaping force of a new dynamics of space, as will be borne out most dramatically in *Au Bonheur des Dames*.

Dissecting the Boulevard

Perhaps surprisingly, it is only in the final chapter of *La Curée* that a boulevard under construction is directly depicted. Saccard, alongside four other members of the Compensation Authority, visits 'the large demolition site that was to become the Boulevard du Prince-Eugène' (K 7.247), where the destruction he described to Angèle has been realised:

> tall, gutted buildings, displaying their pale insides, opened to the skies their wells stripped of stairs, their gaping rooms suspended in mid-air like the broken drawers of a big, ugly piece of furniture. Nothing could be more forlorn than the wallpaper of these rooms, blue and yellow squares hanging in tatters, marking the positions, five or six storeys high, right up to the roofs, of wretched little garrets, cramped holes that had once contained, perhaps, a whole human existence. [. . .] The gap yawned still wider in the midst of these ruins, like a breach opened by cannon. (K 7.247–8)

The buildings are like dissected corpses, their 'pale insides' exposed to view. The 'suspended' rooms recall the 'fragments of unfinished walls and arches' (DS 68) in Staggs's Gardens. This is an exposure of the working-class interior like that which Dickens's 'good spirit' is imagined to bring about, or which James Kay hoped to produce in Manchester, except that here there are no human inhabitants. Only their traces remain, like the squares of wallpaper which indicate where rooms used to be. These form ghostly impressions of vanished lives, such that architecture is inscribed as the site of loss, or a negative image of the human, making it like Eugène Atget's (1857–1927) photographs of 'deserted Paris streets', which Benjamin reads as if they were crime scenes.[42]

An inspector draws attention to one of these traces of habitation: 'It's extraordinary [. . .] Saccard, look at that kitchen up there; there's an old frying pan still hanging over the stove. I can see it quite clearly' (K 7.248). This sign of domesticity is isolated and effectively unreadable. Although it can be seen 'quite clearly', it signifies absence. Like a Benjaminian fragment, the frying pan breaks out of historical chronology, existing in a state of suspension which is both spatial (it is literally 'hanging') and temporal, since it is only visible now, at this precise moment when the buildings are being destroyed. The yawning 'gap' or break (*la trouée*) between the buildings, which marks the line of the future boulevard, also represents spatio-temporal suspension, recalling the gap in the street which Dombey's house becomes in chapter 23 of *Dombey and Son*, before being restored to bourgeois luxury, as will also happen here. The traces of former existence which have been briefly exposed mean this gap is not an absolute blank, but rather a negative presence of the lives and buildings which are on the verge of erasure. Another inspector, a former knife-grinder, spots the room where he lived many years earlier through a 'breach in the wall' (K 7.250), making him 'stop short' (K 7.249). Memory is exposed in this moment along with the domestic interior, so that the boundaries between the city and the self temporarily break down:

> You see the cupboard; that's where I put by three hundred francs, sou by sou. And the hole for the stovepipe, I can still remember the day I made it. There was no fireplace, it was bitterly cold, all the more so because I was often on my own. (K 7.250)

By contrast, Saccard's response is that of the cynical improver: 'There's nothing wrong with pulling these old hovels down. We're going to build fine freestone houses in their place. [. . .] There's nothing to stop you taking up residence on the new boulevard' (K 7.250). His reply, of course, excludes all the former residents of the street who, unlike the inspector, have not made their fortune, and who therefore do have something to stop them moving to the new boulevard. The only presence of these others remains the fragile traces which the new houses will soon replace.

Saccard's own memory does also return amidst these ruins of the old Paris, as he recalls the dinner with Angèle on the Buttes Montmartre where he dreamt of the new boulevards. For him, though, this is a cause for joy rather than melancholy:

> The realization of his prophecy delighted him. He followed the cutting with the secret joy of authorship, as though he himself had struck the first blows of the pickaxe with his iron fingers. He skipped over the puddles, reflecting that three million francs were waiting for him beneath a heap of rubble, at the end of this stream of mire. (K 7.251)

Saccard claims 'the secret joys of authorship' (*des joies secrètes d'auteur*) of this building work, imagining that he not only foresaw the reconstruction of the city but actively produced it. This concept of authorship has a wider significance, hinting that Paris is shifting from an unintentional to an intentional city: one which is planned and authored by those with access to capital and influence. The memory also helps Saccard protect himself from the destruction and ruin around him, allegorically transforming it into a source of fantastical wealth, as he previously did on Montmartre. This time, he contemplates the three million francs he will earn in compensation for his ownership of the buildings, an alchemical transformation of waste into money that parallels the wealth generated by the dust heaps in *Our Mutual Friend*. Saccard's world is not wholly secure, however, since the structure his money creates is unstable: 'The golden stream had a source at last. But it was not yet a solid, established fortune, flowing with an even continuous current' (K 7.253). Saccard's wealth remains transitory, vulnerable and ephemeral, as *L'Argent* (1891), Zola's novel of financial speculation, will show. This opening up of the city is thus also a closing down, as Paris becomes increasingly defined in terms of money and the goods money can buy, so that the promotion of visibility we see in this part of the novel enables the reproduction of a culturally and economically homogeneous world. As the following section will explore, this new kind of invisible architecture, in which transparency is inextricable from enclosure, is not only a feature of the boulevards, but is taken to its most extreme point in Zola's glass and iron department store.

Au Bonheur des Dames and the Commodified World

If the ruin in chapter 7 of *La Curée* seems to be the opposite of Saccard's fantastical hothouse, and by extension of the modern department store of *Au Bonheur des Dames*, this is true only in the way that fashion and death are opposites for Benjamin, as two sides of the same dialectical image which turn into one another. Fashion, says Benjamin, satisfies the desire for a 'new tempo of life', so that it seems linked to active vitality, yet it also 'stands in opposition to the organic. [. . .] To the living, it defends the rights of the corpse.'[43] In the same way, ruin haunts the department store, undermining the appearance of totality which the store works to bring about. Such a dialectical opposition of ruin and totality is found in the final sentence of Benjamin's 1935 exposé for the *Arcades*: 'With the destabilizing of the market economy, we begin to recognize the monuments of the bourgeoisie as ruins even before they have crumbled.'[44] Economic destabilisation is a feature of both *La Curée* and *Au Bonheur des Dames*. In the latter case it is a precept expounded explicitly by the store's owner, Octave Mouret, who tells Baron Hartmann (a version of Haussmann) that his new mode of business is 'based on the rapid and continuous turnover of capital, which had to be converted into goods as many times as possible within twelve months' (LP 3.74). The department store is a bourgeois monument in Benjamin's terms precisely because of this dynamic instability, which makes it anti-monumental in the conventional sense, since it persists only through continual change and reinvention. In this way, the store replicates the commodities which fill it. Zola's novel, as I show in this section, tracks the process by which the store takes on the character of the commodity. It shows how architecture utilises and reproduces the commodity's illusions of transparency on a grand scale, aided by iron, glass and a vast expansion of the spatial logics of Renée's dressing room.

Rather than any particular character, it is the store itself, based largely on the Bon Marché, where Zola did extensive research, that occupies the centre of *Au Bonheur des Dames*. It dominates the narrative and symbolic space of the novel in the same way as it dominates the streets around it. In doing so it displays a dialectical doubleness, being both a part that represents a whole (one building containing the entire world) and a whole made out of many parts (consisting of many different departments and goods), in a similar way to the World Exhibitions. This is a new kind of urban totality, one whose strength comes from its malleability, and which is linked from the start with the store's transparent but visually overwhelming architecture. As the novel opens, Denise Baudu, the main human protagonist, has arrived in Paris to seek work in a draper's shop. Her first view of the Bonheur des Dames department store is one of infinite visual excess:[45]

> With its series of perspectives, with the display on the ground floor and the plate-glass windows of the mezzanine floor, behind which could be seen all the intimate life of the various departments, the spectacle seemed to Denise to be endless. (LP 1.4)

Like Saccard's hothouse, the store turns itself inside out, its plate-glass windows allowing its goods to metaphorically spill onto the street and accost passers-by. The view appears to Denise to be 'endless', yet is also broken up into a 'series of perspectives' and 'various departments'. As Brian Nelson observes, the Ladies' Paradise is 'a microcosm of capitalist society', whose departments (including haberdashery, perfume and ladieswear, where Denise will find a job) compete with one another as if they are separate businesses, as do the individual employees, who work on commission; yet these semi-autonomous regions are nonetheless part of a greater whole.[46] In this way the store spatially embodies the duplicity of spectacular society described by Debord:

> The origin of the spectacle lies in the world's loss of unity [. . .] Spectators are linked only by a one-way relationship to the very center that maintains their isolation from one another. The spectacle thus unites what is separate, but it unites it only *in its separateness*.[47]

In the spectacle, an illusion of unity is produced not in spite of but through the separation of spectators from one another. Similarly here, the simultaneous unity and separation Denise perceives in the shop window is both an indication of the structure by which the store operates and a reflection of her own position within capitalist distributions of space.

Octave Mouret, the store's owner, embodies this uniting/separating centre that makes spectacular culture possible. This is evident in the panoptical viewpoint he adopts during the first of the three great sales that take place in the novel: 'Mouret [. . .] planted himself beside the hall balustrade. From there he dominated the whole shop, for he had the mezzanine departments around him, and could look down into the ground-floor departments' (LP 4.94). The customers he surveys are focused not on each other but on the commodities laid before them; they are united only in the ambiguous and mediated form of being oriented towards a shared object. Mouret is thus the emissary of the commodity-as-image and department store culture, whose axiom, according to Giedion, is 'Welcome the crowd and keep it seduced!'[48] Mouret is the novel's great seducer of women, being 'entranced and affectionate in their presence' (LP 1.33), but also displaying 'brutality' and 'disdain' (LP 3.77) towards them.

It is the internal architecture of the store that allows Mouret to adopt his pseudo-panoptical position. Michael Miller describes the new openness which glass and iron had produced in the Bon Marché, after its reconstruction in 1869 by L. A. Boileau and Gustave Eiffel, an event that inspired chapters 8 and 9 of Zola's novel:

> Together they devised a plan that would employ a framework of thin iron columns and a roofing of glass skylights to work to the best advantage of a giant retail operation. The role of the iron was to provide for open, spacious bays in which large quantities could readily be displayed and through which vast crowds could move with ease. The skylights,

capping what in effect was a series of interior courts, were to permit a maximum influx of natural light, which was deemed necessary for display purposes.[49]

The transparency of the store's public areas gives the impression that everything is open to view, yet it is balanced by a 'provision for central offices on the top floors and a depot that could send and receive packages and store merchandise in a first-level basement', and by the machinery for heating hidden in a second basement.[50] As part of his research, Zola employed an architect, Frantz Jourdain, to produce a full architectural plan of his fictional building in 1882. The plan involved extensive use of iron, glass and colourful decoration, and even 'specif[ied] what materials were to be used, disposition of interior spaces, type of decoration, even cost estimates'.[51] Jourdain later used it as the basis for the Samaritaine department store, which he designed between the 1880s and 1920s.[52] The openness of the design allows Mouret to see and 'dominate' the store while also maximising the visible accumulation of goods, creating a situation where, as Mouret puts it, 'the customer found herself snared [. . .] she bought a whole set of clothes, then got caught by unforeseen attractions, yielding to the need for all that is useless and pretty' (LP 3.75). Mouret becomes a surrogate for modern capitalism, seducing the overwhelmingly female customers of the store while remaining wholly indifferent to them.

The customers' pliability in the face of capitalism leads to their transformation into objects. One of the most telling instances of this reification, as critics have noted, is the mannequins with 'round bosoms' and 'wide hips' (LP 1.6), both also characteristics of the female statues that adorn Saccard's mansion, whose heads have been replaced with price tags.[53] Mirrors 'reflect the dummies, multiplying them endlessly, seeming to fill the street with these beautiful women for sale with huge price tags where their heads should have been' (LP 1.6). For Jean, Denise's adolescent brother, these commodity-women are 'amazing' (LP 1.6), embodiments of desire which make him 'pink with pleasure' (LP 1.6), his pinkness recalling Renée's bath suite. Jean, who has 'the beauty of a girl' (LP 1.6), is another of Zola's effeminate, sexualised male characters, like Maxime. More significant than the fact of Jean's desire, though, is that the store openly displays the commodification of women, and that it gains rather than loses as a result. Women are invited to buy into, and hence become, the very commodities that produce an illusory and unattainable image of femininity, leading them to participate in their own reification.

Strangely enough, when Eisenstein quotes this passage as an example of ecstatic montage, he reads it in the opposite way, as an instance of things becoming people rather than people becoming things, stating that 'the mannequins not only come alive but are incarnated into women'.[54] This telling choice suggests that Eisenstein's ideal of true (that is, socialist) montage, in which *'everything speaks'*, to use Rancière's formulation, in a kind of radical democracy, is not the opposite of capitalist spectacle, but rather its inverse side, so that the two are always liable to turn into one another.[55] The dichotomy between mannequins becoming women and women becoming mannequins is not, in the end, oppositional but complementary, so that utopia and ideology inhere inside one another here.[56]

The Store as Transfigured Landscape

In *Au Bonheur des Dames*, architectural transparency helps make visible the competition between stores taking place in Paris, in its role as the capital of nineteenth-century consumption. Such competition appears at first to empower consumers, in the account Mouret gives to Hartmann:

> Now competition was taking place before the public's very eyes, people had only to walk past the shop-windows to ascertain the prices, and every shop was reducing them, content with the smallest possible profit; there was no cheating [. . .] just continuous business, a regular profit of so much per cent on all goods, a fortune put into the smooth running of a sale, which was all the larger because it took place in full view of the public. (LP 3.75)

Customers can see and assess the store's commodities, able to benefit from open, transparent pricing visible in every window. But this comes at the expense of being seen and assessed as commodities themselves, as several critics have pointed out. Hennessy comments that 'from the outset, Zola conflates the shopper and the merchandise she covets', while Nicholas Rennie notes that 'the individual becomes one of myriad shoppers and commodities'.[57] As Mouret's panoptical gaze shows, the visual field is not in fact neutral but a pervasive network of power relations. When Hartmann responds to Mouret by calling him the 'inventor of a machine for devouring women' (LP 3.77), it is clear that the machine in question is the store itself, whose architecture perversely turns women into the architects of their own destruction. They become like the goods that enter the chute leading to the store's receiving department, which is depicted as a consuming mouth: 'Everything entered through this yawning trap; things were being swallowed up all the time, a continual cascade of materials falling with the roar of a river' (LP 2.36).[58]

This 'river' of commodities rolling into the store invites comparison with a later passage, describing a display of silks:

> material was streaming down like a bubbling sheet of water, falling from above and spreading out on to the floor. [. . .] And at the bottom, as if in a fountain-basin, the heavy materials, the damasks, the brocades, the silver and gold silks, were sleeping on a deep bed of velvets [. . .], their shimmering flecks forming a still lake in which reflections of the sky and the countryside seemed to dance. Women pale with desire were leaning over as if to look at themselves. Faced with this wild cataract, they all remained standing there, filled with the secret fear of being caught up in the overflow of all this luxury and with an irresistible desire to throw themselves into it and be lost. (LP 4.104)

The allusion here is to the myth of Narcissus, undone by his love for his own reflection.[59] In the department store, though, the viewer is gendered as female, and in place of a reflection she sees only commodities, which are somehow both 'still' and 'wild'. As with the mannequins, the truth of what is happening is not hidden but located openly on the surface; the women see commodities in place of their reflections because that is what the shop incites them to become. The wish to 'throw themselves into [the river] and be lost' is the desire to become part of the ideal commodity world, which as Debord shows, no single, purchasable commodity can in fact encompass.[60] This desire to be consumed rather than consume seems realised when, in an Eisensteinian 'leap' from one image to another, the crowd symbolically becomes the river: 'a compact mass of heads was surging through the arcades, spreading out like an overflowing river into the middle of the hall' (LP 4.108). The crowd now joins the concentration of commodities, becoming part of the landscape of the store, in an extension of Benjamin's observation that the flâneur cannot really stay separate from the scenes he contemplates, but is 'in the same situation as the commodity', of which he is unaware, but which fills him with 'the intoxication of the commodity immersed in a surging stream of customers'.[61] Zola's novel extends and heightens this connection to the point of ecstatic exhaustion.

The passage quoted also metaphorically mimics a pastoral scene, which is among a number of spatial metaphors used by Zola in the novel. Another, the machine, has been indicated already, and others – battlefield, temple, bedroom, palace and phalanstery – are used elsewhere, as the following paragraphs will show. Taken together, these metaphors reveal that the store is fundamentally multiple in its architectural legibility. It embodies a new kind of instability, distinct from that found in *Dombey and Son* or *Our Mutual Friend*, where buildings still generally relate to the relatively fixed models of home and office, even while they disrupt those models; here, by contrast, there is no centre from which to deviate. The 'unnatural' no longer only takes the place of the 'natural', but has become indistinguishable from it. The shop's architecture has taken on the flexibility of consumer capitalism, so that, as Rachel Bowlby observes, it is 'a model in miniature of an entirely new form of existence', ceaselessly creating new seasons, new times and new places.[62] It is an early form of what Debord calls 'the diffuse form of the spectacle', which is 'associated with the abundance of commodities', so that it is defined from the start as excess and multiplicity.[63] Such architecture seems to be at once everywhere and nowhere, both a totality and a profusion of fragments.

Despite this tendency to diffuseness, the metaphor of the machine is a leitmotif throughout the text. It provides an alternative means of interpreting the store, representing the base economic reality of exploitation rather than the superstructure of dreamlike display; although, since this too is a metaphor, the store never fully moves outside literary representation, it is always an imaginary as well as physical construction. The machine is first introduced when the shop appears to Denise as 'regulated and organized with the remorselessness of a machine: the vast horde of women were as if caught in the wheels of an inevitable force' (LP 1.16). The store here recalls the manufacturing landscape of industrial Manchester, seeming like the 'confused interior of a factory' to Denise (LP 1.28), and also the train of *Dombey and Son*, which dashes Carker to death under its wheels, since like the train it is compared to a 'monster' (LP 2.49). In Zola's railway novel, *La Bête Humaine* (1890), Jacques Lantier's locomotive, La Lison, carries a similar destructive force: when it crashes, witnesses see 'the train rearing up in the air, seven carriages climbing one on top of the other, and then everything falling back with most dreadful splintering sound into a jumbled mass of wreckage'.[64] This risk of destruction is extended in another metaphor in *Au Bonheur des Dames*, that of the 'battlefield still hot from the massacre of materials' after the first great sale, where 'half-destroyed stacks of cloth were still standing, like ruined houses about to be carried away by an overflowing river' (LP 4.117). War and desire coexist in this scene, with clothes heaped up like 'the greatcoats of disabled soldiers', while discarded silks and underclothes give 'the impression that an army of women had undressed there haphazardly in a wave of desire' (LP 4.117).

Zola's relentless evocation of female desire is also central to the metaphors of the store-as-temple and the store-as-palace. These are found in the window display, which resembles a 'chapel built for the worship of beauty and grace' (LP 1.6), and Mouret's claim to Hartmann that he is 'building a temple to Woman, making a legion of shop assistants burn incense before her' (LP 3.77). Here we see the production of Woman as goddess, desirable but unattainable, in an ideological process which, once again, is not hidden but laid open to view. In the final sale the process reaches its apotheosis, as the temple becomes a bedroom, with a tent made of curtains that is 'evocative both of the tabernacle and the bedroom. It looked like a great white bed, its virginal whiteness waiting, as in legends, for the white princess, for she who would one day come' (LP 14.398). The pinkness of Renée's dressing room has been elevated into whiteness, such that Woman is idealised as both virginal and sexual, and imagined as racially transcending the skin colour of female European bodies to become the essence of whiteness as an ideal form, evoking the eroticism but also lifelessness of classical statuary. Real women are absented from the source of Woman's supposed seat of power, since the only woman appropriate to this interior is a legend or a dream, an impossible 'princess' who will nonetheless 'one day come'. Such a woman is what the store implies or promises as a guarantee of its present and future solidity, but is in the final analysis a fantasy that is nowhere in fact incarnated.

The store-as-palace metaphor is invoked most fully following the shop's renovation. Here, the main gallery comes to resemble the speculative dream-city described by Gogol in his 1835 essay on present-day architecture, which I discuss further in Chapter 4. Gogol writes that domestic architecture could in future acquire an 'ethereal quality', if

> whole stories could be suspended, or if daring arches could be constructed, if whole columns, bunched together, could appear on transparent, cast-iron supports, if a house could have columns, girded from top to bottom with patterned iron railings and if hanging iron embellishments,

in thousands of different designs, could surround it with delicate filigree through which the house would look as though through a transparent veil.⁶⁵

Eisenstein sees Gogol's essay as 'probably the closest approximation of how Piranesi forces [architecture] to live and tremble in his etchings', so looking back to Giovanni Battista Piranesi's (1720–78) prison engravings from the 1740s, which Eisenstein read as ecstatically exploding perspective. But he also sees it as looking forwards to modernist architecture:

> if his [Gogol's] idea of 'the transparency' of architecture was solved, not by his castiron 'transparent veils', but by . . . glass, then – it was the glass of the American (Frank Lloyd Wright), 'father of transparent houses', and the conception of his 'beautiful tower' – is Tatlin's tower.⁶⁶

Like the railway in *Dombey and Son*, Gogol gives us a Benjaminian monad. Benjamin quotes the essay in the *Arcades*, finding in it 'a divinatory representation of architectural aspects of the later world exhibitions', and one which requires to be read as a dialectical image comprising both Gothic enclosure (Piranesi) and modern transparency (Frank Lloyd Wright), making it an instance of invisible architecture.⁶⁷ Closer to Gogol's own time than either of these, his dream seems to be realised in the reinvented *Ladies' Paradise*:

> It was like the concourse of a station, surrounded by the balustrades of the two upper storeys, intersected by hanging staircases, and with suspension bridges built across it. The iron stair cases, with double spirals, opened out in bold curves, multiplying the landings; the iron bridges, thrown across the void, ran straight along, very high up; and beneath the pale light from the windows all this metal formed a delicate piece of architecture, a complicated lacework through which the daylight passed, the modern realization of a dream-palace, of a Babel-like accumulation of storeys in which halls opened out, offering glimpses of other storeys and halls without end. (LP 9.249)

This is architecture as both ornament and arabesque, dominated by 'spirals', 'lacework', the 'accumulation of storeys' and 'halls without end'. It can be taken as an inversion of Piranesi's drawings, transferring them from the underground to the sky, or of Staggs's Gardens, which is also compared to 'Babel'. Industrial infrastructure ('like the concourse of a station') and the fantastical ('a dream-palace') come together here, suturing the various spatial metaphors of the store and making its simultaneously ideological and utopian nature apparent. This combination is anticipated earlier in the novel with the metaphor of the phalanstery, when employees are said to be 'nothing but cogs, caught up in the workings of the machine, surrendering their personalities, merely adding to the mighty common whole of the phalanstery' (LP 5.134). The phalanstery was Charles Fourier's (1772–1837) socialist utopia, projected to 'accommodate about 2,000 people in a communal organisation', in vast buildings operating as 'cities in miniature', complete with amenities including 'pathways over roofs [. . .] to give access to the natural open-air environment'.[68] Benjamin suggests that

> The phalanstery can be characterized as human machinery. This is no reproach, nor is it meant to indicate anything mechanistic; rather, it refers to the great complexity of its structure <*Aufbau*>. The phalanstery is a machine made from human beings.[69]

The phalanstery transforms the rationalism of industrial capitalism into a utopian project, hinting that utopia and capitalist ideology share the same conceptual and architectural space, making it appropriate to Zola's department store. The store, like the phalanstery, creates a sense of totality by transforming people into machinic parts of its structure, drawing on the alienation of industrial society but reversing its polarity, so that becoming part of a vast human machine is reimagined as a collective affirmation.

Commodity Architecture

The store's internal structure is also associated with another phenomenon: the piling up of goods. This transforms commodities into architecture, and commodifies architecture, as well as multiplying visibility until it becomes overwhelming. In a reversal of the hidden surplus labour of Gaskell's Manchester, we now have the profligate display of surplus commodities, not as a by-product but as an economic and structural principle. Mouret tells Hartmann that his business's strength is 'multiplied tenfold by accumulation, by all the goods being gathered together at one point, supporting and boosting each other' (LP 3.75). This is evident when Mouret rearranges a silk display constructed by Hutin, a sales clerk, saying 'but why are you trying to make it easy on the eye? [. . .] Don't be afraid, blind them . . .

Here! Some red! Some green! Some yellow!' (LP 2.48). The dazzling effect of Mouret's display is symbolic of the general ideological effect produced by the store and its commodities, as the opening up of the visual field acts to disrupt vision by erasing all details, leaving only the experience of being overwhelmed. This is extended beyond the walls of the building, since it is the store's relentless visibility, as well as its ongoing expansion, that overwhelms the smaller businesses surrounding it. Such expansion realises the fear of Denise's uncle Baudu, who runs a small draper's shop, that 'the neighbourhood was being gradually overrun and devoured' (LP 1.24). The old shops cannot overcome the realities of the outside world as the Ladies' Paradise can; when it rains, water seems to run 'right up to the counters' (LP 1.27). Later, Baudu's shop is 'overcome by the somnolence of ruin; empty corners formed dark cavities' (LP 8.209), making it invisible in comparison with the store's colonising brightness.

More explicitly, the transformation of goods into architecture is literally realised in the department store's displays, as when Denise is first attracted by a window display where 'umbrellas, placed obliquely, seemed to form the roof of some rustic hut, beneath which, suspended from rods and displaying the rounded outlines of calves, were silk stockings' (LP 1.4). This replacement of architecture by the products of industrial capitalism is also a return to architecture's earliest origins ('a rustic hut'). Such logic is taken to its limit in chapter 4, where Mouret's first great sale features an oriental hall which realises the original goal of architecture as defined by Gottfried Semper, author of *The Four Elements of Architecture* (1851):

> The architect's general task is to provide a warm and liveable space. Carpets are warm and liveable. He decides for this reason to spread out one carpet on the floor and to hang up four to form the four walls. But you cannot build a house out of carpets. Both the carpet on the floor and the tapestry on the wall require a structural frame to hold them in the correct place. To invent this is the architect's second task.[70]

Although Semper's history of architecture, which dreams of an impossible house of carpets, is speculative, Mouret really does create one:

> First of all, the ceiling was covered with carpets from Smyrna, their complicated designs standing out on red backgrounds. Then, on all four sides, were hung door-curtains: door-curtains from Kerman and Syria, striped with green, yellow and vermilion; door-curtains from Diarbekir, of a commoner type, rough to the touch, like shepherds' cloaks; and

> still more carpets which could be used as hangings, long carpets from Ispahan, Teeran and Kermanshah, broader carpets from Schoumaka and Madras, a strange blossoming of peonies and palms, imagination running riot in a dream garden. On the floor there were still more carpets; thick fleeces were strewn there, and in the centre was a carpet from Agra, an extraordinary specimen with a white background and a broad border of soft blue, through which ran purplish embellishments of exquisite design. [. . .] Visions of the Orient floated beneath the luxury of this barbarous art, amid the strong odour which the wools had retained from lands of vermin and sun. (LP 4.87–8)

In this montage-like scene, commodities are no longer contained within architecture, but become architecture. As in Saccard's hothouse, they bring a dreamlike, intoxicating orientalism into the heart of Paris. The designs of the carpets are arabesques, compared to 'imagination running riot in a dream garden', and so adding to the visual profusion of the store's displays. If the original dream of architecture, as Semper suggests, is not to provide structure but to produce a condition of total enclosure, then the department store's achievement is to bring about this enclosure while simultaneously appearing to open itself up into endless vistas.

In such scenes, *Au Bonheur des Dames* brings to a head the simultaneous enclosure and transparency inaugurated by *La Curée*. As we have seen, in both novels the bourgeois city produces ideological enclosure and utopian promise simultaneously, aided by Zola's adoption of montage techniques that are at once ecstatic in Eisenstein's terms and spectacular in Debord's. If it is typical of Zola's *Rougon-Macquart* cycle that the part stands in for the social whole, generating an impression of totality, while at the same time the whole fractures into an apparently endless series of parts, then in the boulevard and the department store such instability is shown to be not a weakness but a strength. This culminates in commodity architecture, which allows the department store to ceaselessly reinvent itself, following the pattern of modern capitalism. Holding to the past is no longer a form of defence against the modern city, as it was at least temporarily for Alice Wilson in industrial Manchester, but a route to rapid obsolescence.

* * *

In the chapters to come I move away from the focus on individual authors and their cities which has defined the first part of this book. Instead, I examine three ways in which the features of invisible architecture discussed so far are manifested in spatial forms that cut across cities, authors and decades. This second part develops the implications of the first, including by returning to previously discussed authors in new ways. Each chapter presents a different perspective on urban space and literature in the nineteenth century, but in each case I argue for the value of reading through a combination of the three moments of architecture outlined in the Introduction: mobility, concealment and transparency.

Notes

1. Sergei Eisenstein, *Nonindifferent Nature*, trans. by Herbert Marshall (Cambridge: Cambridge University Press, 1987), p. 62. The extent of unity within *Rougon-Macquart* has been a topic of debate. David Bell suggests that 'the structure of Second Empire society as Zola conceives it possesses an underlying and encompassing logic that unifies initially distinct domains in a surprisingly tight manner', but Rachel Bowlby contends that Zola's different spheres are 'inconceivable as a single unified whole'. David Bell, *Models of Power: Politics and Economics in Zola's Rougon-Macquart* (Lincoln: University of Nebraska Press, 1988), p. xi; Bowlby, p. 14.
2. Georg Lukács, 'Narrate or Describe?', in *Writer and Critic*, ed. and trans. by Arthur Kahn (London: Merlin, 1970), pp. 110–48.
3. *Nonindifferent Nature*, p. 65.
4. *Nonindifferent Nature*, p. 59.
5. *Nonindifferent Nature*, p. 85. François Vanoosthuyse discusses the privileged status of Zola's novels as 'supporting columns' for Eisenstein in 'Zola dans l'Optique d'Eisenstein', *Les Cahiers Naturalistes*, 87 (2013), 311–29.
6. For a sustained study of the visual in Zola, see William Berg, *The Visual Novel: Émile Zola and the Art of His Times* (University Park: Pennsylvania State University Press, 1992).
7. Jacques Rancière, *The Future of the Image*, trans. by Gregory Elliott (London: Verso, 2007), p. 48.
8. *Antinomies of Realism*, p. 54.
9. *Antinomies of Realism*, p. 54. See *Order of Things*, pp. 51–85.
10. Berg, p. 224. A counterpoint to Berg is Moretti's observation that 'Zola's Paris novels are mostly confined to very small spaces, whose boundaries are crossed only on special occasions'. Moretti, *Atlas*, p. 90. Taking Berg and Moretti together, we might say that no novel fully represents the city but each attempts in some way to symbolise it.
11. Émile Zola, *The Kill*, trans. by Brian Nelson (Oxford: Oxford University Press, 2004), p. 3. Further references provided in the main text.
12. Lehan, p. 62. Hamon, p. 91.

13. *Arcades*, p. 196.
14. *Arcades*, p. 175.
15. *Arcades*, p. 175.
16. On Haussmannisation, see Philippe Panerai et al., *Urban Forms: The Death and Life of the Urban Block*, trans. by Olga Samuels (Oxford: Architectural Press, 2004), pp. 1–29 and Sharon Marcus, pp. 135–65.
17. P. M. Wetherill, 'Flaubert, Zola, Proust and Paris: An Evolving City in a Shifting Text', in *Émile Zola*, ed. by Harold Bloom (Broomall, PA: Chelsea House, 2004), pp. 151–64 (p. 152).
18. Alison Walls, *The Sentiment of Spending: Intimate Relationships and the Consumerist Environment in the Works of Zola, Rachilde, Maupassant, and Huysmans* (New York: Peter Lang, 2008), p. 7.
19. Honoré de Balzac, *Père Goriot*, trans. by A. J. Krailsheimer (Oxford: Oxford University Press, 1991), p. 263.
20. *Arcades*, p. 252.
21. Zola's great novel of painting is *L'Ouevre* (1886), but his connection with art begins much earlier, his first article in defence of Manet being published in 1866. Monet's seminal *Impression: Sunrise* was not painted until 1872, and first shown in 1874, both after *La Curée* was written, but William Berg suggests Zola 'undertakes in literature a visual revolution like that of Manet and the impressionists in painting – against the precept and prejudice of abstract thought'. Berg, pp. 31–3, p. 47. Rancière has similarly argued that Zola forms part of an 'aesthetic revolution' across art and literature, beginning around 1850, which disrupts the 'order of stable relations between the visible and the invisible'. Jacques Rancière et al., 'Aesthetics and Politics Revisited: An Interview with Jacques Rancière', *Critical Inquiry*, 38.2 (2012), 289–97 (p. 292); *Future of the Image*, p. 12. On Zola and Manet see also F. W. J. Hemmings, *The Life and Times of Émile Zola* (London: Elek, 1977), pp. 52–67.
22. Brian Nelson, 'Introduction' to *The Kill*, pp. vii–xxix (p. x).
23. Charles Baudelaire, *The Flowers of Evil*, trans. by James McGowan (Oxford: Oxford University Press, 1993), pp. 168–9. Louis Thomas quoting Georges Barral, in *Arcades*, p. 242.
24. Hamon, p. 75.
25. *Arcades*, p. 407.
26. Masha Belenky, 'Disordered Topographies in Zola's *La Curée*', *Romance Notes*, 53.1 (2013), 27–37 (p. 30).
27. *Arcades*, p. 419.
28. *OED*, masquerade, n. and adj. *OED Online*, Oxford University Press, <www.oed.com/view/Entry/114657>. Accessed 11 March 2022. Brigid Delaney, 'The "Colportage Phenomenon of Space" and the Place of Montage in *The Arcades Project*', *Germanic Review: Literature, Culture, Theory*, 81.1 (2006), 37–64. See also the previously quoted *Arcades*, p. 406.

29. *Arcades*, p. 419.
30. Sharon Marcus, p. 169.
31. *Arcades*, p. 419.
32. Patrick Bray, *The Novel Map: Space and Subjectivity in Nineteenth-Century French Fiction* (Evanston, IL: Northwestern University Press, 2013), p. 177.
33. Nikolai Gogol, *Arabesques*, trans. by Alexander Tulloch (Ann Arbor: Ardis, 1982), p. 126.
34. *Arcades*, p. 214.
35. *Nonindifferent Nature*, p. 64.
36. Émile Zola, *The Ladies' Paradise*, trans. by Brian Nelson (Oxford: Oxford University Press, 1995), p. 260. Further references in main text.
37. MacPhee, p. 70.
38. Guy Debord, *The Society of the Spectacle*, trans. by Donald Nicholson-Smith (New York: Zone, 1995), p. 12.
39. *Society of the Spectacle*, p. 32.
40. Émile Zola, *The Belly of Paris*, trans. by Brian Nelson (Oxford: Oxford University Press, 2007), p. 187. On this scene see *Future of the Image*, p. 43.
41. Peter Brooks, *Realist Vision* (New Haven: Yale University Press, 2005), p. 127, p. 128.
42. *The Work of Art*, p. 27.
43. *Arcades*, p. 65. 'Paris, the Capital' [1935], p. 8.
44. 'Paris, the Capital' [1935], p. 13.
45. Michael Miller, *The Bon Marché: Bourgeois Culture and the Department Store, 1869–1920* (Princeton: Princeton University Press, 1981), p. 5 and throughout.
46. Brian Nelson, *Zola and the Bourgeoisie: A Study of Themes and Techniques in Les Rougon-Macquart* (Totowa, NJ: Barnes and Noble, 1983), p. 28. On employee competition in the Bon Marché, see Michael Miller, p. 81.
47. *Society of the Spectacle*, p. 22.
48. Giedion quoted in *Arcades*, p. 40.
49. Miller, p. 42. Janet Beizer suggests the renovation makes the store 'the potential home of the *Unheimlich*'. 'Au (delà du) *Bonheur des Dames*: Notes on the Underground', *Australian Journal of French Studies*, 38.1 (2001), 393–406 (p. 403).
50. Miller, p. 42.
51. Meredith Clausen, *Frantz Jourdain and the Samaritaine* (Leiden, Netherlands: Brill, 1987), p. 20.
52. Clausen, pp. 44–9.
53. Danielle Bishop discusses the metaphorical significance of 'losing one's head' in '*Au Bonheur des Dames*: A Novel of Construction, Constructors, and the Constructed', *Excavatio*, 23.1-2 (2008), 243–54 (pp. 250–1). Alison Walls notes the violence and loss of identity in

this image (Walls, p. 72), as does Susie Hennessy in 'Consumption and Desire in *Au Bonheur des Dames*', *French Review*, 81.4 (2008), 696–706 (p. 699). For Bowlby, the dummies represent a descent into image and fragmentation under capitalism. Bowlby, p. 73.
54. *Nonindifferent Nature*, p. 67.
55. *Future of the Image*, p. 15.
56. Fredric Jameson has extensively explored the relationship between utopia and ideology in ways partly indebted to Benjamin. See especially *Archaeologies of the Future: The Desire Called Utopia and Other Science Fictions* (London: Verso, 2005).
57. Hennessy, p. 699. Nicholas Rennie, 'Benjamin and Zola: Narrative, the Individual and Crowds in an Age of Mass Production', *Comparative Literature Studies*, 33.4 (1996), 396–413 (p. 408). See also Bowlby, pp. 66–82.
58. Consumption and the underground are connected elsewhere in Zola, including in the mine entrance in *Germinal* and the market of Les Halles, which is the city's belly in *Le Ventre de Paris*.
59. Bowlby also makes the link with Narcissus. Bowlby, p. 72.
60. 'The already questionable satisfaction allegedly derived from the *consumption of the whole* is adulterated from the outset because the real consumer can only get his hands on a succession of *fragments* of this commodity heaven – fragments each of which naturally lacks any of the *quality* ascribed to the whole.' *Society of the Spectacle*, p. 43.
61. Benjamin, *The Paris of the Second Empire in Baudelaire*, in *The Writer of Modern Life*, p. 85. For a brief literary history of the flâneur, see Ben Moore, 'The Flâneur', in *The Palgrave Encyclopedia of Urban Literary Studies*, ed. by Jeremy Tambling (Cham: Palgrave, 2022), pp. 661–6.
62. Bowlby, p. 42.
63. *Society of the Spectacle*, p. 42.
64. Émile Zola, *La Bête Humaine*, trans. by Roger Pearson (Oxford: Oxford University Press, 1996), p. 289.
65. *Arabesques*, pp. 133–4.
66. *Nonindifferent Nature*, p. 160, pp. 123–36, p. 165.
67. *Arcades*, p. 198. Benjamin appears not to have read the whole essay but to have become aware of it through Wladimir Weidlé's book *Les Abeilles d'Aristée* (1936).
68. George Kohlmaier, *Houses of Glass: A Nineteenth-Century Building Type*, trans. by Barna von Sartory (Cambridge, MA: MIT Press, 1986), p. 15.
69. *Arcades*, p. 626.
70. Semper, quoted in Mark Wigley, *White Walls, Designer Dresses: The Fashioning of Modern Architecture* (Cambridge, MA: MIT Press, 1995), p. 13.

II: Spatial Forms

Chapter 4

Gothic Architecture and Urban Modernity

Gothic architecture has often been positioned as antithetical to urban modernity. In *Contrasts: or, A Parallel between the Noble Edifices of the Fourteenth and Fifteenth Centuries and Similar Buildings of the Present Day; Shewing the Present Decay of Taste* (1836), A. N. W. Pugin lays out the view that European Gothic was the pinnacle of Christian architecture and, in a related way, of unified social order, in contrast to the degraded and fragmented modern city. Before the English Reformation, it was 'the faith, the zeal, and, above all, the unity, of our ancestors, that enabled them to conceive and raise those wonderful fabrics that still remain to excite our wonder and admiration', but once 'schism' and 'avarice' took over, 'the spell was broken, the Architecture itself fell with the religion to which it owed its birth, and was replaced by a mixed and base style'.[1] For Pugin, the restoration of Gothic architecture must be accompanied by 'a restoration of the ancient feelings and sentiments that motivated' its creators, otherwise 'all that is done will be a tame and heartless copy'.[2] Similarly, at the end of Volume 1 of *The Stones of Venice*, which has celebrated Venetian Gothic, Ruskin argues that for city-dwellers, the function of architecture should be 'to tell us about nature', but that this is no longer possible in London, dominated by 'grim railings and dark casements, and wasteful finery of shops, and feeble coxcombry of club-houses'. Ruskin contends that 'the fresh winds and sunshine of the upland' that true Gothic is able to evoke is always 'better than the choke-damp of the vault, or the gas-light of the ball-room', which define the modern city.[3] As Barry Bergdoll observes, 'the notion that Gothic was associated with England's glorious past and cherished institutions was established as early as 1741', generating a form of Gothic nationalism that would later spread across much of Europe, alongside an attempt to 'craft identity through nostalgia for a lost "natural" community'.[4]

This general picture has been nuanced by the recognition that the middle part of the century saw the growth of a 'developmental' school, under which Gothic architecture was gradually modified through a 'slow and accretive adaptation of historical models', accommodating it to some extent with the modern world.[5] My argument in this chapter is more radical, however. I argue that alongside the nostalgic, antimodern approach to Gothic that certainly existed, there was a strain of writing which reinterpreted Gothic as part of the landscape of modernity. This is evident in literary texts including Nikolai Gogol's essay 'On Present-Day Architecture', which appeared in *Arabesques* (1835), Victor Hugo and Émile Zola's reflections on Gothic churches in Paris, and, just after the turn of the century, Henry James's impressions of New York in *The American Scene* (1907).[6]

Henri Lefebvre begins to recognise this Gothic modernity when he writes, during an analysis of his three elements of abstract space, that 'the "logic of visualization" identified by Erwin Panofsky as a strategy embodied in the great Gothic cathedrals now informs the entirety of social practice'. In other words, the modern dominance of vision, which ensures that 'any non-optical impression [. . .] is no longer anything more than a symbolic form of, or a transitional step towards, the visual', was first realised in the Gothic cathedral.[7] In his earlier discussion of Panofsky, Lefebvre characterises this visual logic as shaped especially by height and light: 'the religious edifice, by rising higher, receives more light [. . .] [T]he pillars, small columns and ribbing rise with slender elegance towards the vault'. Lefebvre criticises Panofsky, though, for not recognising the full implication of this logic, which is that 'all should be revealed. All? Yes – everything which was formerly hidden, the secrets of the world.'[8] In this sense, the Gothic cathedral anticipates the open and transparent structures of glass and iron found in modern buildings such as Mouret's department store in *Au Bonheur des Dames*. In theoretical terms, it anticipates Rancière's aesthetic regime, under which art and writing expand in all directions, with the goal of saying everything that can be said.

As valuable as Lefebvre's suggestion is, it does not take us all the way. The concept of invisible architecture can add another dimension to this reading, since although writers certainly did link Gothic architecture with light, height and visibility, there was also an accompanying – and in my view dialectically complementary –

movement of the Gothic tower towards invisibility. This takes place in two main ways: through the recognition that Gothic spires which had previously dominated the city skyline were now relegated to minor and hidden parts of the urban texture, and through descriptions of Gothic towers stretching towards the unseeable and unknowable. In the latter case, the religious ability of Gothic to gesture towards divinity is secularised and reinterpreted, either to imply the future of the modern city (especially the skyscraper), or to indirectly hint at concealed complexities within the urban texture. In this double link to visibility and invisibility, Gothic architecture comes to signify the disjunctive nature of urban modernity in the nineteenth century, of the kind recognised by Benjamin's comments on Baudelaire, who sees modernity as 'marked with the fatality of being one day antiquity'.[9] Out of this conjunction of old and new, visible and invisible, emerges a new conception of the Gothic, one that is never entirely modern, but which nonetheless plays a significant role in nineteenth-century conceptualisations of modernity in the city.

Get Rid of All Disagreeable Views

An 1890 advertising poster for McCaw, Stevenson and Orr's Glacier Window Decoration symbolises the simultaneous modernity and anti-modernity of Gothic in the nineteenth century (Figure 4.1). According to an 1899 edition of *The British Printer*, the 'Glacier' patent dates to the early 1880s, and successfully 'carried the firm's name abroad'.[10] The product was exhibited at the 1893 Chicago World's Fair, nicknamed the White City, as 'a substitute for stained glass'.[11] As the advertisement shows, the company offered sheets of decorated transparent paper which could be applied to ordinary household windows to screen external views and give the impression of stained-glass ornamentation, like that found in a medieval Gothic church. The slogan runs 'Get rid of all Disagreeable Views from your Windows'. In the image, the external view is one of smoking factory chimneys, so that the scene juxtaposes modern urban industrialisation outside with pseudo-medieval decoration within. The same scene is virtually repeated, including the woman of the house applying the decoration, in an advertisement which appeared in the *Graphic* newspaper in 1890 (Figure 4.2). As another company advertisement of 1887 puts it, the product solves the problem that 'many houses in cities have for outlook from the back only a maze of chimneypots, dingy roofs, and the smoking chimneys of manufactories'.[12] Drawing attention to the

Figure 4.1 Advertising leaflet for Glacier Window Decoration (1880s). Alamy.

Figure 4.2 Advertisement for Glacier Window Decoration, *The Graphic* (3 May 1890). Look and Learn.

domesticity of the advert in Figure 4.1, Lori Loeb reads it as signalling a defensive inward turn of the family in the late nineteenth century, in which a 'reluctance to confront the frequent ugliness of the outside world is even given physical manifestation'.[13]

Certainly it seems clear that these advertisements offered a new way of incorporating Gothic design features into the middle-class home, positioning Gothic and a generalised medieval aesthetic as a defence against encroaching urban modernity. By such means, the smoking factories beyond the home are rendered invisible, while at the same time the Gothic church is spectrally evoked as a second form of invisible architecture, now domesticated and commodified. Yet this deployment of medieval Gothic against the city could only happen within a modern system of consumer capitalism, one which is able to utilise sophisticated production techniques. *The British Printer*, for instance, contrasts McCaw, Stevenson and Orr's original association with 'old-style printing', from around 1878, to its expansion and removal in 1894 to Loopbridge, outside Belfast. On this new site, 'the litho machine department covers a large area, and is splendidly equipped with machinery of the best classes'. Of Glacier Window Decoration, the article states that 'nearly a thousand different designs are stocked in large quantities'.[14] Such advanced manufacturing infrastructure, and the vast array of consumer choice it enabled, was in turn transmitted by modern newsprint advertisements, carrying news of this innovative technology to homes across Britain and beyond. This is not, therefore, simply a case of decorative antiquity being opposed to disagreeable modernity, but a new utilisation of Gothic design which transforms it into an aesthetic form that is as modern as it is anti-modern.

A few years later, in 1910, Frank Lloyd Wright's essay 'Organic Architecture' would describe his project as being 'to make of a human dwelling-place a complete work of art'. Wright argued that such an approach ran counter to earlier models, where 'a dwelling was a composite of cells arranged as separate rooms'.[15] His manifesto thus indicates the entrance into domestic architecture of a tendency within nineteenth-century art: the *Gesamtkunstwerk*, or total work of art. This was an idea developed by Wagner, described by James Garratt as 'the collective artwork at the heart of both the Greek polis and the community of the future', and in one essay collection on the topic as 'an aesthetic ambition to borderlessness'.[16] It is the theme of Zola's novel *L'Oeuvre* (1886), where Claude Lantier, based on Paul Cézanne, dreams of painting a masterpiece that would encompass 'Paris in all its glory'.[17] Gogol explores the same idea in 'The Last Day of Pompeii', an essay in *Arabesques* discussing Karl Bryullov's painting of the same name (1830–3, Figure 4.3). Gogol writes that 'Bryullov's painting may be said to be a complete creation of worldwide significance. It includes everything. Within its limits it captures diversity to an extent which nobody previously had managed to capture.' For Gogol this is symptomatic of the nineteenth century, which

Figure 4.3 *The Last Day of Pompeii* (1830–3), Karl Bryullov. Wikiart.

is 'aware of its own terrible process of disintegration and is striving to unite all genres into general groups'.[18] The Gothic cathedral can be seen as a prototype for just such a total work of art, since it was often understood, however idealistically, as a collective dream of organic artistic, religious and social unity. By the time of Wright's work, the combination of unity and variety which Gothic was supposed to achieve, described by Ruskin as 'subtle and flexible like a fiery serpent', was becoming recentred on the modern and proto-modernist home, as an alternative to processes of mainly urban fragmentation and alienation.[19] In a later lecture, Wright would directly acknowledge the organic character of Gothic as an influence on his ideas, along with traditional Japanese buildings and Egyptian architecture: 'The Gothic cathedrals in the Middle Ages had much in them that was organic in character, and they became influential and beautiful, insofar as that quality lived in them which was *organic*.'[20]

This potential modernity of Gothic, in which it comes to represent a set of aesthetic ideals that are not regressive but anticipatory, is also registered in Ernst Bloch's *The Spirit of Utopia* (1916), an idiosyncratic work that sought to recover a revolutionary Marxist and messianic potential within Western art and culture. For Bloch, Gothic represents 'not merely organic but organic-spiritual transcendence', exceeding its physical medium of stone, which becomes 'merely a reinforcing, technically supporting formula'.[21] He goes on to describe this transcendence:

> The Gothic will to render the choir and indeed the entire interior ever more transfigured, the Gothic's upward tendency in its fullness dematerializes all mass: now the obsessive illustrations have room; the laces and tendrils of an unprecedented mason's art shoot up into the crockets and capitals, and mingle filigree and rose into the glowing windows; vaulting, and not simply vaults, rises into the nave and into the choir's depths.[22]

Significant here is the reading of Gothic verticality as 'dematerialising' all mass, releasing ornament to expand in all directions. By contrast, Bloch argues, modern artists have become 'more individual, searching, homeless', though he still finds signs of a persistent desire for transcendence in Cubism and Expressionism.[23] Art after Impressionism, he suggests, begins to 'think in spatial terms', so that 'now things do not merely exist in space, but space exists within things, and space can certainly build a foundation without equal, as in the Roman Pantheon or even in Gothic Cathedrals'.[24] Bloch here echoes what Wright calls the 'central thought of organic architecture', supposedly first expressed by Lao Tze (alternatively Laozi, the reputed author of the *Tao Te Ching*, the central text of Taoism), who claimed that 'the reality of the building does not consist of walls and roof but in the space within to be lived in'.[25]

Bloch's work is a defence of ornament after Adolf Loos's 1908 denunciation of it, seeking to make ornament a means of salvaging, as interiority, forms of utopic transcendence that were previously encountered in architecture.[26] This takes place amidst a crisis of subjectivity, in which

> things [. . .] become like the inhabitants of one's own interior, and if the visible world seems to be crumbling away, to be increasingly emptying itself of its own soul, becoming uncategorical, then in it and through it the sounds of the invisible world correspondingly want to become pictoriality.[27]

This idea that an increase in pictoriality is a symptom of modern crisis brings us back to Lefebvre, and the idea of Gothic cathedrals as anticipating overwhelming visuality. For Bloch, a mystical self-encounter takes place between the subject and modern pictures, which 'strangely familiar, can appear like magical mirrors where we glimpse our future, like the masked ornaments of our inmost shape'.[28] Ornament is hereby reimagined as a source of utopian potential, in a way which draws on energies earlier expressed by Gothic architecture, making Gothic a model for a transformed modern subjectivity rather than something merely archaic.

Gogol's Gothic Modernity

It is not only at the end of the century that this association between Gothic and transcendent modernity can be found. The relationship between the two is present in a nascent but already quite complex form in Gogol's 'On Present-Day Architecture', which like the other essays in the volume *Arabesques* is extremely broad and ambitious, a style described by Donald Fanger as 'all aspiration [. . .] hyperbolic, universalistic, global'.[29] As noted in Chapter 3, Benjamin found in it 'a divinatory representation of architectural aspects of the later world exhibitions', but he does not discuss the essay in detail, unlike Eisenstein, who dedicates several pages to it in *Nonindifferent Nature*.[30]

The main thrust of Gogol's argument is that current European architecture is lacklustre compared to the styles of other times and places, an idea he expresses from the start:

> It makes me sad to look at the new buildings which we are constantly erecting, and on which millions have been squandered and of which few can arrest the startled eye with the majesty of their design or the wilful impertinence of their imagination, or even the luxury and dazzlingly colorful nature of their adornments.[31]

There are two things to note here. Firstly, Gogol's conception of good architecture is fundamentally visual: he wants buildings that will 'arrest the startled eye'; and secondly, this arresting of the eye is to be achieved through design and ornamentation that is not only varied but 'majest[ic]', 'wilful' and 'dazzling'. Visuality is important throughout Gogol's work, as many critics have recognised, including Fanger, who calls the essay 'panoramic', as well as William Rowe, Andrei Bely, Eisenstein, Anne Nesbet and Susanne Fusso.[32] Here as elsewhere, he makes visual monotony the great error to be overcome.

As the essay continues, Gogol weighs up the qualities of different historical styles, beginning with medieval Gothic, a form that he, like

Pugin, sees as the highpoint of Christian design, but one which has now been lost:

> Those centuries have passed when faith, fiery passionate faith, directed all thought, all minds and all activity towards one goal, when an artist strived to raise his creation higher and higher up to heaven, striving for it alone and, almost in sight of it, beneficently raising his imploring hand to it. His edifice soared up to heaven; the narrow windows, columns and arches stretched endlessly upwards; the transparent spire, almost lace-like, hovered transparently above it, like smoke, and the magnificent temple would seem so immense by comparison with the ordinary dwellings of the people; so great are the demands of the soul compared to those of the body.[33]

There is a desire for unity here, but also a suggestion of the ultimate unattainability of the goal Gothic architecture strives for. The Gothic tower, as it fades from view, leads towards an invisible divinity whose presence it can only imply. It is the 'transparent' nature of the Gothic cathedral that allows this. Only by rendering itself invisible can it reveal its true purpose, which is to point towards a whole or absolute that cannot be directly signified. Unlike in Pugin, though, the tower's transparency suggests something modern and ephemeral, especially in the comparison to 'smoke'.

There is an influence from German Romanticism evident in this attempt to locate a divine truth or 'absolute' in the chaotic world of appearance, which probably comes from Gogol's contact with the *Lyubomudry* ('Lovers of Wisdom') circle, who took their cues from Schelling in particular. This group included Vladimir Pavlovich Titov, author of 'A Few Thoughts about Architecture' (1827), which V. V. Gippius identifies as an inspiration for Gogol.[34] It is perhaps unsurprising, therefore, that Gogol seems to echo Friedrich Schlegel's 'Principles of Gothic Architecture' (1804–5), where Schlegel writes of one church spire in Cambrai, France: 'wonderful style of architecture! springing from the highest story of the tower, it seems to pierce the clouds like a transparent obelisk, or pyramid of open tracery!'[35] Like Gogol, Schlegel associates Gothic with open transparency and verticality, but Schlegel's focus in what is essentially a travelogue is much more firmly on European history than on how architecture might develop in the future. Nonetheless, he concludes, in a fairly conventional Romantic way, by critiquing the transitory 'modern world' of Paris, where 'luxury is the all-absorbing deity that governs the hasty revolutions of the fleeting day, amid a universal irregularity of existence, buildings, garments, and the ornamental refinements of life, interrupted only by the fantastic caprice of ever-varying fashion'. The essay ends with the hope that this 'irregularity' will be overturned, and 'sublimity and beauty become once more attainable', but offers no clear sense of exactly how Gothic architecture might be utilised to achieve this.[36]

Unlike Schlegel, Gogol attempts to rethink the role of the Gothic, in conjunction with other forms of architecture, in ways which are not only historical but also oriented towards the future. One method is to emphasise the overwhelming scale and verticality of the Gothic tower:

> Gothic architecture should be reserved for use only in very tall, towering churches and buildings. [. . .] Build it as it should be built; build its walls higher and higher, until they are as high as possible [. . .] And remember the most important thing, there must be no comparison between height and width. The word 'width' should disappear. The one dominant idea must be – height.[37]

For Gogol, the great example here is Cologne Cathedral, which is nothing 'but perfection and majesty' (A 124). When Gogol was writing, the cathedral had lain incomplete for centuries, but proposals for its completion began to circulate during the Napoleonic wars, supported by Schlegel, who wrote in 1804–5 that 'a third part only of the body of the church, and half of one tower, are yet completed', but even so, 'one glance at the immense height of the choir fills every beholder with astonishment'.[38] In 1823, Goethe would write that Cologne Cathedral, which he visited in an 'unfinished and prodigious' state, had reawakened his earlier state of delight at seeing Strasbourg Cathedral. The choir, one of the few completed parts, left him 'happily amazed' and 'joyously startled'.[39]

Appropriately, the later history of Cologne Cathedral provides an example of the re-eruption of Gothic in the nineteenth century in a hybrid form, neither solely medieval nor solely modern, but both at once. As Robin Lenman points out, when the south tower was finally completed in August 1880, after work had been suspended in 1560 and eventually restarted in 1842, Cologne Cathedral became the tallest structure on earth.[40] It would be supplanted in this title nine years later by the Eiffel Tower, in a symbolic replacement of Gothic stone and a project many generations in the making by a modern iron building designed for a single event, the *Exposition Universelle* of 1889, and completed in little over two years. There was an outpouring of nationalist historicism around the cathedral's completion, culminating in a pageant attended by Emperor Wilhelm I, where 'about 1,000 people in period costumes, 400 horses and 8 floats symbolically re-created Cologne's history from the thirteenth century'.[41] Yet at the same time, as Lenman observes, the cathedral can paradoxically 'be seen as a symbol of modernity'.[42] During the inauguration it was illuminated by floodlights that relied on new Siemens dynamo technology, while the construction process drew heavily on modern techniques and materials:

> The entire roof-framework of the new nave was an iron skeleton weighing over 180 tons, and the original wooden rafters of the choir were also eventually replaced with iron struts. The 63-metre ridge turret, weighing 214 tons and supported inside the roof on tubular legs, was one of the largest all-iron structures of its time.[43]

Moreover, through the location and surrounding infrastructure it became integrated, like the Crystal Palace at Sydenham, with modern architectures of transport:

> Practically and symbolically, too, the cathedral was closely linked to the railway. [...] Trains transported stone and manufactured components for the cathedral, and on his last visit in 1855 Friedrich Wilhelm IV not only celebrated the completion of the south transept façade but also laid the foundation-stone of Cologne's first fixed bridge across the Rhine, a combination of iron lattice-work and crenellated stone towers.[44]

This combination, or collision, of iron and stone makes the cathedral act as a Benjaminian dialectical image, in which medieval and modern come together not through smooth historical progression, but as fracture and discontinuity. It can be compared to the opening of *Our Mutual Friend*, where Hexam's boat floats 'between Southwark Bridge which is of iron, and London Bridge which is of stone' (OMF 1.1.1), suggesting both temporal regression, since the movement is from iron to stone, and a disjunctive confrontation between the modern and the medieval.

Such a collision of old and new runs through Gogol's essay too, defining his treatment of verticality, which he presents as producing a shock effect that is at once modern, medieval and prehistoric. The Gothic cathedral has the power to regress the observer to a primal state, as its grandeur 'plunges the common man into a kind of numbness which is the only spring moving a wild man'.[45] A few pages earlier,

Gogol argues that 'a building should tower to an incalculable height above the head of the on-looker; it should stop him in his tracks, struck by sudden amazement and scarcely able to see the top'.[46] This paralysing shock effect is associated with both the prehistoric (the 'wild man') and medieval religious awe. Shock also, however, evokes the experience of modern city living, as in descriptions of Manchester as the 'shock city' of the 1840s.[47] Eisenstein makes this link with modernity explicit, suggesting that Gogol's descriptions seem 'to have "guessed" . . . the skyscraper (although of medium height)'.[48]

These linkages between religious feeling and shock, the Gothic cathedral and the skyscraper, are captured in a 1916 painting by the relatively minor artist Glyn Philpot, held by the Victoria Art Gallery in Bath (Figure 4.4). In this painting, a young man gazes off towards something that cannot be seen, located behind, above and to the left of our perspective. His face, which indicates shock, reverence or awe, is lit up from the direction in which he gazes, and his hat is held before his chest in a prayer-like gesture of respect or solemnity. He stands against a plain dark background. Only the title, *The Skyscraper*, indicates what the man looks at. For the viewer of the painting, this is a literal instance of invisible architecture. It suggests what Rem Koolhaas claims of Manhattan, that it 'inspired in its beholders *ecstasy about architecture*', and effectively illustrates the effect Gogol wished Gothic architecture to produce – especially since, according to Eisenstein, Gothic architecture was the 'most ecstatic' of all styles for Gogol.[49] Making the absent skyscraper an unseen point of light also activates a mode of perception associated with biblical revelation, which rather than representing God directly shows signs of His presence, such as a burning bush or an angel, as for instance in Fra Angelico's Annunciation paintings of the 1430s–50s. In this way, what is most modern is presented as simultaneously medieval and/or biblical; and indeed these possibilities are layered on top of one another. If the temporal relationship I am locating in this painting is one where modernity reactivates past forms of aesthetic and affective response, in Gogol's essay that relationship is inverted, so that the Gothic tower, as the sign of a lost past, evokes a half-imagined future, which will become the skyscraper. In both Gogol and Philpot, the shock or ecstasy of the tower is accompanied by non-representability, since Philpot's skyscraper is not shown, while Gogol's tower fades into invisibility.

As well as carrying features of transparency, verticality and shock effect, Gogol's Gothic becomes modern, or even anticipates the postmodern, in the way it does not remain as a totalising unity but

Figure 4.4 *The Skyscraper* (1916), Glyn Philpot. Victoria Art Gallery, Bath and North East Somerset Council/Bridgeman Images.

becomes part of an ornamental multiplicity. We see this when Gogol describes his ideal town of the future:

> A city should consist of many different styles of building, if we wish it to be pleasing to the eye. Let as many contrasting styles combine there as possible! Let the solemn Gothic and the richly embellished Byzantine arise in the same street, alongside colossal Egyptian halls and elegantly proportioned Greek structures![50]

Here we find the dream of an architecture which would truly arrest the eye, with Gogol imploring 'let the houses fuse into a single, even, monotonous wall as seldom as possible, but let some lean upwards and some downwards. Let multifarious towers give a varied aspect to the streets as often as possible'.[51] In the same Convolute where he quotes this passage, Benjamin cites an 1830 proposal for urban planning in Paris, which, like Gogol, foreshadows the 'architecture of future exhibitions':

> It would be advisable to vary the forms of the houses and, as for the districts, to employ different architectural orders, even those in no way classical – such as the Gothic, Turkish, Chinese, Egyptian, Burmese, and so forth.[52]

In both cases, the city resembles the world exhibitions, or the department store, in the way all architectures of the world are laid out side by side like products, either intermingled 'in the same street' (for Gogol) or placed in separate 'districts' (for the Paris planners). Such intermingled architecture is a feature of Gogol's approach to history, as in a separate essay on the Middle Ages where he describes the period as a 'huge building', with walls

> composed of different materials, both ancient and modern, so that Gothic fleeces can be seen on one brick, while on others the Roman giltwork gleams; Arabian carvings, a Green cornice, a Gothic window – all have stuck together to form a mottled tower.[53]

The Gothic capacity for improvisation and reinvention identified by Ruskin ('if they wanted a window, they opened one; a room, they added one; a buttress, they built one; utterly regardless of any established conventionalities of external appearance') is now extended beyond Gothic, so that it becomes part of a conglomeration of different architectures, which is paradoxically both symbolic of the Middle Ages and the sign of an approaching future.[54]

Despite replacing Gothic with a multiplicity of styles, Gogol's ideal town retains its traumatic effect:

> A town should be built in such a way that each part, each group of houses, taken separately, should present a striking landscape. A group of houses must be given scope, if one may use such an expression, to toy with sharp features so that it will scratch its way into the memory and torment the imagination. There are those views which one remembers

for a lifetime, but there are also those which, however one tries, one cannot retain in one's memory.⁵⁵

Gogol might almost be talking of the picturesque when he describes a 'striking landscape' emerging amidst the city; indeed, he has already referred to the 'unexpected views' found in 'an English garden'.⁵⁶ Susanne Fusso comments on this link, suggesting that the text of *Arabesques* functions like a picturesque garden, aiming to 'avoid monotony at all costs'.⁵⁷ Yet the effect Gogol outlines in this passage is not pleasurable contemplation but trauma. The city scratches its way into the mind of the viewer, becoming either impossible to forget or impossible to recall. For Freud, trauma combines both these effects, overwhelming the subject's ability to register and remember the traumatic experience, even though such events are always liable to return in the form of repetition.⁵⁸ For Gogol, then, Gothic represents the central ecstatic principle which he believes modern architecture should make visible, including in new forms of iron and glass (as discussed in Chapter 3), yet also recedes from prominence to become part of a larger collection, or colportage, of architectural forms. At play as well is the idea of Gothic as overwhelming, generating a shock effect which future cities should emulate.

In French literature of the nineteenth century, however, there is a tradition of writing, running from Hugo to Zola, which seems to describe the opposite to Gogol. It presents a vision in which Gothic architecture is overwhelmed and replaced by modernity within the city. As I will show in the next section, though, these writers in fact locate a paradoxical modernity within the Gothic even as they contemplate its demise.

Will This Kill That?

In *Notre Dame de Paris* (1831), Victor Hugo retrospectively prophesises the death of the Gothic cathedral in the face of printing in the fifteenth century. The title of the well-known chapter, 'This Will Kill That', refers to two ideas: first that 'the printing press will kill the Church' and second that 'printing will kill architecture'.⁵⁹ For Hugo's narrator, speaking as if with the voice of the medieval church, 'during the first six thousand years of the world's existence, from the most immemorial pagoda of Hindustan down to Cologne Cathedral, architecture was the great script of the human race'.⁶⁰ Architecture is a form of writing, then, and indeed the most privileged form of writing, reaching its height in the Gothic cathedral, where, in line with Ruskin in 'The Nature of Gothic', Hugo identifies a 'privilege fully comparable with our present freedom of the press'.[61] The suspension of work on Cologne Cathedral in 1560 marks the symbolic end of this period (Hugo was writing before building work was restarted). Before this time, 'anyone who was born a poet became an architect', so that up until Gutenberg architecture was 'the main, the universal form of writing'.[62]

After the advent of printing the metaphor is reversed, so that rather than architecture being the ultimate form of writing, the book becomes a new form of architecture. It absorbs 'all the life ebbing out of architecture', now become 'just skin and bones', concealed behind 'stiff' and 'glacial' facades.[63] Printing creates a structure which is even more multiform than the 'visible majesty' of the architecture it replaces. This new invisible architecture of the printed word has 'a thousand storeys' and 'on its surface art brings forth a visible luxuriance of arabesques, rose-windows and tracery', including eruptions such as 'the cathedral of Shakespeare' and 'the mosque of Byron'. It is a structure where the 'harmony' of the whole emerges from the chaos of many parts, as 'countless towers jostle in disorder on this metropolis of universal thought'.[64] The word metropolis (*métropole*) is significant, as it implicitly makes this chapter a theory of the development of the modern European city, which shifts from being dominated by churches and cathedrals to becoming a landscape of writing, as was increasingly the case in the 1830s through the growing presence of newspapers, advertising and other forms of text.[65] It is clear that the Gothic cathedral is the height of an art form that is doomed to collapse. Nonetheless, the 'freedom' and variety of Gothic becomes a metaphor to understand the world of printing, reimagined as a vast, overwhelming building. Even as it is superseded, Gothic architecture provides the best means to conceptualise the printed word. Thus, within the symbolic economy of the chapter, architecture is in the end not so much destroyed by the word as integrated within it.

Gogol's essay makes a similar comparison between architecture and books, but reverses its direction. This takes place in a fascinating footnote, which I quote here in full:

> A very strange thought occurred to me: I thought that it wouldn't do any harm to have in a city one such street which would act as a chronicle of architecture. It should begin at one end with heavy, somber gates, passing through which an observer would see on both sides the

towering majestic buildings of the original, uncultivated style which is common to all proto-nations. Then he would see the gradual change into various styles: the lofty transformation into the colossal Egyptian style so imbued with simplicity, then into the beautiful Greek style, then the lascivious Alexandrian and Byzantine style with smooth cupolas, then the Roman style with rows of arches, further on descending again to uncultured times and suddenly ascending again with the unique luxury of the Arabs, then the uncultured Gothic, then the Gothic-Arabian, then the purely Gothic, the crown of art, emanating from Cologne cathedral, then the ancient Greek in a new guise and finally, so that the whole street should end with gates, redolent with the elements of the new style. This street would then become, in certain respects, the history of the development of style, and anyone too lazy to leaf through thick tomes would only have to walk along it to find out everything.[66]

This footnote has a parergonal status to the main text; while apparently marginal and secondary, it also encapsulates the central idea of the essay, acting as a manifesto for what it hopes to achieve. When placed in relation to Hugo, it is striking that Gogol imagines his street as a 'chronicle', an alternative to leafing through 'thick tomes', so making it a replacement for the book. In Gogol's account, though, the book is no longer sufficient to understand history or the city, necessitating a return to architecture. At the same time, this fantasy evokes new visual technologies, especially the panoramas, which for Benjamin 'prepare the way not only for photography but for <silent> film and sound film'.[67] In this sense, Gogol's turn towards architecture is 'really' an anticipation of cinema, and bears comparison with Benjamin's imagined cinematic compression of Paris, where the city's history is contained not in a single street, but in half an hour:

> Couldn't an exciting film be made from the map of Paris? From the unfolding of its various aspects in temporal succession? From the compression of a centuries-long movement of streets, boulevards, arcades, and squares into the space of half an hour? And does the flâneur do anything different?[68]

In both cases, time and space are compressed, enabling new forms of perception to emerge. Rather than modernity involving the replacement of architecture by the book, as Hugo seems to suggest, reading Hugo alongside Gogol and Benjamin instead produces an unsettling of temporality in which the architecture of the past, especially the Gothic, re-emerges as part of the landscape of modernity.

This temporal unsettling is extended by Zola, since Hugo's confrontation between Gothic architecture and modernity is explicitly recast in *Le Ventre de Paris* (1873), translated as *The Belly of Paris*, where the late medieval Gothic church Saint-Eustache (built between 1532 and 1632) has been enveloped by the new iron and glass marketplace Les Halles (constructed 1853–70, under the direction of Victor Baltard, who also oversaw the restoration of Saint-Eustache in 1846–54). 'It's an odd mixture', says Claude Lantier, Zola's modern painter, 'that section of the church framed by an avenue of cast iron. The one will destroy the other. The iron will kill the stone.'[69] Following this near-quotation of Hugo, Claude makes the claim that 'Saint-Eustache is done for!', before anticipating Sigfried Giedion's reading of engineering as the architectural unconscious of the nineteenth century with the words, 'since the beginning of the century, only one original building has been built that has not been copied from anywhere else and has sprung naturally from the spirit of the times, and that is Les Halles'.[70] Despite the confidence of this statement, the picture is somewhat more complicated. For a start, the idea of Les Halles springing organically from 'the spirit of the times' borrows from Hugo's conceptualisation of Gothic architecture, since after the changes brought by the Crusades, Hugo says, 'the face of architecture changes too. Like civilization it has turned the page, and the new spirit of the times finds it ready to write at its dictation', so that Les Halles conceptually imitates what it is supposed to replace.[71]

My point is that the market has not, in fact, replaced the church but rather combined with it to form a new assemblage. It is the combination of the church, now fragmented and presented to view in a new way, with the market buildings that creates a 'symbol' of modern art for Claude:

> Do you believe in chance, Florent? I don't think it was some chance that put one of the rose windows of Saint-Eustache right in the middle of Les Halles. No, it's an entire manifesto in itself! It's modern art, realism, naturalism – whatever you want to call it! And it has grown up in the face of traditional art, don't you agree?[72]

In a more or less unconscious way, Claude registers that modernity is not a feature of the iron alone, but of the iron's 'odd mixture' with the stone, so that modernity is only fully realised in the jarring confusion of different architectures and different temporal moments.[73] This idea is famously confronted by Baudelaire in 'Le Cygne' (1861), or 'The Swan', which reflects on Haussmann's transformations with the lines 'Paris may change, but in my melancholy mood | Nothing has budged!' The spaces of Haussmann's Paris are most modern when they are juxtaposed with the poet's memories, which remain, 'heavier than stone', as Saint-Eustache too remains, though surrounded by new buildings.[74] It is specifically Claude's view of the rose window amidst Les Halles that becomes a 'manifesto' for realism or naturalism, making it a counterpart to Gogol's 'strange thought', if we take that as a manifesto, and to Zola's own manifesto 'The Experimental Novel' (*Le Roman Experimental*), to be published in 1880. Whereas Zola appeals to science in his later essay, especially the biology of Claude Bernard (1813–78), Claude Lantier's manifesto here is purely aesthetic. Ironically, but appropriately for the reading I am pursuing, Les Halles would be entirely demolished by 1973, whereas the church of Saint-Eustache still remains intact. In a twist which echoes the return of architecture as a replacement for the book in Gogol, the apparently outmoded building has outlasted that which superseded it.

As noted in the Introduction, Jacques Rancière revisits Hugo's 'book of stone' in *Mute Speech*, seeing it as a precursor to Flaubert's 'book about nothing'.[75] This is especially the case because Hugo demonstrates a 'correspondence between the arts' which does away with external forms of measurement (such as God). The cathedral becomes a 'poem of stone' that is 'the common power of the Word made visible', so that, according to Rancière, Hugo retrospectively reframes the building as an architectural embodiment of the aesthetic regime.[76] This leads to what Rancière calls, echoing Derrida's commentary on Hegel and Bataille, a move 'from restricted to general poetics'.[77] Such a general poetics is an aestheticising of the world in which all arts become 'languages', and hence translatable to one another. Commodity capitalism either contributes to or, read more cynically, exploits this condition, including in *The Ladies' Paradise*, where, as Rancière puts it, 'as poeticized by Zola, the cascade of fabrics in Octave Mouret's shop window is indeed the poem of a poem, the poem of the double, "sensible-supersensible" being that Marx defines as the commodity'.[78] What I am suggesting is that the Gothic cathedral is not exempt from this literary shift towards 'general poetics', but is instead incorporated within the newly aestheticised landscape that blends the sensible and super-sensible.

Looking beyond Zola, such aesthetic blending is also evident in the opening of Dickens's unfinished final novel, *The Mystery of Edwin Drood* (1870):

An ancient English Cathedral Tower? How can the ancient English Cathedral tower be here! The well-known massive gray square tower of its old Cathedral? How can that be here! There is no spike of rusty iron in the air, between the eye and it, from any point of the real prospect. What is the spike that intervenes, and who has set it up? Maybe it is set up by the Sultan's orders for the impaling of a horde of Turkish robbers, one by one. It is so, for cymbals clash, and the Sultan goes by to his palace in long procession. Ten thousand scimitars flash in the sunlight, and thrice ten thousand dancing-girls strew flowers. Then, follow white elephants caparisoned in countless gorgeous colours, and infinite in number and attendants. Still the Cathedral Tower rises in the background, where it cannot be, and still no writhing figure is on the grim spike. Stay! Is the spike so low a thing as the rusty spike on the top of a post of an old bedstead that has tumbled all awry? Some vague period of drowsy laughter must be devoted to the consideration of this possibility.[79]

This vision arises before John Jasper, who is lying in an opium den in London. The building he seems to see is Cloisterham Cathedral, based on Rochester, built mainly in a Norman style but also with Gothic features from the fifteenth century, including the prominent west window. In Jasper's confused perception, the cathedral is combined with a scene of oriental fantasy which, as Giles Whiteley shows, quotes from Robert Southey's *The Curse of Kehama* (1810).[80] As Nicholas Royle points out, despite the visuality of the scene, 'there is no sense here of a single unified "point of view"', so that there is no possibility for mastery, meaning the spike that cuts through the image becomes a 'spiking of narrative voice'.[81] Similarly, Whiteley reads the spike as an instance of Lacanian 'impediment, failure, split', opening up a partial glimpse into the unconscious, as in Chapter 2 I argued the river Thames does in *Our Mutual Friend*. In Jasper's dream-vision, the Gothic is more implicit than explicit, suggested partly by the imposing height of Cloisterham Cathedral's tower, which is emphasised elsewhere (in chapter 7, Mr Neville states that his sister has 'come out of the disadvantages of our miserable life, as much better than I am, as that Cathedral tower is higher than those chimneys', and in chapter 9, a musical service 'pierced the heights of the great tower').[82] Anticipating the fate of Gothic churches themselves in the later nineteenth- and twentieth-century city, in *The Mystery of Edwin Drood* Gothic no longer dominates, but (as in Gogol) comes to form part of a varied poetic and aestheticised assemblage.

Although a certain fading from prominence of the Gothic cathedral is registered in both Zola and Dickens, this is accompanied by a reincorporation within new forms of aesthetic urban modernity.

More speculatively, I want to suggest that aesthetic modernity takes on features associated with the Gothic in nineteenth-century literary discourse – its free play, its unity in variety, its book-like or language-like character – so that Gothic spectrally persists within the modern city, continuing to shape its development in ways that are not only regressive. Similarly, the verticality of the Gothic spire anticipates and heralds, even as it is exceeded by, modern structures such as the Eiffel Tower and the skyscraper. As the next section shows, these characteristics come together in Henry James's *The American Scene*, a book that dwells on the radically changing face of New York in the years shortly after 1900.

The Extinction of Trinity

In the original 1907 London edition of Henry James's *The American Scene*, each double page is headed with a subtitle, one of which, in the chapter 'New York Revisited', is 'The Extinction of Trinity'.[83] This refers to the Gothic Revival building Trinity Church, at the intersection of Broadway and Wall Street. The structure James knew still stands today, and was the third to be built on this site, in 1839–46, after a first version (built 1698) was destroyed by fire in 1776, and a second version (built 1788–90) was damaged by heavy snowfall in 1838–9. Until 1869, Trinity Church was the tallest building in the United States, and it remained the tallest in New York until 1890, when, shortly after the Eiffel Tower superseded Cologne Cathedral, it was topped by the New York World Building, which was the headquarters of the *New York World* newspaper and one of the first generation of skyscrapers. Even the word 'skyscraper' itself was still new at this point; the *OED*'s first citations for its modern meaning come from just a few years earlier, in 1883.[84]

James turns to Trinity after reflecting on what he calls the 'tall buildings', or 'multitudinous sky-scrapers', that confront him from the bay of New York.[85] These buildings seem to exist only in the present, being 'crowned not only with no history, but with no credible possibility of time for history', because they are designed purely for commercial purposes.[86] They also lack beauty, which is, by contrast, 'the aim of the creator of the spire of Trinity Church, so cruelly overtopped and so barely distinguishable, from your train-bearing barge, as you stand off, in its abject helpless humility'. This 'abject humility' comes from the concealment of the tower's original verticality amidst the changing skyline. 'Where', James asks, is the felicity of simplified Gothic, of noble pre-eminence, that once made of this highly-pleasing edifice the pride of the town and the feature of Broadway? The answer is, as obviously, that these charming elements are still there, just where they ever were, but that they have been mercilessly deprived of their visibility.[87]

The church's 'wretched figure' is 'the fault of the buildings whose very first care is to deprive churches of their visibility'. As a result, the Gothic church, whose very principle according to Panofsky is its overwhelming visuality, has in New York been rendered invisible, a 'poor ineffectual thing'.[88] James's language is highly emotive and affective in this section, making the fate of Gothic the subject of pathos, even tragedy.

Yet James's impressions do not end here. He acknowledges that these skyscrapers, though 'monsters of the mere market', are also

the element that looms largest for me through a particular impression, with remembered parts and pieces melting together rather richly now, of 'down-town' seen and felt from the inside. 'Felt' – I use that word, I dare say, all presumptuously, for a relation to matters of magnitude and mystery that I could begin neither to measure nor to penetrate, hovering about them only in magnanimous wonder, staring at them as at a world of immovably-closed doors behind which immense 'material' lurked, material for the artist, the painter of life, as we say, who shouldn't have begun so early and so fatally to fall away from possible initiations.[89]

As Whiteley points out, impression is the appropriate term here (and is often repeated elsewhere), since James 'admits that a space such as New York cannot be known, but can only be discerned in its "effect"'.[90] The imagined 'painter of life' is in one sense James himself, who regrets his exclusion from the wealth of artistic and literary material contained within these buildings, as a result of his self-imposed exile to Europe (this American visit of 1904–5 was his first since 1883).[91] For my purposes, though, what is most important is the way the affective impressions of these 'monsters' come to replicate effects associated with the Gothic cathedral. These include variety ('parts and pieces melting together'), impenetrable divinity ('matters of magnitude and mystery that I could begin neither to measure nor to penetrate'), and a sense of suspension or transcendence ('hovering about them only in magnanimous wonder'). James thus captures at the dawn of the skyscraper, as Gogol did proleptically in the 1830s, a blurring between it and the Gothic cathedral, centred on the affective responses the skyscraper produces, as captured in Philpot's depiction of 1916. In this way, James's text implicitly contests any simple model of linear progress and obsolescence, even as he bemoans the fate of the cathedral.

New York, James suggests, would have been the ideal material for Émile Zola, though on a scale beyond perhaps even his capabilities:

> my thought went straight to poor great wonder-working Emile Zola and his love of the human aggregation, the artificial microcosm, which had to spend itself on great shops, great businesses, great 'apartment-houses', of inferior, of mere Parisian scale. His image, it seemed to me, really asked for compassion – in the presence of this material that his energy of evocation, his alone, would have been of a stature to meddle with. What if *Le Ventre de Paris*, what if *Au Bonheur des Dames*, what if *Pot-Bouille* and *L' Argent*, could but have come into being under the New York inspiration?[92]

This is especially significant because the following paragraph returns to Trinity Church, but now as part of an assemblage – an 'odd mixture' to use Claude Lantier's term, or a dialectical image to use Benjamin's – with the skyscraper that will replace it. The following lines should therefore be read as in conversation with Claude's view of Saint-Eustache and Les Halles in *Le Ventre de Paris*, and before that with Hugo on Notre-Dame:

> The reflecting surfaces, of the ironic, of the epic order, suspended in the New York atmosphere, have yet to show symptoms of shining out, and the monstrous phenomena themselves, meanwhile, strike me as having, with their immense momentum, got the start, got ahead of, in proper parlance, any possibility of poetic, of dramatic capture. That conviction came to me most perhaps while I gazed across at the special sky-scraper that overhangs poor old Trinity to the north – a south face as high and wide as the mountain-wall that drops the Alpine avalanche, from time to time, upon the village, and the village spire, at its foot; the interest of this case being above all, as I learned, to my stupefaction, in the fact that the very creators of the extinguisher are the churchwardens themselves, or at least the trustees of the church property. What was the case but magnificent for pitiless ferocity? – that inexorable law of the growing invisibility of churches, their everywhere reduced or abolished presence, which is nine-tenths of their virtue, receiving thus, at such hands, its supreme consecration. This consecration was positively the greater that just then, as I have said, the vast money-making structure quite horribly, quite romantically justified itself, looming through the weather with an insolent cliff-like sublimity.[93]

The building that 'overhangs' Trinity is the Trinity Building (Figure 4.5), newly built in 1905 and extended in 1907. It was in fact designed by Francis Kimball to echo the church, adopting some of its Gothic design features. James at first suggests that such buildings exceed the possibility of 'dramatic capture', in which case they put art and literature in a state of shock, and of belatedness, unable to adequately comprehend or keep up with them. This is reinforced by calling the Trinity Building both 'monstrous' and sublime, hence unrepresentable, understandable only as a great 'mountain-wall' that is also, like Mouret's department store in *Au Bonheur des Dames*, an enormous heap of capital, a 'vast money-making structure'. (We might note in passing that James's use of a Romantic metaphor to describe the building means he seems to disavow the impossibility of dramatic capture of the skyscraper as soon as he has uttered it.) James's language choices here echo, perhaps unconsciously, his comments on *Le Ventre de Paris* in a 1903 essay on Zola, where he writes that that novel addresses the 'alimentation of the monstrous city [. . .]. Paris richly gorged, Paris sublime'.[94] Zola's Paris is

Figure 4.5. *Trinity Church and Office Buildings*, New York (between 1910 and 1920), Detroit Publishing Co. Library of Congress, Washington, DC.

transplanted onto New York, but just as in *Le Ventre de Paris* the sublimity of the scene only works because the church and the skyscraper appear together; it is a function of their relationship, not the new building alone. It is perhaps partly for this reason that Christoph Lindner suggests that in James's text, as opposed to Baudrillard or Certeau, 'the uncanny ultimately comes to dominate much more forcefully over the sublime', in an instance of Vidler's 'architectural uncanny'.[95] The point appears more starkly from our present vantage point, because the avalanche never has in fact dropped, so that, like Saint-Eustache, Trinity continues to exist up the present day, in a state of perpetual disjunction from the city but never wholly subsumed by it.

In James's tableau, then, the impression of Gothic immensity is transferred from Trinity Church to the skyscraper, which also happens to utilise Gothic design. The connection between the opposed elements is emphasised by James's 'stupefying' – and hence shocking or traumatising, as the Gothic is for Gogol – discovery that the trustees of the church are themselves responsible for the building that overhangs it.[96] The church has willed its own extinction, so to speak. Perhaps it is in the working out of this apparent death drive that the vastness which was the preserve of the Gothic is transferred to the skyscraper, where it begins to become transformed by what Koolhaas calls the logic of 'bigness', meaning size and verticality drained of all content other than modernisation, arriving in the wake of the modern.[97] This developing logic might be what James recognised in turn-of-the-century New York, and what horrified him about it.

James's *American Scene* marks the final coordinate in the relationship between Gothic architecture and urban modernity that I have been tracing in this chapter, running from Schlegel to Gogol, Hugo to Zola, and even Wright to Bloch. Despite his rejection of the 'tall buildings' of New York for their vulgar expression of capitalism and the way they render the Gothic church invisible, James also recognises a powerful aesthetic and affective force in the skyscraper, one which (though he does not admit this) replicates the Gothic. His vision of Trinity Church confronted by Trinity Building intertextually repeats, in an altered form, the dynamic of both Hugo's 'this will kill that' and Zola's 'the one will destroy the other'. Of the writers discussed in this chapter, though, it is in the end Gogol who pushes furthest the question of what Gothic might one day become. At the limit of his essay on present-day architecture, the Gothic has been transformed into something quite different, which is not fully conceptualised, but which, taking a clue from the title of his book, we might associate with the arabesque. In the next chapter I push this speculation further by addressing the network of historical and theoretical ideas activated by the term 'arabesque', in order to posit the concept of the 'arabesque city' as an appropriately multifarious way to read urban modernity in the nineteenth century.

Notes

1. Augustus Welby Pugin, *Contrasts: or, A Parallel between the Noble Edifices of the Fourteenth and Fifteenth Centuries and Similar Buildings of the Present Day; Shewing the Present Decay of Taste* (London: n.p., 1836), p. 3. The book was also substantially reworked for an 1841 edition.
2. Pugin, p. 22.
3. John Ruskin, *The Stones of Venice, Volume I* (London: Smith, Elder and Co., 1851), p. 343, p. 344.
4. Barry Bergdoll, *European Architecture: 1750–1890* (Oxford: Oxford University Press, 2000), p. 144, p. 170.
5. Bergdoll, pp. 197–8.
6. Although Benjamin comments on Gogol's essay, as noted in Chapter 3, I have located only four texts in English which address it in detail: William Keyes, 'Meditations on Form and Meaning in Gogol's "On Present-Day Architecture"', *Russian History*, 37 (2010), 378–88; Anne Nesbet, 'Gogol, Belyi, Eisenstein and the Architecture of the Future', *Russian Review*, 65 (July 2006), 491–511; Melissa Frazier, 'Arabesques, Architecture and Painting', in *Russian Subjects: Empire, Nation and the Culture of the Golden Age*, ed. by Monika Greenleaf and Stephen Moeller-Sally (Evanston, IL: Northwestern University Press, 1998), pp. 277–95; and Susanne Fusso, 'The Landscape of *Arabesques*', in *Essays on Gogol: Logos and the Russian Word*, ed. by Susanne Fusso and Priscilla Meyer (Evanston, IL: Northwestern University Press, 1992), pp. 112–25. This comparative lack of attention is partly because the essays in *Arabesques* have only been available in English since Alexander Tulloch's 1982 edition, and partly because critics have viewed the essays as less important than the book's Petersburg tales. Gogol himself omitted the essays from his 1842 collected works. See Fusso, pp. 112–13; Frazier, p. 277.
7. Lefebvre, p. 286. Alongside the '*optical (or visual) formant*' (p. 286), Lefebvre's other two elements of abstract space are '*the geometric formant*' (p. 285) and '*the phallic formant*' (p. 286).
8. Lefebvre, p. 259.
9. *Arcades*, p. 22.
10. *The British Printer*, vol. 12 (London: Raithby, Lawrence & Co., Ltd, 1899), p. 221.

11. *The Royal Commission for the Chicago Exhibition 1893: Official Catalogue of the British Section* (London: William Clowes and Sons, n.d.), p. 222.
12. Glacier Window Decoration advertisement, 13 June 1887.
13. Lori Anne Loeb, *Consuming Angels: Advertising and Victorian Women* (Oxford: Oxford University Press, 1994), p. 26.
14. *British Printer*, p. 221, p. 222.
15. Frank Lloyd Wright, 'Organic Architecture (Excerpt)', in *Programs and Manifestoes on 20th-Century Architecture*, ed. by Ulrich Conrads, trans. by Michael Bullock (Cambridge, MA: MIT Press, 1971), p. 25.
16. James Garratt, *Music, Culture and Social Reform in the Age of Wagner* (Cambridge: Cambridge University Press, 2010), p. 166. Anke Finger and Danielle Follett, 'Introduction' to *The Aesthetics of the Total Artwork*, ed. by Anke Finger and Danielle Follett (Baltimore: Johns Hopkins University Press, 2011), p. 3.
17. Émile Zola, *The Masterpiece*, trans. by Thomas Walton (Oxford: Oxford University Press, 1993), p. 211.
18. *Arabesques*, p. 205.
19. John Ruskin, *The Stones of Venice, Volume II* (Boston: Estes and Lauriat, 1851), p. 179. As this quotation suggests, it is possible to read a modernity into Ruskin's account of the Gothic, as Rancière does when he writes 'the Ruskinian concept of the gothic is thus far more than another stone added to the romantic nostalgia for the faith of medieval artisans. It is not simply the concept of a form of historically situated art. It proposes an idea of art equally capable of inspiring the art workers of a secular republic and the rational engineers of modern life' (*Aisthesis*, p. 142).
20. Frank Lloyd Wright, *An Organic Architecture: The Architecture of Democracy* (Cambridge, MA: MIT Press, 1970), p. 11. This book collects four lectures given to the Royal Institute of British Architects in May 1939.
21. Ernst Bloch, *The Spirit of Utopia*, trans. by Anthony Nassar (Stanford: Stanford University Press, 2000), p. 25.
22. Bloch, p. 26.
23. Bloch, p. 27.
24. Bloch, p. 29.
25. *Organic Architecture*, p. 3. Richard Sennet reads the same quotation in relation to the 'massiveness of medieval churches'. Richard Sennet, *The Conscience of the Eye: The Design and Social Life of Cities* (New York: Norton, 1990), p. 12.
26. Hilde Heynen argues that 'although Loos's name is not mentioned, his criticisms are so clearly addressed to the theses about ornament and the applied arts advocated by Loos that there is every reason to assume that Loos was Bloch's direct target here'. Heynen, p. 122.
27. Bloch, p. 32.

28. Bloch, p. 32.
29. Donald Fanger, *The Creation of Nikolai Gogol* (Cambridge, MA: Belknap Press, 1979), p. 63. According to V. V. Gippius, Gogol dated the essay as 1831 but it was written in 1833. Tulloch gives the date of completion as February 1834 (*Arabesques*, p. 261). Gogol's perhaps intentionally inaccurate dating makes sense if he wanted to distance himself from *Arabesques*, as suggested by an 1835 letter to M. A. Maximovich which describes *Arabesques* as a 'mishmash' or 'mixture of everything'. See V. V. Gippius, *Gogol*, trans. by Robert Maguire (Durham, NC: Duke University Press, 1989 [1924]), p. 193, p. 41; see also Fanger, p. 58.
30. *Arcades*, p. 198. *Nonindifferent Nature*, pp. 159–65.
31. *Arabesques*, p. 115.
32. Fanger, p. 64. See William Rowe, *Through Gogol's Looking Glass: Reverse Vision, False Focus, and Precarious Logic* (New York: New York University Press, 1976); Andrei Bely, *Gogol's Artistry*, trans. by Christopher Colbath (Evanston, IL: Northwestern University Press, 2009); Sergei Eisenstein, *Selected Works, Volume 2: Towards a Theory of Montage*, trans. by Michael Glenny (London: BFI, 1991), pp. 262–3, pp. 354–5; Nesbet; and Susanne Fusso's comments on Gogol and optic lenses (Fusso, pp. 114–15).
33. Gogol, p. 115.
34. Gippius, pp. 42–4. For an overview of the *Lyubomudry* group, see Victoria Frede, *Doubt, Atheism and the Nineteenth-Century Russian Intelligentsia* (Madison: University of Wisconsin Press, 2011), pp. 21–53. According to John Kopper, Gogol was influenced by a simplified form of German philosophy; see 'The "Thing-in-Itself" in Gogol's Aesthetics: A Reading of the *Dikanka* Stories', in *Essays on Gogol*, pp. 40–62 (p. 54).
35. Friedrich Schlegel, 'Principles of Gothic Architecture', in *The Aesthetic and Miscellaneous Works of Frederick von Schlegel*, trans. by E. J. Millington (London: Henry G. Bohn, 1849), pp. 149–99 (p. 155).
36. 'Principles of Gothic Architecture', p. 198, p. 199.
37. *Arabesques*, p. 124.
38. 'Principles of Gothic Architecture', p. 172, p. 173.
39. Johann Wolfgang von Goethe, *Essays on Art and Literature*, ed. by John Gearey, trans. by Ellen von Nardroff and Ernest von Nardroff (Princeton: Princeton University Press, 1986), p. 12.
40. Robin Lenman, *Artists and Society in Germany: 1850–1914* (Manchester: Manchester University Press, 1997), p. 16.
41. Lenman, p. 17.
42. Lenman, p. 22.
43. Lenman, p. 22.
44. Lenman, p. 22.
45. *Arabesques*, p. 125.

46. *Arabesques*, p. 121.
47. Briggs, p. 51.
48. *Nonindifferent Nature*, p. 164. Simon Karlinsky also notes this association with skyscrapers in *The Sexual Labyrinth of Nikolai Gogol* (Chicago: University of Chicago Press, 1996), pp. 106–7.
49. Koolhaas, p. 4. *Nonindifferent Nature*, p. 160.
50. *Arcades*, p. 198.
51. *Arabesques*, pp. 130–1.
52. *Arcades*, p. 201.
53. *Arabesques*, p. 32.
54. *Stones, Volume II*, p. 179.
55. *Arabesques*, p. 131.
56. *Arabesques*, p. 123.
57. Fusso, p. 121.
58. See, for instance, Sigmund Freud, 'Inhibitions, Symptoms and Anxiety' [1926], in *The Standard Edition, Volume XX (1925–1926)*, ed. by James Strachey (London: Vintage, 2001), pp. 77–175.
59. Hugo, p. 192, p. 193.
60. Hugo, p. 194.
61. Hugo, p. 197.
62. Hugo, p. 197, p. 198.
63. Hugo, p. 203.
64. Hugo, p. 192, p. 194, p. 205, p. 206.
65. See for instance Sara Thornton, *Advertising, Subjectivity and the Nineteenth-Century Novel: Dickens, Balzac and the Language of the Walls* (Houndmills: Palgrave Macmillan, 2009).
66. *Arabesques*, pp. 132–3.
67. *Arcades*, p. 5.
68. *Arcades*, p. 83.
69. *The Belly of Paris*, p. 186. For a discussion of Zola's depiction of Les Halles, including a map that features Saint-Eustache, see Geoff Woollen, 'Zola's Halles, A *Grande Surface* Before Their Time', *Romance Studies*, 18.1 (2000), 21–30.
70. *The Belly of Paris*, p. 186.
71. Hugo, p. 196.
72. *The Belly of Paris*, p. 186.
73. See Hugo, pp. 192–206.
74. *The Flowers of Evil*, p. 175.
75. *Mute Speech*, p. 50.
76. *Mute Speech*, p. 53, p. 54, p. 55.
77. This is the title of Part 1 of *Mute Speech*. For comparison see Jacques Derrida, 'From Restricted to General Economy: A Hegelianism Without Reserve', in *Writing and Difference*, trans. by Alan Bass (London: Routledge and Kegan Paul, 1978), pp. 251–300.
78. *Mute Speech*, p. 64.

79. Charles Dickens, *The Mystery of Edwin Drood*, ed. by Margaret Caldwell (Oxford: Oxford University Press, 1982), p. 1.
80. Whiteley, p. 95.
81. Nicholas Royle, *The Uncanny* (Manchester: Manchester University Press, 2003), p. 265. Whiteley, p. 95.
82. *Edwin Drood*, p. 46, p. 72.
83. Henry James, *The American Scene* (London: Chapman and Hall, 1907), p. 83.
84. *OED*, skyscraper, n.6. *OED Online*, Oxford University Press, <www.oed.com/view/Entry/181180>. Accessed 9 September 2022. Peter Collister's footnote to James suggests instead that the term skyscraper first came into use in 1891. Henry James, *The American Scene*, ed. by Peter Collister (Cambridge: Cambridge University Press, 2019), p. 89 n. 7. Further references to James are to this edition.
85. *American Scene*, p. 89.
86. *American Scene*, p. 90.
87. *American Scene*, p. 91.
88. *American Scene*, p. 91.
89. *American Scene*, pp. 93–4.
90. Whiteley, p. 212.
91. Collister in *American Scene*, p. xxii.
92. *American Scene*, p. 96.
93. *American Scene*, pp. 96–7.
94. Henry James, 'Emile Zola' [*sic*], in *Documents of Literary Realism*, ed. by George Becker (Princeton: Princeton University Press, 1963), pp. 506–34. In the same essay, James also reads Zola as architectural, anticipating Eisenstein (see Chapter 3): 'If we remember that his design was nothing if not architectural, that a "majestic whole", a great balanced façade, with all its orders and parts, that a singleness of mass and a unity of effect, in fine, were before him from the first, his notion of picking up his bricks as he proceeded becomes, in operation, heroic' ('Emile Zola', p. 512).
95. Christoph Lindner, *Imagining New York City* (Oxford: Oxford University Press, 2015), p. 45, p. 46.
96. Peter Collister notes that 'Trinity Church had acquired large amounts of land in Manhattan, part of a royal grant from Queen Anne; having sold off much of this real estate, it became (and remains) an unusually rich church.' Collister in *American Scene*, p. 97 n. 27.
97. Rem Koolhaas, Bruce Mau and OMA, *S,M,L,XL*, 2nd edn (New York: Monacelli Press, 1998), p. 499.

Chapter 5

The Arabesque City

By naming his 1835 collection of essays and stories *Arabesques*, Gogol connected it to an aesthetic form at the intersection of architectural design and literature – not to mention music, art and dance – as well as a set of debates that had animated German Romanticism in the preceding decades. Taking Gogol's usage as inspiration, this chapter ranges across art, design, architecture, literature, philosophy and theory in order to argue for the value of the arabesque as a concept for reading the nineteenth-century city. In my readings, the arabesque functions partly as a metaphor which attracted increased attention in Europe and America at exactly the period modern cities were developing, and partly as a form with direct links to urban architecture and writing.

The arabesque's value as a conceptual framework for the modern city is due firstly to its persistent links with 'movement and multiplicity', as articulated in different ways by Kant, Goethe and Schlegel, and secondly to its position on the border between meaning, order and structure on the one hand, and meaninglessness, chaos and the unnatural on the other.[1] At the risk of oversimplification, we might say that Western responses to the arabesque have tended to raise the question of whether it is purposive or non-purposive, and if purposive, whether this is in the Kantian sense of purposiveness which exists 'apart from a purpose'.[2] As Winfried Menninghaus observes, 'without directly using the concept, Kant's *Critique of Judgement* (1790) formulates and elaborates a philosophy of the arabesque that then serves as a major touchstone for the reevaluation of the arabesque in early Romanticism'.[3] Kant associates the arabesque with 'free beauty', which exemplifies purposiveness-without-a-purpose, when he writes that 'designs *à la grecque*, foliage for framework or on wall-papers, etc., have no intrinsic meaning; they represent nothing – no object under a determinate concept – and are free beauties'.[4] Free beauty does not conform to a particular purpose or structure, but instead activates the imagination (as opposed to pure or practical reason). It formally imitates nature, but does not reproduce it. Yet a little later, and not usually acknowledged by commentators, Kant seems to recognise the potential for the arabesque to turn into the grotesque, and hence break with beauty, in these lines:

> English taste in gardens, and baroque taste in furniture, push the freedom of imagination to the verge of what is grotesque – the idea being that in this divorce from all constraint of rules the precise instance is being afforded where taste can exhibit its perfection in projects of the imagination to the fullest extent.[5]

Assuming that we can align Kant's examples here with the arabesque (baroque furniture, for instance, was dominated by Hogarth's arabesque 'line of beauty'), it is a form that seems to lie on the border between free beauty and the grotesque.[6] Though emerging from natural laws, the arabesque approaches the limit of this category and is on the 'verge' of becoming something else, which is unnatural, even monstrous. Already within Kant, then, there is an internal tension regarding the aesthetic and symbolic meaning of the form.

In what follows, I propose that this internal tension is not secondary or accidental but fundamental to the arabesque, such that in its division between structure and disorder, beauty and the grotesque, purposiveness and non-purposiveness it becomes an equivalent to the underground man's categorisation of cities as intentional or unintentional in *Notes from Underground*, as discussed in Chapter 1. In the arabesque, it is as if the intentional and unintentional have been collapsed onto one another, so that either might dominate at any given time. As a result, the arabesque embodies one of the central tensions of the developing modern city: the question of whether it is fundamentally structured, like a great machine or organism, or something that works against structure, even against nature, to adopt J. K. Huysmans's novel title of 1884. The questions provoked by the arabesque are therefore also applicable to the city. Does its surface point to a deeper meaning? Does it signify an intentionality or aesthetic order, an underlying invisible architecture, or is it instead a deceptive facade covering a fundamental lack? Alternatively – and this is where literature becomes important – does the non-signifying, multitudinous form of the arabesque offer a fitting resource for writing in, of and about the city?

The tensions that define the arabesque are exacerbated by the etymological and conceptual ambiguity of the term, which was first used in the European Renaissance to describe a recurring ornamental pattern or decoration, often interchangeably with 'moresque' and 'grotesque'. Raphael (1483–1520) is particularly associated with the earliest modern arabesques. The arcade he designed at the Vatican for Pope Leo X features 'curled and involuted shoots, from whose foliage animals emerge and cause the difference between animal and vegetable forms to be eliminated'. Wolfgang Kayser distinguishes the arabesque from the moresque because it uses perspective, is 'more profuse, so that the background is often completely hidden' and 'avails itself of patterns composed of more realistic shoots, leaves and blossoms, to which animal forms are occasionally added', but he also admits that 'the three terms were often used indiscriminately' up to the eighteenth century.[7] Complicating this picture further, the name suggests an influence from Islamic art, alongside the acknowledged Greek and Roman inheritance, as becomes evident in the range of meanings listed for 'arabesque' by the *OED*, which include 'Arab or Arabian in character, appearance, or style'; 'Ornate, intricate, or complex. Also: fantastical; strangely mixed'; 'The Arabic language'; 'A decorative pattern consisting of flowing lines (typically of branches, leaves, and flowers) that scroll or interlace'.[8] The term, then, brings together Arabic culture and design, a connection to language, a generic association with the 'fantastical', and ornamentality, as well as being a Renaissance revival of a classical design mode.[9]

This concatenation of meanings is especially significant in a context like that of nineteenth-century Britain, where Islamic design was being newly (re)imported by works such as Owen Jones's *The Grammar of Ornament* (1856), discussed below. In such a case, the arabesque complicates chronology and geography, since it is both European and Islamic, associated with both traditional Arabic forms and Renaissance design, both an established design feature and a newly reappraised (in Northern Europe at least) style and concept, especially in the wake of the German Romantics. The arabesque is therefore in the nineteenth century an unsettled, entangled and mobile term, one that contests the more linear and teleological conceptions of Western modernity, what Heynen calls 'programmatic' as opposed to 'transitory' modernity.[10] Reading through the arabesque can instead open up a perspective on what Haomin Gong, writing in the context of contemporary China, calls 'uneven modernity', which he argues is not secondary but an 'intrinsic *feature* of modernity', a 'dynamical *problematic* rather than [. . .] a dismissible *problem*'.[11] Benjamin makes a similar point when he writes that 'the "modern" [. . .] is as varied in its meaning as the different aspects of one and the same kaleidoscope'.[12] If we put this character of the arabesque at the forefront of our reading, then rather than being a confused or imprecise term it comes to stand for the temporal, spatial, conceptual and architectural disjunctions to which European cities, partly through an entanglement with the Islamic world, gave rise in the nineteenth century.

The arabesque tradition I am concerned with in this chapter culminates with Art Nouveau and Jugendstil during the *fin de siècle*, a period when Western Europe became 'obsessed with the arabesque'.[13] For Benjamin, Jugendstil is both 'an advance' and 'a regression', a failed 'attempt on the part of art to come to terms with technology', and so represents a kind of threshold condition of bourgeois life, one in which the bourgeoisie dreams it is 'out of bed and getting dressed', despite still being asleep.[14] On one level, therefore, the sections that follow constitute a fore-history of Jugendstil, showing how the contradictions that run through it are already at work earlier in the century.

Arabesque on the Threshold

The German Romantic debate concerning the arabesque opened up issues around truth, ornamentation and representation that have continued to animate critical discussion. In particular, Schlegel's linkage with the literary and Hegel's discussion of architecture widened the parameters of the arabesque in important ways. Before these interventions, and before Kant, Goethe's essay 'von Arabesken' (1789) was one of the first major statements on the topic. Goethe distinguishes between arabesques in antiquity, which he sees not as superfluous but an efficient form of decoration, and those of Raphael, which become more excessive and Dionysian: 'An den Wänden sieht man kleine Genien und ausgewachsene männliche Gestalten, die auf Schnörkeln und Stäben gaukeln und sich heftiger und munterer' ('On the walls one sees little genii and full-grown male figures swaying on curlicues and sticks, and moving quite vigorously and briskly').[15] This idea of the (early) modern arabesque as defined by movement and fantastical imagination is extended by Schlegel, who in *Gespräch über die Poesie* (1800) applies the concept to writers including Diderot, Cervantes and above all Lawrence Sterne. Schlegel states of such writing: 'Freylich ist es keine hohe Dichtung, sondern nur eine – Arabeske. Aber eben darum hat es in meinen Augen keine geringen Ansprüche; denn ich halte die Arabeske für eine ganz bestimmte und wesentliche Form oder Außerungsart der Poesie' ('Certainly there is no high poetry but one – Arabesque. But for that reason it has in my eyes no small claim; because I take the arabesque for a very specific and essential form or expression of poetry').[16] As Melissa Frazier points out, Schlegel identifies a shared capacity in the novel and the arabesque to bring together the part and the whole, the finite and the infinite.[17] For Schlegel, the arabesque draws us towards the Absolute, not despite but because of its mutability and multiplicity, through which it gestures towards what cannot be directly signified or made manifest. This idea is followed through in Gogol's *Arabesques*, where as Fusso notes the fragment is always important, signified by Gogol's repeated use of the word *drob'* (fragment).[18] In this light, Gogol's essay 'Thoughts on Geography (for children)' from the book is suggestive. He claims that

> One must never teach the size of the world by calculations in square miles. The only way to appreciate its size is to look at a map. It is a good idea to cut out each separate state individually so that it can be seen as a separate entity, and, being linked to the others, can be seen as being part of the world.[19]

A whole philosophical project is expressed here: the world must be sliced up into separate pieces, but only in order for the connection between part and whole to become apparent. It is aesthetic and spatial perception rather than pure rationality that leads to an appreciation of totality. Elsewhere in Gogol's writing, however, stories such as 'The Overcoat' place this form of totality into question, in ways which Schlegel's concept of the arabesque as a form of literary language can help illuminate, as I will return to later.

A few decades after Schlegel, Hegel's *Aesthetics* (lectures 1818–29; published 1835) discusses the arabesque as a feature of architecture, symptomatic of 'the transition out of a natural organic form used by architecture to the more severe regularity of architecture proper'. The arabesque emerges first from natural forms, including 'columns originating in the greatest variety from plant-formations' in Egyptian palaces and temples, but already 'the imitation is not true to nature; on the contrary; the plant-forms are distorted architecturally, brought nearer to the circle, the straight line, and what is mathematically regular'. The arabesque is thus on the threshold between the organic ('plants, leaves, flowers, and animals') and the 'inorganic and geometrical', and it is only in the latter that architecture begins to express itself as an independent and 'free' art form ('free' here both recalling Kant's 'free beauty' and referring to the unconstrained expression of human spirit through art).[20] The 'geometrically ordered purposiveness' of architecture is however ultimately only a stage in its movement back towards the organic in a different form, as an expression of spirit.[21] Again the arabesque is linked to the free play of imagination, and so in psychoanalytic terms to a loosening of repression, or a partial suspension of conscious control. This cannot be its whole purpose, however, since if arabesque becomes mere ornament, with no integral relation to architecture, it leads towards the 'stiff and untrue', whereas, when used architecturally, 'everything that might be viewed as a distortion, and unnaturalness and stiffness in the plant-forms is essentially to be regarded as an appropriate transformation for strictly architectural purposes'.[22] The arabesque therefore lies on the border between the necessary and the superfluous; it is the natural made unnatural, recalling Dickens's narrator in *Dombey and Son*, who asks of Nature in the city whether 'in the enforced distortions so produced, it is not natural to be unnatural' (DS 47.683). Gray Kochhar-Lindgren, who argues of Hong Kong that 'the city is an arabesque-in-motion', reads the arabesque in Hegel as 'a counter-thrust to the natural', associated with duty and proportion, but one that never fully breaks with nature, so that 'the arabesque is an entwined movement that undoes all oppositions between nature and culture, spirit and materiality'.[23] While I broadly agree with Kochhar-Lindgren, his Deleuzian reading tends to see the arabesque as undoing oppositions entirely, whereas in its nineteenth-century form, at least, I want to instead argue that these oppositions subsist in unresolved dialectical tension with one another.

In recent years there has been something of a resurgence of critical interest in the arabesque, of which Kochhar-Lindgren's book is a part (and the most interested in the urban). Building on earlier work such as Rae Gordon's *Ornament, Fantasy, and Desire in Nineteenth-Century French Literature* (1992), books by Gurminder Bhogal (2013), Heba Barakat and Muhammad Waley (2018, the latter as editor), Cordula Grewe (2021), Anne Leonard (as editor, 2022, and featuring essays from both Bhogal and Grewe), and to some extent Jacob Berman (2012), have all re-examined the cultural and aesthetic significance of the form.[24] This work has tended to emphasise the complexity and multiplicity of arabesque. Gordon, for instance, calls the arabesque a 'uniquely polysemic figure', while Leonard refers to 'the definitional instability that seems inherent to the arabesque'.[25] As Leonard and the contributors to her collection point out, this instability comes partly from a cultural transformation in Europe, through which misinterpretation or disregard of Islamic practices – such as the integration of spirituality, writing and decoration in architecture – made the arabesque into something both more extractable and reusable as a fragment (and so appropriable by commodity capitalism) while at the same time becoming more closely associated with 'improvisation and free movement', rather than with repetition as a way to approach the infinite nature of God.[26] This association with individual imagination is evident in Matisse, for instance, who in 1952 called the arabesque 'the most synthetic way to represent oneself in all one's aspects', an 'impassioned impulse' that is present even in 'certain cave drawings'; Debussy, Mallarmé and Loie Fuller would also be relevant here.[27] As I have already begun to indicate, however, there are also ways in which the Islamic associations with repetition, writing and the infinite/absolute return or persist in European (and American) usage in the nineteenth century, alongside the shift towards imaginative freedom and non-signifying ornamentation.

One approach to thinking about this double nature of the arabesque is offered by Bertrand Éveno's article on 'multicolored arabesques' in Carl Jung's *The Red Book*. Éveno, the publisher of the French edition of Jung's dreamlike volume, composed between approximately 1915 and 1930, finds in its 'undulating' and 'serpentine' arabesques, taken to be a sub-category of Jung's illustrations, a dialectic between 'fragmented chaos' and 'an organizing factor'.[28] This description is close to Kochhar-Lindgren's description of Hong Kong, citing Coole and Frost, as a system that seems 'structured yet unpredictable'.[29] In both cases we find a combination of the intentional (the organised) and the unintentional (the chaotic). In Jung's case this is also a psychical topography, a border between conscious and unconscious, since Éveno argues that his arabesques form 'the fabric, the skin, or even the very bodily substance' of figures encountered in the unconscious.[30] For this reason Éveno links the images to those which appear in Henry James's story 'The Figure in the Carpet' (1896), since they similarly serve 'to hide or mask other living figures that are not immediately visible, either underneath the skin or upon another surface, begging to be discovered or deciphered'.[31] The arabesque thereby becomes a symptom of an invisible architecture, evoking a structure that is never fully revealed. This association is reinforced by Donald Winnicott's reading of Jung as performing 'a constant building and rebuilding followed always by the staging of an earthquake and the destruction of the building', a process that is literally at work in *Dombey and Son* and Zola's Parisian novels, as discussed in Chapters 2 and 3.[32]

Éveno, however, seems to take 'The Figure in the Carpet' as a relatively unproblematic encouragement to read further and deeper, whereas, as J. Hillis Miller has shown, the story in fact problematises the whole dynamic of critical reading, so that to try and say what it is about is 'to succumb to the lure, to take the bait'. Instead, it 'dramatizes the experience of unreadability'.[33] This dramatising of unreadability takes place primarily through the image of a 'complex figure in a Persian carpet', employed as a metaphor for the secret meaning supposedly concealed within the novels of the author Vereker, if only one can find the right perspective to recognise it.[34] This meaning is, of course, never revealed to either narrator or reader, and all those privy to it die during the course of the narrative. Hillis Miller reads the story in light of references to fabric and embroidery elsewhere in James's prefaces, which conceptualise (though ultimately misleadingly) literary narrative as

> separate flowers side by side, extending outward in every direction on a canvas which, at first a figure for the finite surface enclosed within the charmed circle the artist has drawn by that 'geometry of his own', now must become 'boundless' once more, since it is the paradoxical unfolding of the infinite implicit in the finite.[35]

This is finally an impossible scheme, but with this idea of the infinite in the finite, Hillis Miller's reading of James gives us a version of the arabesque that brings it back to both the Islamic sense of evoking divinity through repetition, and to Schlegel's conception of a digressive, repetitious form of literary arabesque which – as in *Don Quixote* or *Tristram Shandy*, where the story is never truly completed – always resists closure, and hence finitude.

To begin to think further about how this oscillating or dialectical figure of the arabesque helps us read architecture and the city in the nineteenth century, I turn now to Owen Jones's *The Grammar of Ornament*, one of the most significant British texts to engage with the arabesque in the period, and to George Eliot's short but significant review of it, as well as Jones's Alhambra Court, created for the Crystal Palace at Sydenham in 1854.

Owen Jones and George Eliot: The Alhambra and the Interior

Owen Jones (1809–74) was a British architect and designer whose 1834 and 1837 studies of the Alhambra in Granada (published 1842–5) would become immensely important for both his own work, including *The Grammar of Ornament*, and those he went on to influence,

180 Invisible Architecture in Nineteenth-Century Literature

Figure 5.1 Frontispiece to *The Grammar of Ornament* (1856), Owen Jones. The Metropolitan Museum of Art, New York, Gift of Friends of the Thomas J. Watson Library.

including Alois Riegl (1858–1905), whose *Stilfragen* (1893) includes an important chapter on the arabesque, William Morris, Frank Lloyd Wright, Le Corbusier and others.[36] In 1851, Jones was in charge of the decoration for the Crystal Palace, and also worked on the exhibition arrangements, then in 1854 he designed a replica of the Alhambra, originally built in the thirteenth to fourteenth century, for the newly relocated Crystal Palace at Sydenham (Figure 5.2). This was one of over twenty-five courts in total, and ten Fine Art Courts, each representing 'a specific style of architecture ranging from antiquity to modern times', so that Jones in effect contributed to realising Gogol's dream of a street 'which would act as a chronicle of architecture'.[37] As Murphy suggests, though, immersion in each place or period was never total:

> Overall, the effect would have been that of a number of distinct spatial logics all competing, in some cases disjunctively co-existing with each other in the same space; an iron girder clashing with an Egyptian column; the seeming solidity of the walls compared with the timber floor creaking three stories up in the air.[38]

Phillips's 1854 guide to the Crystal Palace at Sydenham, discussed in the Introduction, describes the Alhambra Court as an interruption to the general 'architecture sequence', 'one of those offshoots from a parent stem which flourished for a time, and then entirely disappeared', so that it seems this space was regarded at least by some as disjunctive, a monument to a relatively transitory or secondary culture.[39] This is perhaps because, as Kathryn Ferry notes, Jones was 'unprecedentedly placing Islamic art on a par with the other great artistic traditions'.[40] Phillips goes on to describe the stark distinction in Moorish architecture between the exterior, built of 'plain, simple masonry', and the interior, which is 'literally covered, from end to end, with rich arabesque work in coloured stucco, and adorned with mosaic pavements, marble fountains, and sweet-smelling flowers'.[41] Here, the idea of arabesque as an architecture of the interior, which becomes important in *The Grammar of Ornament*, and Eliot's review of it, is prominent, although the part of the Alhambra reproduced by Jones (the Court of the Lions and the Tribunal of Justice) did in fact feature decoration on the outside, consisting of 'inscriptions in Arabic character, of conventional representations of flowers and of flowing decoration, over which the eye wanders'.[42] As Ferry explains, this apparent contradiction came about because the 'the blank red castellated walls of the original monument were not a suitable sign to attract visitors', so Jones 'created a façade that was simultaneously

Figure 5.2 *The Alhambra Court* (1854), photograph by Philip Henry Delamotte. © Victoria & Albert Museum, London.

internal *and* external', modifying the original form of the building.[43] In doing so he exemplified Benjamin's point about the nineteenth-century city, that the interior moves outside, so that 'the street becomes room and the room becomes street'.[44] Jones thus brought to London an arabesque architecture of the interior which unfolded outwards into exteriority while still ultimately remaining enclosed within the larger structure of the Crystal Palace itself.

Jones published his own book about the court, *The Alhambra Court in the Crystal Palace* (1854), part of which is reproduced in *The Grammar of Ornament*. Here, Jones overtly overlays the Alhambra onto the Crystal Palace, and vice versa, by opening with part of a poem that appears 'on the walls of the Hall of the Two Sisters in the Alhambra [. . .] in honour of its builder, the Imán Ibn Nasr' (Abu Abdullah Muhammad ibn Yusuf ibn Nasr, or Muhammad I of Granada, 1195–1273). The lines run as follows:

> Look attentively at my elegance, thou wilt reap the benefit of a commentary on decoration.
> For, by Allah! the elegant buildings by which I am surrounded surpass all other buildings in the propitious omen attending their foundation.

Apartments are there enfolding so many wonders, that the eyes of the spectator remain for ever fixed upon them; provided he be gifted with a mind to estimate them.

How many delightful prospects – how many objects in the contemplation of which a highly gifted mind finds the gratification of its utmost wishes.

Markets they are where those provided with money are paid in beauty, and where the judge of elegance is perpetually sitting to pronounce sentence.

This is a palace of transparent crystal; those who look at it imagine it to be a boundless ocean.

Indeed we never saw a palace more lofty than this in its exterior, or more brilliantly decorated in its interior, or having more extensive apartments.

And yet I am not alone to be wondered at, for I overlook in astonishment a garden, the like of which no human eyes ever saw.[45]

As Jones writes:

> it would be difficult to find a more appropriate introduction to a visit to the Crystal Palace at Sydenham, than these eloquent words of an Arabian poet of the thirteenth century in honour of a building which appears to have been the glory of his age, as the Crystal Palace may become of our own.[46]

The lines about contemplating and evaluating the wonders contained within are emphasised by Jones, but it is the phrase 'this is a palace of transparent crystal' that is most striking. While there may be an element of creative translation at work, at least as relayed by Jones the poem makes the Alhambra an equivalent of the Crystal Palace. Though Jones is clear that this is a harmonic similarity, one could equally read it as a temporal disjunction in which the past speaks back to this most modern building, making it appear no longer original but rather an imitation of the work of the medieval Moors. In this case the role of the replica is displaced, redirected from the Alhambra court to the building that contains it.[47] In Benjamin's terms, we can read the relationship between the two as a dialectical image in which past and present uncannily coincide, complicating the question of what kind of architecture defines the modern, and where it originates. In this context it is worth recalling that the Alhambra was not just a fortress or a palace, but what Robert Irwin calls 'a palace-city', whose walls enclosed 'perhaps as many as six palaces, a barracks, a congregational mosque, and a small town, as well as a zoo, an aviary and industrial workshops', accommodating up to 40,000 people. Arabic sources described it 'not as a *qasr* (palace), but as a *madina* (town)'.[48] If on one level the relationship is between the Alhambra and the Crystal Palace, then on another it is between the Alhambra and London, two very different cities brought into conjunction. As with all such conjunctions between the ruined or outmoded and the new, including Doré's image of the New Zealander discussed in Chapter 2, this puts London in a state of belatedness, existing anachronistically with itself.

While Jones does not say so explicitly, the opening line quoted above, 'look attentively at my elegance, thou wilt reap the benefit of a commentary on decoration', might equally apply to his most famous work, *The Grammar of Ornament*, in which case like the Crystal Palace the book becomes an imitation of the Alhambra, a translation of architecture into words. Indeed, an emphasis on architecture is present from the start, with Proposition 1 of Jones's 'General Principles in the Arrangement of Form and Colour, in Architecture and the Decorative Arts, which are Advocated throughout this Work' (of 37 in total) stating that 'the Decorative Arts arise from, and should be properly attendant upon, Architecture'. The arabesque is central too, in a conjunction that recalls Hegel, as a feature of coherent structure rather than free imagination: 'beauty of form is produced by lines growing out one from the other in gradual undulations: there are no excrescences; nothing could be removed and leave the design equally good or better' (Proposition 6). Arabesque ornament is structural rather than arbitrary, part of an efficient architectural framework. In an associated way, as the title suggests, Jones approaches architectural design as a language with its own grammatical structure, which must be uncovered and utilised, but without simply replicating the styles of the past: 'The principles discoverable in the works of the past belong to us; not so the results. It is taking the end for the means.'[49] This repeats sentiments expressed in the Alhambra Court volume, where Jones, writing against the historical eclecticism of his time, condemns

> the folly of attempting to adapt to new wants styles of architecture which have ever been the expression of the wants, faculties, and sentiments of the age in which they were produced, instead of seeking in every style for those general principles which survive from generation to generation.

The goal, then, is to examine ornamentation, and above all the arabesque, in order to uncover the hidden messages, the 'eternal' truths behind the 'local or temporary' fashions manifested by different cultures.[50] This leads to the search for an invisible architecture of ornament, a Kantian purposiveness that can be discovered by gathering together enough varying fragments of design; and so Jones's book includes 112 illustrated plates containing 2,350 representative samples, ranging from 'Ornament of Savage Tribes' to 'Leaves and Flowers from Nature', via eighteen other categories.[51]

George Eliot's highly favourable review of *The Grammar of Ornament*, written on the occasion of a new 1865 edition, is important because it both reflects on the dynamic between interior and exterior that emerges from Jones's work and puts it into relation to urban industrialism. Her approval is perhaps unsurprising given that Jones was a friend of G. H. Lewes and had decorated the house he and Eliot bought together in 1863.[52] After first praising 'the men who are trying to banish ugliness from our streets and our homes, and to make both the outside and inside of our dwellings worthy of a world where there are forests and flower-tressed meadows', Eliot writes:

> Think of certain hideous manufacturing towns where the piety is chiefly a belief in copious perdition, and the pleasure is chiefly gin. The dingy surface of wall pierced by the ugliest windows, the staring shop-fronts, paper-hangings, carpets, brass and gilt mouldings, and advertising placards, have an effect akin to that of malaria; it is easy to understand that with such surroundings there is more belief in cruelty than in beneficence, and that the best earthly bliss attainable is the dulling of the external senses. For it is a fatal mistake to suppose that ugliness which is taken for beauty will answer all the purposes of beauty; the subtle relation between all kinds of truth and fitness in our life forbids that bad taste should ever be harmless to our moral sensibility or our intellectual discernment; and – more than that – as it is probable that fine musical harmonies have a sanative influence over our bodily organization, it is also probable that just coloring and lovely combinations of lines may be necessary to the complete well-being of our systems apart from any conscious delight in them. A savage may indulge in discordant chuckles and shrieks and gutturals, and think that they please the gods, but it does not follow that his frame would not be favorably wrought upon by the vibrations of a grand church organ. One sees a person capable of choosing the worst style of wall-paper become suddenly afflicted by its ugliness under an attack of illness. And if an evil state of blood and lymph usually goes along with an evil state of mind, who shall say that the ugliness of our streets, the falsity of our ornamentation, the vulgarity of our upholstery, have not something to do with those bad tempers which breed false conclusions?[53]

The 'hideous manufacturing towns' and 'ugliness of our streets', but also bad wallpaper and upholstery, are associated with disease, savagery (repeating colonial stereotypes), immorality, falsity and an 'evil state of mind'. This ugliness is visible in violent disharmonic conjunctions ('the dingy surface of wall pierced by the ugliest windows') as opposed to architectural beauty, which is assumed to have a positive influence over 'our bodily organization', comparable to 'fine musical harmonies'. The industrial town is here discordant and chaotic, lacking any sense of purpose or coherent meaning. In this context, Eliot suggests, it is much faster and easier to bring 'artistic reform' to 'our interior decoration than to our external architecture'. What is significant about Jones is that he 'has zealously vindicated the claim of internal ornamentation to be a part of the architect's function'.[54] What was first framed as a problem that traverses exterior and interior is now apparently resolved through the transformation of 'internal ornamentation' alone. This turn to the domestic interior as an arena to overcome wider social problems through the protection and nourishment of the subject repeats features of Gaskell and Dickens's writing, as discussed in Chapters 1 and 2, though in those texts the interior is always in some way opened out, exteriorised or penetrated (as in the auction of Dombey's possessions, for instance, or the permeable and unprotective cellar of the Davenports).[55] Ornament in Jones, inspired by the Alhambra's interweaving of interior and exterior across its various spaces, even while it maintains a separation from the outside world, seems to offer the possibility of folding interior and exterior together to counter the potential vulnerability of domestic space. Eliot's review, therefore, though arguing for the modernisation of design, also maintains a belief in 'dwelling' of the kind that Lefebvre diagnoses, referring to Bachelard and Heidegger, as nostalgic. In Bachelard, Lefebvre suggests, 'the relationship between Home and Ego [. . .] borders on identity', which is a sign of the nostalgia that frequently accompanies modernity, manifested as the desire to take shelter within a spatial imaginary formed by sensory memories. Such a desire shows that 'the modern world's brutal liquidation of history and of the past proceeds in a very uneven manner', since a drive towards the preservation of tradition coexists alongside the most radical transformations of social space.[56]

While there are certainly notes of nostalgia in Eliot (as with the repeated return to the scenes of her childhood in her novels), she is also arguing here for a globalised and universalised understanding of ornament drawn from Jones. *The Grammar of Ornament* is not intended, she says, 'to present a collection of models for mere copyists', but to help us identify 'a logic of form which cannot be departed from in ornamental design without a corresponding remoteness from perfection; unmeaning, irrelevant lines are as bad as irrelevant words or clauses, that tend no whither'.[57] Ornament is a form of language, but in an opposite way to the arabesque in Schlegel; rather than free imagination, it leads us to recognise universal structures in design, something broadly similar to Noam Chomsky's universal grammar in language. Jones's sweeping review of styles from a wide range of places and periods asserts that there is a shared structure behind each surface manifestation, a figure in the carpet to be identified and followed. Moorish design is the highest example in this respect, because the Moors 'worked as nature worked', yet without directly copying it, so drawing out more fully than other styles the Kantian purposiveness-without-a-purpose that is at the heart of beauty.[58] What is reassuring in all this, and Eliot's response to it, is the proposition that there is after all a grammar to ornament, architecture and nature to be discovered, and that this can be utilised to counter the disordered and 'savage' pandemonium of urban life.

Elsewhere in Eliot's writing, though, there are places that put this hope of uncovering a unifying deep structure into question. In 'The Lifted Veil' (1859), for instance, the narrator supernaturally sees behind the surface appearance of other people, but this is a curse rather than a blessing. In his perception,

> the rational talk, the graceful attentions, the wittily-turned phrases, and the kindly deeds, which used to make the web of their characters, were seen as if thrust asunder by a microscopic vision, that showed all the intermediate frivolities, all the suppressed egoism, all the struggling chaos of puerilities, meanness, vague capricious memories, and indolent make-shift thoughts, from which human words and deeds emerge like leaflets covering a fermenting heap.[59]

Here it is surface appearance, imagined as a veil or 'web', which is rational, orderly and moral, whereas the unconscious or preconscious mind below is a 'struggling chaos' of fragments and 'capricious memories'. Surface appearance is not a clue to a deeper grammar but a paper-thin covering of leaflets atop a 'fermenting heap'. The narrator nonetheless desires to see the mind of his future wife Bertha, the only person whose thoughts are still hidden from him. But when the 'terrible moment of complete illumination' comes, he finds 'that the darkness had hidden no landscape from me, but only a blank prosaic wall [. . .] I saw all round the narrow room of this woman's soul'.[60] What is horrifying is not that Bertha conceals a hidden secret, but the fact that there is no secret. The awful truth is that there is no depth to be revealed. This narrator is, of course, a study in rancour and *ressentiment*, but nonetheless the story points to another side of ornament and the arabesque from that celebrated by Jones: the possibility that the play of surface decoration generates only the impression of a deep grammar which does not in fact exist.

In *The Grammar of Ornament*, too, there is a moment that puts the presumption of universal structure into question, and it comes from the arabesque's connection to the grotesque. Though I have been discussing the material on Moorish architecture as the main example of the arabesque, it is in the chapter on Italian Ornament, written by the architect Matthew Digby Wyatt (1820–77), where the word is explicitly used. As is often the case, arabesque is linked to Raphael, with Wyatt referring to his less-discussed designs for the Villa Madama as well as the Vatican (see Figure 5.3). However, Wyatt then offers a critique of the arabesques of Giulio Romano (1499–1546), Raphael's pupil. In Giulio's work in Mantua, Wyatt finds a 'tendency to caricature', which becomes almost grotesque, in 'the bustle of line, the fluttering ribbons, and vague jewelled forms of No. 5, and in the monotonous masques and foolscaps of No. 1' (the numbers referring to images on the illustrated plates). Giulio's 'vanity intoxicated him', asserts Wyatt, and his art became excessive. In one image, 'a scroll ornament freely dashed out is entirely spoilt by the ludicrous object from which it springs', that object being a partial human figure, while in another 'the ridiculous masques seem sneering at the graceful forms which surround them'. In these examples, it is especially masks and human or human-like figures that are criticised, as well as the supposed maltreatment of nature ('he gathered flowers from her bosom only to crush them in his rude grasp'), suggesting that bodies and unrefined natural forms begin to intrude and disrupt the purity of the arabesque only a few years after its modern emergence with Raphael.[61] Yet I would suggest that it is exactly in these moments when the arabesque becomes ludicrous and caricatural that we see its other face, which is a counterpoint to the geometrical order of the Alhambra. This unbalanced, non-purposive element of the arabesque is the unintentional discord that cannot finally be separated from the intentional order Jones is seeking to find in ornament. As a hybrid mode, both Islamic and European, the arabesque is always liable to be double and self-contradictory in this way. Indeed, it is precisely this grotesque exuberance which allies the arabesque most strongly with the literary writing of authors such as Poe, Gilman and Gogol, as I will go on to explore in the remaining sections of this chapter.

Figure 5.3 Plate 86 from *The Grammar of Ornament* (1856), Owen Jones. The Metropolitan Museum of Art, New York, Gift of Friends of the Thomas J. Watson Library.

Literary Arabesques I: Poe and Gilman

A route into the specifically literary arabesque is offered by Walter Scott's 1827 essay on E. T. A. Hoffman, 'On the Supernatural in Fictitious Composition', which as Gabrielle Rippl points out influenced Edgar Allan Poe's understanding of the arabesque. Poe uses the term in the title of his short story collection, *Tales of the Grotesque and Arabesque* (1840), and it is also important in his short essay 'The Philosophy of Furniture' from the same year. Scott's reading of Hoffman seems to pick up almost exactly where Wyatt's reading of Giulio Romano ends, since Giulio's intoxicating vanity in his own creations points towards madness, while Hoffman, says Scott, was 'so nearly on the verge of actual insanity, as to be afraid of the beings his own fancy created'. Scott expands:

> the grotesque in his compositions partly resembles the arabesque in painting, in which is introduced the most strange and complicated monsters, resembling centaurs, griffins, sphinxes, chimeras, rocs, and all other creatures of romantic imagination, dazzling the beholder as it were by the unbounded fertility of the author's imagination.[62]

The arabesque runs together with the grotesque here, as the sign of a madly excessive poetic imagination, which might explain why critics have found it so difficult to separate the 'grotesque' from the 'arabesque' in Poe's stories. At the same time, in its role as pure imagination the arabesque seems to become drained of semantic content. This is certainly the case in 'The Philosophy of Furniture', which like Eliot's review positions the interior as the locus for tasteful self-expression. Poe emphasises the importance of having 'distinct circular figures, *of no meaning*' on carpets, noting that 'all upholstery of this nature should be rigidly Arabesque'.[63] The arabesque is placed in contrast to the American (as opposed to British) preference for '*glare*' and '*glitter*', especially in 'gas and glass'. Mirrors, for instance, present 'a continuous flat, colourless, unrelieved surface' that is a kind of anti-arabesque.[64] The wallpaper of Poe's ideal apartment, by contrast, is 'of a glossy, silvery hue, intermingled with small Arabesque devices of a fainter tint of the prevalent crimson', while the paintings that cover it are 'chiefly landscapes of an imaginative cast, such as the fairy grottoes of Stanfield, or the Lake of the Dismal Swamp of our own Chapman'.[65] Clarkson Stanfield (1793–1867) illustrated travel books and novels, and was known for his images of castles and ancient houses, while John Gadsby Chapman (1805–89) painted *The Lake of the Dismal Swamp* in 1831, based on a poem by the Irish poet Thomas Moore (1779–1852) which probably inspired Poe's 1827 poem 'The Lake'.[66] Both examples can be interpreted as grotesques, especially if we note the etymology of grotesque as descending from *grotta* (cave), so linking it to Stanfield's 'fairy grottoes',[67] although, according to Benjamin, 'the word is not derived from *grotta* in the literal sense, but from the "burial" – in the sense of concealment – which the cave or grotto expresses'.[68] Appropriately in this case, Chapman's swamp painting is dark and melancholy, the only sign of animal life it presents being a bird that sits ominously on a branch, possibly anticipating Poe's 'The Raven' (1845). In this way, we get a speculative topology for Poe's *Tales* of 1840: the arabesque is the background of non-signifying imagination which lies behind, like a spatial unconscious, and gives rise to the dreamlike grotesque images that stand out upon it. This reading of the arabesque as background would of course complicate the idea of it as a feature of the surface, but then such a complication is appropriate to the mobility and doubleness of the arabesque, its status as both an incidental border decoration (background) and what draws the eye (foreground), in the manner of Derrida's parergon.

In Poe's stories the semantic emptiness associated with the arabesque is what allows it to be particularly stimulating to the imagination, to generate multiple overlapping impressions that hover between the objective and the subjective. This is the case in 'Ligeia' (1838), for instance, where a 'heavy and massive-looking tapestry' that covers the walls of a bridal chamber is 'spotted all over, at irregular intervals, with arabesque figures, about a foot in diameter, and wrought upon the cloth in patterns of the most jetty black'. These arabesques are anamorphic images which are 'changeable in aspect', so that from 'simple monstrosities' they appear to shift as the visitor walks through the room, becoming 'an endless succession of the ghastly forms which belong to the superstitions of the Norman, or arise in the guilty slumbers of the monk', creating a 'phantasmagoric effect [that] was vastly heightened by the artificial introduction of a strong continual current of wind behind the draperies'.[69] The arabesque is not only figuratively but literally in motion. Moreover, as in Mouret's department store, the fabric almost literally becomes a form of architecture, since not only is the tapestry hung 'from summit to foot', but the same material features as a carpet, a covering for the furniture, a canopy for the bed and a set of curtains.[70]

In one way this scene of Gothic interiority seems far away from urban life, but in another the 'phantasmagoric effect' of constant change that holds the eye but also resists interpretation is deeply urban, and is closely repeated in Poe's evocation of the London crowd in 'The Man of the Crowd' (1839), which was of so much interest to Benjamin.[71] In that story, the narrator's opening description of the changing crowd outside his coffee-house echoes the movement of the arabesque tapestry in 'Ligeia', as well as the increase of monstrosity and guilt as the visitor progresses into the room. At first, we hear that 'the tumultuous sea of human heads filled me [. . .] with a delicious novelty of emotion', but a little later,

> As the night deepened, so deepened to me the interest of the scene; for not only did the general character of the crowd materially alter (its general features retiring in the gradual withdrawal of the more orderly portion

of the people, and its harsher ones coming out into bolder relief, as the late hour brought forth every species of infamy from its den,) but the rays of the gas-lamps, feeble at first in their struggle with the dying day, had now at length gained ascendancy, and threw over every thing a fitful and garish lustre.[72]

The harsher features of the crowd that come out in 'bolder relief' repeat the increase of 'ghastly forms' in 'Ligeia', while the 'fitful and garish lustre' of the gas-lamps generates a similar phantasmagoric effect. As Benjamin notes, 'the appearance of the street as an *intérieur* in which the phantasmagoria of the flâneur is concentrated is hard to separate from the gas lighting', though Poe's critique of gas-light in the furniture essay might complicate this observation.[73] Even the disproportionate significance of a single detail, present here in the face of the 'decrepid old man', which 'arrested and absorbed my whole attention, on account of the absolute idiosyncrasy of its expression', is typical of the arabesque, as in Wyatt's complaint that Giulio's decoration is entirely spoilt by the 'ludicrous object' from which it springs.[74] Baudelaire also seems to view the arabesque in this way when he describes the struggle within modern painters between 'the will to see all and forget nothing and the faculty of memory, which has formed the habit of a lively absorption of general colour and of silhouette, the arabesque of contour'; as a result, 'many a trifle assumes vast proportions; many a triviality usurps the attention', but only as part of a state of 'anarchy' where 'all hierarchy and all subordination vanishes'.[75] In Poe this struggle is present in the juxtaposition between the narrator's insistence on the significance of the man he follows, and the man's failure to acknowledge or recognise the narrator when confronted by him: 'I [. . .] gazed at him steadfastly in the face. He noticed me not, but resumed his solemn walk.' Though the man of the crowd has acted as a provocative foreground image for most of the narrative, from his perspective the narrator who is his shadow or double is no more than an irrelevant background detail. This turns the conclusion away from any possibility of reading intention or meaning in the man of the crowd's actions: 'it will be in vain to follow; for I shall learn no more of him, nor of his deeds'.[76] In this way, the story effectively captures not only the phantasmagoric and anamorphic potential of the arabesque, but its combination of intentionality and unintentionality, meaning and meaninglessness, foreground and background.

As Rippl has argued, Poe's interest in the arabesque is developed and transformed by Charlotte Perkins Gilman in 'The Yellow Wallpaper' (1890), where a woman postnatally prescribed a 'rest cure' (as Gilman was) narrates her gradual turn towards madness while contemplating the repulsive yellow wallpaper in her room, decorated with 'one of those sprawling flamboyant patterns committing every artistic sin', later described as 'interminable grotesques' and 'florid arabesque'.[77] Rippl reads Poe as pursuing an 'anticlassical (or anticlassicist) agenda' in which the grotesque and arabesque work against mimesis and order, through the use of 'many conspicuous repetitions' on the level of sound, language and character, so that his writing takes on 'the qualities of a continuous incantation'.[78] Gilman's short story builds on this, but also acts as a 'metatext that takes the constructedness of literary texts as its subject and that demonstrates how readings of such texts are inconclusive', so resembling James's 'The Figure in the Carpet'.[79] For Rippl, the narrator's approach to reading is 'feminine' and 'arabesque', moving in 'undirected and phantasmagorical fashion' and assuming 'polysemantic meaning', as opposed to the fixed, rational and 'masculine' reading method of her doctor husband.[80] Rippl thus reads the narrator's struggle between reading the wallpaper as polysemantic on the one hand, and decoding its meaning (as James's narrator also wishes to do) on the other, as one between feminine and masculine styles of reading, which ultimately 'ends with complete identification between the protagonist and her doubles', as she peels off the wallpaper and becomes one of the 'great many women', or perhaps 'only one', that seem to hide behind the surface pattern, making this a 'unidimensional' and 'masculine' ending.[81]

I would add to this, however, that at another level the conflict Rippl finds between rational (masculine) structure and polyvalent (feminine) disorder is itself characteristic of the arabesque. When Rippl points out that in the evening the pattern transforms, so that 'meaningless in themselves, the arabesques now become an endless series of grotesques, that is, objects that by definition are meaningful', this underestimates the way that the arabesque is already itself a play between meaning and lack of meaning, not merely one coordinate within this dynamic.[82] In fact, a vacillatory movement between the two poles is fundamental to the wallpaper, as in these lines:

> Looked at in one way each breadth stands alone, the bloated curves and flourishes – a kind of 'debased Romanesque' with *delirium tremens* – go waddling up and down in isolated columns of fatuity.
> But, on the other hand, they connect diagonally, and the sprawling outlines run off in great slanting waves of optic horror, like a lot of wallowing seaweeds in full chase.[83]

Isolation and connection exist simultaneously, in the same way as the narrator is both separate from and connected to the patterns she views, blurring subject/object distinctions. This relates to what is perhaps the most significant innovation made by Gilman's story in the context of the history of the arabesque: the fact that what lies behind the arabesque, occupying the place of the Absolute in Schlegel or purposiveness in Kant, is a (female) subject who is simultaneously single and multiple, as in these lines:

> The front pattern *does* move – and no wonder! The woman behind shakes it!
>   Sometimes I think there are a great many women behind, and sometimes only one, and she crawls around fast, and her crawling shakes it all over.[84]

The conclusion of the story, where the narrator peels off 'the top pattern', which is to say the wallpaper, in order to release the woman/women trapped behind, does not so much settle the arabesque's meaning into one form, as Rippl suggests, as release its indeterminacy and mobility onto the figure of the subject and narrator. The woman who crawls is, like the figure in the carpet in James, not in the end a being behind the surface, but rather another layer of patterning: 'I didn't realize for a long time what the thing was that showed behind, that dim sub-pattern, but now I am quite sure it is a woman.'[85] The comma after 'behind' is telling; the point is that the sub-pattern is the woman: they are one and the same. This is why the narrator must move continually (but repetitively) in the final pages of the story, and why she must remain within the interior rather than going outside ('outside you have to creep on the ground [. . .] But here I can creep smoothly on the floor, and my shoulder just fits in that long smooch around the wall'): because she has now become the pattern, or sub-pattern, that was simultaneously on and behind the surface of the wallpaper; she has become arabesque.[86]

Literary Arabesques II: Gogol

While Gilman's text is not an urban one, the concept of the arabesque subject that emerges from it, which I take to be a subject that physically or linguistically embodies the arabesque, can be usefully reapplied to city texts elsewhere in the nineteenth century. In the last section of this chapter, I read Gogol's 'The Overcoat' (1842) as an example of such a text, despite it not being published in *Arabesques* (where the Petersburg Tales 'Nevsky Prospect', 'The Portrait' and 'Diary of a Madman' first appeared). Whereas in Gilman's story the main character is also the narrator, in Gogol's text a third-person narrator describes the experiences of Akaky Akakievich, a junior clerk in the St Petersburg civil service who desperately needs a new coat, which he eventually acquires and then has stolen from him, only to finally die and haunt his previously unsympathetic superior. Both narrator and character in the tale speak an arabesque language characterised by hesitation, gaps, digression and repetition. Their intentionality is always accompanied by an unintentionality or uncontrollability that exceeds or escapes what is expressed, so that the story both demonstrates and works against the notion of Petersburg as a purely 'abstract and intentional' city, anticipating the double-voiced discourse of Dostoevsky's underground man.[87]

As Charles Bernheimer notes, the tale opens with a digression: 'in the department of ... but it would be better not to say in which department. There is nothing more irascible than all these departments, regiments, offices – in short, all this officialdom.'[88] Victor Brombert reads this tendency as both playful and subversive of authorial authority, showing 'the arbitrariness of any fictional structure'. Gogol, says Brombert, seems caught 'between the conviction that writing is the only salvation, and that it is powerless to say the unsayable'.[89] More than this, we can see that Petersburg itself contributes to this 'unsayability', confusing the possibility of coherent narrative:

> Precisely where the clerk who had invited [Akakievich] lived, we unfortunately cannot say: our memory is beginning to fail us badly, and whatever there is in Petersburg, all those houses and streets, has so mixed together in our head that it is very hard to get anything out of it in a decent fashion.[90]

The effect of the city 'going into' the narrator's head works against anything, especially language, getting 'out of it in a decent fashion'. Fragmentation thus defines both the story's language and the experience of living in Petersburg. Janet Tucker suggests that this fragmentation extends to the generic make-up of 'The Overcoat', which like *Arabesques* is a patchwork of different forms of writing, including 'hagiography, the physiological sketch, the gothic tale, bureaucratic prose plus the oral tale, and the society tale'.[91]

Fragmentation and digression are hallmarks of arabesque writing, especially if, as Schlegel proposes, Lawrence Sterne is taken as the archetypal arabesque writer, since *Tristram Shandy* (1759–67) famously consists of almost nothing but digression. Such writing has an affinity with Baroque, a form, like Gothic and arabesque, that is both architectural and literary. For Gavriel Shapiro, Baroque forms the basis of Gogol's writing, characterised by 'figures of language based on repetition, cumulation, and wordplay', echoing the writing of Cervantes.[92] Bely combines the architectural and literary forms of Baroque when he compares Gogol's writing to 'an asymmetrical Baroque structure surrounded with a colonnade of repetitions'.[93] Similarly, Strathausen suggests that a genuine translation of the arabesque into writing should be expected to use 'ellipses, redundancies, [. . .] alliterations [. . .] repetitive phrases, and so forth'.[94] All these features, especially repetition, characterise Akakievich. Like Melville's Bartleby the Scrivener, Akakievich's sole job is to copy documents, an activity which dominates his life. Unlike Bartleby, though, he derives a peculiar pleasure from copying:

> There, in that copying, he saw some varied and pleasant world of his own. Delight showed in his face; certain letters were his favorites, and when he came to one of them, he was beside himself: he chuckled and winked and helped out with his lips, so that it seemed one could read on his face every letter his pen traced.[95]

Bernheimer identifies in this pleasure a Kierkegaardian freedom, which recalls Kant's description of free beauty: '"repetition", writes Kierkegaard, "signifies freedom itself, . . . a transcendency, a religious movement by virtue of the absurd, which comes to pass when it has reached the borders of the marvellous"'.[96] Such a movement beyond the absurd and marvellous repeats Scott's reading of Hoffmann and anticipates Gilman's narrator, and recalling Kant we might align it with the grotesque. What is most significant here is the way that repetition and writing rather than unrestricted imagination signifies a (peculiar) form of freedom, returning us to features of the Islamic form of the arabesque, where writing and ornament are integrated, and where repetition evokes the infinity of God. Repetition, indeed, is embedded in Akaky's name, since he was christened after his father, taking his patronymic as his given name. In Russian, notes Brombert, this is emphasised, since his name suggests the syllable *kak*, meaning 'like', as well as indicating absurdity and inferiority by sounding like a child's term for excrement. The story is also written using 'seemingly endless variations' on the same Russian words, heightening the repetitive effect.[97] This is repeated in Akaky's speech, which is marked by ellipses, redundancies and digressions, making it highly non-referential:

> It should be known that Akaky Akakievich expressed himself mostly with prepositions, adverbs, and finally such particles as have decidedly no meaning. If the matter was very difficult, he even had the habit of not finishing the phrase at all, so that very often he would begin his speech with the words 'That, really, is altogether sort of . . .' after which would come nothing, and he himself would forget it, thinking everything had been said.[98]

Such Shandean language is typical of the arabesque according to Schlegel, but in Gogol's hands it becomes an urban and abstracted form, mimetically signifying the abstraction of the city of St Petersburg even as it clashes with its intentionality. These unfinished, interrupted sentences disallow continuity, so expressing in linguistic form the fragmented character of urban life.

In this way, Akaky presents a linguistic patterning of the new form of perambulating movement which the modern city generates, and which can be seen later in Raskolnikov's erratic journeys around Petersburg in *Crime and Punishment* (1866), as when he wanders in a 'state of brooding', 'but when, with a sudden start, he raised his head again and looked around him, he immediately forgot what he had been thinking about a moment ago and even what part of town he had been walking through'.[99] The affinity between Akaky's language and such movement can be observed in a passage that comes after he learns his old coat cannot be fixed:

> When he went outside, Akaky Akakievich was as if in a dream. 'So that's it, that's what it is', he said to himself. 'I really didn't think it would come out sort of . . .' and then, after some silence, he added, 'So that's how it is! that's what finally comes out! and I really never would have supposed it would be so'. Following that, a long silence again ensued, after which he said, 'So that's it! such an, indeed, altogether unexpected, sort of . . . it's altogether . . . such a circumstance!' Having said this, instead of going home, he went in the entirely opposite direction, without suspecting it himself.[100]

Akaky's erratic language becomes erratic movement. Both are arabesques, generated out of and in reaction to the modern city. The influence the city exerts is attuned with the bureaucracy which continually passes Akaky new documents to copy, and which is part of the city's invisible architecture, since it is not described directly, but only in its effects. This invisible architecture works to repress both Akaky's desires and his expression of those desires, which nonetheless emerge in the story's conclusion, when Akaky's ghost appears to take on the form of his superior. Yet at the same time it is this architecture of bureaucracy that generates the peculiar freedom Akaky exhibits in his copying. In a similar way, the gaps in Akaky's language (which parallel the gaps in Mrs Skewton's speech in *Dombey and Son*) can be taken as signifying both repression and an opening up of unexpected and unknown arenas of thought and action, such as the capacity for ghostly vengeance.

This combination of control and freedom, organisation and randomness is, as this chapter has argued, definitional of the arabesque subject and the arabesque city. In addition to the multiplicity and mobility that have been often remarked upon as features of the arabesque, and which are unquestionably significant, it is this doubleness in particular that gives it a dialectical character which aligns it with the characteristics of invisible architecture. In the following chapter, I propose a similar reading of spatial and architectural whiteness in the nineteenth century, arguing that it too represents – in a somewhat different manner – a complex of meaning and non-meaning that proves generative as a way of conceptualising the uneven modernity of city life and literature in this period.

Notes

1. Carsten Strathausen, 'Eichendorff's *Das Marmorbild* and the Demise of Romanticism', in *Rereading Romanticism*, ed. by Martha Helfer (Amsterdam: Rodopi, 2000), pp. 367–88 (p. 375 n. 15).
2. Immanuel Kant, *Critique of Judgement*, trans. by James Creed Meredith, ed. by Nicholas Walker (Oxford: Oxford University Press, 2007), p. 52.
3. Winfried Menninghaus, *In Praise of Nonsense: Kant and Bluebeard*, trans. by Henry Pickford (Stanford: Stanford University Press, 1999), p. 77. Frazier and Strathausen also make similar points.
4. Kant, p. 60.
5. Kant, p. 73.
6. William Hogarth, *The Analysis of Beauty* (London: W. Strahan, 1772), p. x.
7. Wolfgang Kayser, *The Grotesque in Art and Literature*, trans. by Ulrich Weisstein (Gloucester, MA: Peter Smith, 1968), p. 20, p. 22, p. 23.
8. *OED*, arabesque, n. and adj. *OED Online*, Oxford University Press, <www.oed.com/view/Entry/10073>. Accessed 16 May 2023.

9. For a more detailed history of the arabesque, see Gurminder Kaur Bhogal, *Details of Consequence: Ornament, Music, and Art in Paris* (Oxford: Oxford University Press, 2013), pp. 64–114.
10. Heynen, p. 11.
11. Haomin Gong, *Uneven Modernity: Literature, Film, and Intellectual Discourse in Postsocialist China* (Honolulu: University of Hawai'i Press, 2012), p. 2.
12. *Arcades*, p. 545.
13. Bhogal, p. 67. Although as a counterpoint to this chronology, see William Audsley and George Audsley's *Popular Dictionary of Architecture and the Allied Arts, Volume II* (New York: G. P. Putnam's Sons, 1881), pp. 5–14, whose entry on the arabesque culminates with the Renaissance, rather than seeing it as a current art form.
14. *Arcades*, p. 559, p. 557, p. 551.
15. Johann Wolfgang von Goethe, *Sämtliche Werke*, vol. 30 (Stuttgart: J. G. Cotta, 1895), p. 173. My translation.
16. Friedrich Schlegel, *Gespräch über die Poesie* (Stuttgart: J. B. Metzlersche, 1968), p. 331. My translation.
17. Frazier, p. 278.
18. Fusso, pp. 112–13.
19. *Arabesques*, p. 199.
20. G. W. F. Hegel, *Aesthetics: Lectures on Fine Art, Volume II*, trans. by T. M. Knox (Oxford: Clarendon, 1975), p. 658.
21. Hegel, p. 659.
22. Hegel, p. 658, p. 659. Interpolation in original text.
23. Gray Kochhar-Lindgren, *Urban Arabesques: Philosophy, Hong Kong, Transversality* (London: Rowman and Littlefield, 2020), p. 33, p. 45.
24. See Rae Beth Gordon, *Ornament, Fantasy, and Desire in Nineteenth-Century French Literature* (Princeton: Princeton University Press, 1992); Bhogal; Heba Barakat (author) and Muhammad Waley (editor), *The Arabesque: An Introduction* (Kuala Lumpur: Islamic Arts Museum Malaysia, 2018); Cordula Grewe, *The Arabesque from Kant to Comics* (Abingdon and New York: Routledge, 2021); Anne Leonard, ed., *Arabesque Without End: Across Music and the Arts, from Faust to Shahrazad* (New York: Routledge, 2022); Jacob Berman, *American Arabesque: Arabs, Islam, and the 19th Century Imaginary* (New York: New York University Press, 2012).
25. Gordon, p. 34. Anne Leonard, 'Introduction: The Arabesque Aesthetic', in *Arabesque Without End*, pp. 1–18 (p. 3).
26. Leonard, p. 4.
27. 'Interview with André Verdet, 1952', in Jack Flam, *Matisse on Art* (Berkeley and Los Angeles: University of California Press, 1995), pp. 209–16 (p. 210). See Elizabeth McCombie, *Mallarmé and Debussy: Unheard Music, Unseen Text* (Oxford: Oxford University Press, 2003), especially pp. 40–4, pp. 95–154; Rancière, *Aisthesis*, pp. 93–110.

28. Bertrand Éveno, 'Jung's "Multicolored Arabesques": Their Renderings and Intentions in the Pictorial Vocabulary of *The Red Book*', trans. by Leslie de Galbert, *Psychological Perspectives*, 58.1 (2015), 5–33 (p. 17).
29. Kochhar-Lindgren, p. 13.
30. Éveno, p. 23.
31. Éveno, p. 25. Hédi Jaouad also links the arabesque to 'A Figure in the Carpet', via Robert Browning: see Hédi Jaouad, *Browning upon Arabia: A Moveable Feast* (Cham: Palgrave, 2018), p. 26.
32. Winnicott quoted in Éveno, p. 30.
33. J. Hillis Miller, 'The Figure in the Carpet', *Poetics Today*, 1.3 (1980), 107–18 (p. 113).
34. Henry James, 'The Figure in the Carpet', in *Complete Stories 1892–1898* (New York: Library of America, 1996), pp. 572–608 (p. 586).
35. 'The Figure', p. 110.
36. For an overview see John Jespersen, 'Originality and Jones' *The Grammar of Ornament* of 1856', *Journal of Design History*, 21.2 (2008), 143–53.
37. Kathryn Ferry, 'Owen Jones and the Alhambra Court at the Crystal Palace', in *Revisiting Al-Andalus: Perspectives on the Material Culture of Islamic Iberia and Beyond*, ed. by Glaire Anderson and Mariam Rosser-Owen (Leiden: Brill, 2007), pp. 227–46 (p. 228). *Arabesques*, p. 132.
38. Murphy, p. 31.
39. Phillips, p. 57.
40. Ferry, p. 228 n. 2.
41. Phillips, p. 58.
42. Phillips, p. 58. The reproduction was, however, imperfect due to considerations of space; see Ferry, pp. 230–2.
43. Ferry, p. 232.
44. *Arcades*, p. 406.
45. Owen Jones, *The Alhambra Court in the Crystal Palace* (London: Crystal Palace Library and Bradbury & Evans, 1854), p. 5, pp. 5–6. These lines and others quoted by Jones were 'translated by Mr Gayangos, from our casts taken in 1837', *Alhambra Court*, p. 48.
46. *Alhambra Court*, p. 6.
47. Temporal disjunction also played a role in other ways: Ferry reproduces an 1861 letter that appeared in *The Times* from Mohammed Lamate, a Muslim living in London, complaining about the 'wanton desecration' of including on the floor an inscription that featured the name of God, which could easily be trodden upon. This was in fact the 'only surviving example of medieval flooring' in the Alhambra, which Jones faithfully reproduced, but this oldest fragment of the palace is instead interpreted by Lamate (and, he claims, the 'Moorish Ambassador') as 'carelessness or ignorance' by modern English artists. Ferry, p. 242.

48. Robert Irwin, *The Alhambra* (London: Profile Books, 2004), p. 21.
49. Owen Jones, *The Grammar of Ornament* (New York: Van Nostrand Reinhold, 1972 [1856]), p. 5, p. 8.
50. *Alhambra Court*, p. 7.
51. *Grammar*, p. 9, p. 12. Jespersen, p. 147.
52. Jespersen, p. 147.
53. George Eliot, *The Essays of George Eliot*, ed. by Nathan Sheppard (New York: Funk and Wagnells, 1883), p. 272, pp. 272–3.
54. *Essays*, p. 273.
55. On the fraught dynamic of public and private space in industrial novels as a crisis of realism, see Catherine Gallagher, *The Industrial Reformation of English Fiction: Social Discourse and Narrative Form, 1832–1867* (Chicago: University of Chicago Press, 1985).
56. Lefebvre, p. 121, p. 122.
57. *Essays*, p. 274.
58. *Grammar*, p. 70.
59. George Eliot, *The Lifted Veil and Brother Jacob* (Oxford: Oxford University Press, 1999), p. 14.
60. *Lifted Veil*, p. 32.
61. Wyatt in *Grammar*, p. 145.
62. Gabrielle Rippl, 'Wild Semantics: Charlotte Perkins Gilman's Feminization of Edgar Allen Poe's Arabesque Aesthetics', in *Soft Canons*, ed. by Karen Kilcup (Iowa City: University of Iowa Press, 1999), pp. 123–40. Walter Scott, 'On the Supernatural in Fictitious Composition; and Particularly on the Works of Ernest Theodore William Hoffman', *Foreign Quarterly Review*, 1 (July 1827), 60–98 (p. 81, pp. 81–2).
63. Edgar Allan Poe, 'The Philosophy of Furniture', *Burton's Gentleman's Magazine*, 6.5 (May 1840), 243–5 (p. 244).
64. 'Philosophy', p. 244.
65. 'Philosophy', p. 245.
66. C. T. Walters, 'Poe's "Philosophy of Furniture" and the Aesthetics of Fictional Design', in *Edgar Allan Poe: Beyond Gothicism*, ed. by James Hutchisson (Newark: University of Delaware Press, 2011), pp. 1–16 (pp. 6–7). T. O. Mabbott, ed., *The Collected Works of Edgar Allan Poe, Vol. 1: Poems* (Cambridge, MA: Belknap Press, 1969), p. 83.
67. Kayser, p. 19.
68. *Origin*, p. 171.
69. Edgar Allen Poe, *Selected Tales* (Oxford: Oxford University Press, 1998), p. 34.
70. *Selected Tales*, p. 34.
71. See *The Paris of the Second Empire in Baudelaire* and 'On Some Motifs in Baudelaire', in *Writer of Modern Life*, pp. 79–85, pp. 186–8.
72. *Selected Tales*, p. 84, p. 87.
73. *Writer of Modern Life*, p. 81.

74. *Selected Tales*, p. 88.
75. *Painter of Modern Life*, p. 16.
76. *Selected Tales*, p. 91.
77. Charlotte Perkins Gilman, *The Yellow Wallpaper and Selected Writings* (London: Virago, 2009), p. 6, p. 12, p. 15.
78. Rippl, p. 126.
79. Rippl, p. 128.
80. Rippl, p. 130.
81. Rippl, p. 134, p. 135. Gilman, p. 19.
82. Rippl, p. 133.
83. Gilman, p. 11.
84. Gilman, p. 19.
85. Gilman, p. 16.
86. Gilman, p. 23.
87. *Notes from Underground*, p. 17.
88. Charles Bernheimer, 'Cloaking the Self: The Literary Space of Gogol's "Overcoat"', *PMLA*, 90.1 (1975), 53–61 (p. 54). Nikolai Gogol, 'The Overcoat', in *The Collected Tales of Nikolai Gogol*, trans. by Richard Pevear and Larissa Volokhonsky (London: Granta, 1998), pp. 394–424 (p. 394).
89. Victor Brombert, 'Meaning and Indeterminacy in Gogol's "The Overcoat"', *Proceedings of the American Philosophical Society*, 135.4 (1991), 569–75 (p. 573, p. 575).
90. *Collected Tales*, p. 410.
91. Janet Tucker, 'Genre Fragmentation in Nikolai Gogol's "The Overcoat"', *Canadian–American Slavic Studies*, 46 (2012), 83–97 (p. 84).
92. Gavriel Shapiro, *Nikolai Gogol and the Baroque Cultural Heritage* (University Park: Pennsylvania State University Press, 1993), p. 5.
93. Bely, p. 7.
94. Strathausen, p. 376.
95. 'The Overcoat', p. 397.
96. Bernheimer, p. 57.
97. Brombert, p. 571.
98. 'The Overcoat', p. 402.
99. Fyodor Dostoevsky, *Crime and Punishment*, trans. by David McDuff (London: Penguin, 2003), p. 65.
100. 'The Overcoat', p. 404.

Chapter 6

The Whiteness of the City

This chapter examines spatial and architectural whiteness in the nineteenth-century city, taking it as a final example of invisible architecture in the period. I propose that such whiteness is both a precursor and a counterpoint to the white walls that would come to define modernist architecture in the early twentieth century. In line with a number of critics in recent decades, the chapter therefore reads the nineteenth century, or the 'Victorian Age', as neither hermetically sealed nor uniform, but rather as porous and temporally fractured, while still recognising that it displays recurrent features and patterns which cut across texts and spaces.[1]

I begin from Mark Wigley's suggestion that the hidden logic of modernist architecture is to make decoration and the absence of decoration one and the same while claiming to erase ornament completely, and that this is exemplified by the white wall, where 'having been stripped of decoration, the white surface itself takes over the space-defining role of decorative art'.[2] I argue that in contrast to this erasing role within modernism, nineteenth-century whiteness is strikingly multiple and unsettled, alive with the contradictions which are typically submerged in the white walls of the International Style practised by Gropius, Le Corbusier and their contemporaries. The whiteness of the nineteenth-century city cleanses but also dirties, erases but also exposes, conceals ornamentation but also functions as ornament. Such whiteness is a compelling example of invisible architecture. Like the other forms of invisible architecture discussed in this book, it carries a powerful ideological force yet also retains a utopian aspect, seeming to offer in its blankness the hope of limitless possibilities. Though not itself a space, urban whiteness is nonetheless paradigmatic of the spaces and structures I have considered so far, operating as an aesthetic feature that is both fascinating and disturbing, at once dazzlingly visible and hauntingly empty. To begin to explore these contradictions, I turn first to Herman Melville's *Moby-Dick* (1851) and its celebrated chapter 'The Whiteness of the Whale', which although not concerned directly with the city, acts as a point of departure for the issues I wish to consider.

The Whiteness of the Whale

Melville's chapter on whiteness comes a third of the way through *Moby-Dick*, following chapter 41, which describes Captain Ahab's monomaniacal pursuit of the white whale, leading the narrator Ishmael to the startling recognition that 'it was the whiteness of the whale that above all things appalled me'.[3] Ishmael suggests that while whiteness is often associated with pre-eminence and virtue, as in 'the innocence of brides', the 'ermine of the judge' and the white man's 'ideal mastership over every dusky tribe' – comments which invite us to read the chapter as a layered commentary on sexual relations, law, power, race and colonialism – at the same time 'there yet lurks an elusive something in the innermost idea of this hue, which strikes more of panic to the soul than that redness which affrights in blood'.[4] What is disturbing about whiteness is precisely this 'elusive something', unknown and unseen, which lies below the surface while also constituting part of that surface.

This play of surfaces activated by whiteness suggests that it might be read as either a powerful signifying structure or the breakdown of such a structure, which is how Monika Gehlawat among others interprets the text: 'The whiteness of the whale [...] does not carry any implicit meaning, but in its refusal to signify, it provides a passive, blank space upon which meaning, desire and loss may be inscribed.'[5] This non-signifying signification is evident when Ishmael compares his fear of whiteness to a newborn colt's fear of a buffalo hide, though it has never seen a buffalo:

> Though neither knows where lie the nameless things of which the mystic sign gives forth such hints; yet with me, as with the colt, somewhere those things must exist. Though in many of its aspects this visible world seems formed in love, the invisible spheres were formed in fright.[6]

Whiteness signifies the existence of the inexpressible, like a Gothic tower reaching towards something it cannot represent (see Chapter 4), or Schlegel's conception of the arabesque as a non-representative symbol of the absolute (see Chapter 5). Here, though, what is signified is not an inexpressible presence but an all-consuming absence, the precise nature of which intrigues and disturbs Ishmael:

Is it that by its indefiniteness it shadows forth the heartless voids and immensities of the universe, and thus stabs us from behind with the thought of annihilation, when beholding the white depths of the milky way?[7]

Whiteness seems to operate like the psychoanalytic unconscious, which for Lacan is 'inaccessible to contradiction, to spatio-temporal location and also to the function of time'. As Lacan notes, 'the unconscious is the elusive', and elusiveness is what Melville's text is interested in, centring as it does on the hunt for Moby Dick, the elusive white whale.[8] Just as for Freud the unconscious permits the coexistence of desire and repulsion towards the same object, whiteness brings together visible 'love' and invisible 'fright'.[9] In this respect it evokes the uncanny, where *Heimlich* is always also *Unheimlich*. Like the uncanny, the determining feature of whiteness is its indeterminacy, manifested as the potential 'annihilation' of the perceiving subject, threatened with a collapse of monadic identity in the 'heartless voids' of the universe.

In this dual elusiveness and pervasiveness, the whale's whiteness functions as a symbolic representation of ideology. Toni Morrison has persuasively argued that *Moby-Dick* marks Melville's 'recognition of the moment in America when [racial] whiteness became ideology'.[10] This is a traumatic recognition, since it reveals that 'white racial ideology is savage' and an 'inhuman idea', existing as a means to justify slavery and discrimination by naturalising and celebrating the superiority of whites above blacks, as well as over nature and all other races.[11] In this reading, *Moby-Dick* is a text that brings racial whiteness into visibility, pulling it from the background into the foreground, and so confronting the problem that, as George Yancy puts it, 'whites see themselves, even if unconsciously, as raceless, as abstract minds, spectral beings, as constituting the transcendental norm', a problem that 'has complex historical links with European modernity and imperialism', and with the history of aesthetics, as David Lloyd has pointed out.[12]

As Morrison observes, when Ishmael suggests that 'the invisible spheres were formed in fright', invisibility is aligned with whiteness, so that whiteness-as-invisible is shown to be forged in a state of fear and anxiety. If *Moby-Dick* performs the reverse work of making whiteness visible, it does so only in an ambiguous way, through metaphor and allegory. Race itself remains under the skin, so to speak. In Morrison's reading, this is because Melville is struggling not with describing white people as such, but with 'whiteness idealized', which is something 'gigantic' and terrifying whose contours he cannot properly articulate.[13] More broadly, this terrifying vastness and borderlessness suggests we should read the white whale as standing not only for racial ideology, powerful as it is, but also for ideology in general, in the Althusserian sense of a pervasive structuring force which grasps and constitutes us as subjects, and which marks the limits of subjectivity.[14]

To put it another way, the whale and its whiteness evoke the Lacanian real, which again 'eludes' the analyst and cannot be pinned down.[15] The real is never fully present, but always experienced as a 'missed encounter' or *méconnaissance* ('misrecognition').[16] Such missed encounters are felt as trauma, which cannot be remembered, like John Harmon's 'death' and rebirth in *Our Mutual Friend*. In this sense, the trauma motivating *Moby-Dick* would be the original encounter between Ahab and the whale, which is a missed encounter since it achieved no understanding or resolution; neither party died, though Ahab lost his leg. To turn this missed encounter into a full, authentic encounter – which must end in death, since the real is what annihilates – is Ahab's goal. As Kevin Goddard argues, Ahab makes the whale an overdetermined symbol, his desire to kill it signifying an 'obsession with pinning meaning down, reducing all metaphysical uncertainties to a single tangible object'.[17] Ishmael, by contrast, is open to indeterminacy and uncertainty, these being among the attributes that activate his soliloquy on whiteness.

Lacan argues that the reality system 'leaves an essential part of what belongs to the real a prisoner in the toils of the pleasure principle', meaning that an image or echo of the real forms part of the same screen that blocks us from it.[18] This is, in effect, the conclusion Ishmael reaches when he suggests that whiteness reveals colours and images to be mere forms of painting, behind which subsists a devastating and overpowering reality. The key passage comes at the end of the chapter:

> And when we consider that other theory of the natural philosophers, that all other earthly hues [. . .] are but subtile [*sic*] deceits, not actually inherent in substances, but only laid on from without; so that all deified Nature absolutely paints like the harlot, whose allurements cover nothing but the charnel-house within; and when we proceed further, and consider that the mystical cosmetic which produces every one of her hues, the great principle of light, for ever remains white or colourless in itself, and if operating without medium upon matter, would touch all objects, even tulips and roses, with its own blank tinge – pondering all this, the palsied universe lies before us a leper [. . .]. And of all these things the Albino whale was the symbol. Wonder ye then at the fiery hunt?[19]

Whiteness is a skin or medium, a 'mystical cosmetic' apparently empty or transparent in itself, which nonetheless produces the colours of the world around us. The white whale, though part of this cosmetic, also functions as a gap or split that reveals appearance to be a screen concealing something else, which is deathly and inaccessible.

This screen of whiteness, like ideology or light, is so familiar that it is almost impossible to detect, as Melville indicates when he returns to the subject in chapter 68, 'The Blanket'. Here, Ishmael attempts to define whale skin, finding it to be an almost unachievable task:

> from the unmarred dead body of the whale, you may scrape off with your hand an infinitely thin, transparent substance, somewhat resembling the thinnest threads of isinglass, only it is almost as flexible and soft as satin; that is, previous to being dried, when it not only contracts and thickens, but becomes rather hard and brittle. I have several such dried bits, which I use for marks in my whale-books. It is transparent, as I said before; and being laid upon the printed page, I have sometimes pleased myself with fancying it exerted a magnifying influence. At any rate, it is pleasant to read about whales through their own spectacles, as you may say. But what I am driving at here is this. That same infinitely thin, isinglass substance, which, I admit invests the entire body of the whale, is not so much to be regarded as the skin of the creature, as the skin of the skin, so to speak.[20]

This piece of whale skin has become so insubstantial it is transparent, almost disappearing into nothingness, but it also modifies the way we view the world, acting as 'spectacles' which seem to exert an ideological effect, 'magnifying' certain things, and hence minimising others. Melville raises the possibility that all readers have such 'spectacles' that determine how they read the world, including the text of *Moby-Dick* itself, which implicitly takes its place among Ishmael's volumes as the greatest 'whale-book' of all. In this case, the skin works as what Derrida calls 'white mythology', which he defines, following Nietzsche, as 'metaphysics which has effaced in itself that fabulous scene which brought it into being, and which yet remains, active and stirring, inscribed in white ink, an invisible drawing covered over in the palimpsest'.[21] White mythology is metaphor which has forgotten it is metaphor, making the logos of the white man appear universal, so aligning with Morrison's argument. White mythology acts here in the same way as invisible architecture, by simultaneously shaping ways of seeing and (almost) vanishing from view, like the 'skin of the skin' of the whale.

Defined by indefinability, the whale skin can be understood as a sign of the absence of the real; it is the edge or outer limit of that which we cannot access directly, but which nonetheless haunts our imaginary. In this case Ishmael's whale-books represent an attempt to approach the real by means of the symbolic, which can circle around the object but never grasp it. Indeed, the point is that the supposed object (the whale) is not in the end the thing itself, but only another surface. To posit one last definition of invisible architecture, I would describe it in similar terms, as a name for spatial structures which signify the absence of the real. In this case the texts discussed in the rest of this chapter, and throughout the book, are sites where the traces of this absence can be detected.

Whiteness in the City I: Whitewashing

To return to the nineteenth-century city in the light of Melville, I want to consider three ways in which urban whiteness functions, like the whiteness of the whale, as a surface that simultaneously conceals and reveals, hides and highlights. I will come to whiteness's relationship with ornament, and to the idea of being 'targeted' by whiteness, but I begin with the material and metaphorical resonances of whitewashing, read initially through texts by James Kay and Friedrich Engels first discussed in Chapter 1. Whereas that chapter considered the social and spatial dynamics of working-class invisibility, I focus here on the specific role played by whitewashing as an aesthetic and sanitary concern, which opens out onto a wider set of concerns about truth, falsity and concealment. My aim is to show how whitewashing in nineteenth-century discourse functions to combine, often uneasily, practices of concealment and making visible.

For Kay in *The Moral and Physical Condition of the Working Classes*, whitewashing the buildings of the poor is fundamental to the project of cleansing and socialising industrial Manchester. In one statistical table, alongside 'No. of houses reported as requiring repair' and 'No. of houses wanting privies', he includes 'No. of houses reported as requiring whitewashing'. This prominence suggests that for Kay and the new statistical science he represents, whiteness is an important sign of hygiene and cleanliness, but also visibility, since the desire to survey the houses of the poor coincides with the desire to open them up to the middle classes, as covered in Chapter 2. As I noted there, Kay's survey indicates a desire to redefine the city as abstract space, to make it rational, statistical and measurable.[22] The whitewashing statistics are flawed for this purpose, however, as Kay is aware, remarking that 'this column fails to indicate [the houses'] gross neglect of order, and absolute filth'. Nonetheless, whitewashing does at least start to bring into view what cannot be seen, helping overcome the difficulty of obtaining 'satisfactory statistical results concerning the want of furniture, especially of bedding, and of food, clothing and fuel', by literally and metaphorically presenting such items – or their absence – on a blank field.[23]

Kay returns to the question of whitewashing later on, noting that under the auspices of the Special Board of Health in Manchester, 'more than a thousand houses have been whitewashed', and when laying out advice for the future organisation of the city, he states that 'each habitation should be provided with a due receptacle for every kind of refuse, and the owner should be obliged to whitewash the house, at least once every year'. In both cases, whitewashing is associated with monitoring and regulating the city, in the second case alongside a proposal for the continuance of 'special police regulations' to secure order and the election of 'a body of commissioners' to oversee house construction.[24] Regular whitewashing, Kay implies, is part of a move towards greater surveillance and greater state power. He sees it as antithetical to concealment, aligned with the removal of disorder, waste and criminal activity. Adolf Loos famously claimed that ornament is crime, since it represents 'wasted manpower' and 'wasted capital'; here, the erasure of ornament through whitewashing does away with both crime and waste, leaving behind simplicity and order, enforced through top-down observation.[25]

For Engels in *The Condition of the Working Class in England*, whitewashing holds a quite different moral valence. Rather than cleansing and opening up, it signifies deception and dissimulation. Describing Ashton-under-Lyne, a factory town near Stockport, Engels comments on the stark contrast between its broad, relatively clean streets of new houses and the concealed back lanes behind. Whitewashing plays its part in this facadal structure: 'there are even in Ashton streets in which the cottages are getting bad, [. . .] where the walls have cracks and will not hold the chalk whitewash inside'.[26] As it leaks from the walls whose interior it is supposed to cover, whitewash comes to indicate the falsity of the facade of respectability and comfort which the main streets maintain. These streets, too, will soon begin to crumble, leaving behind only hovels and ruins. Whitewash has the same role in Ancoats, a working-class district of Manchester, in the north-east of which 'lie many newly-built-up streets; here the cottages look neat and cleanly, doors and windows are new and freshly painted, the rooms within newly whitewashed'. Yet, nonetheless, 'cellar dwellings are to be found under almost every cottage; many streets are unpaved and without sewers; and, worse than all, this neat appearance is all pretence, a pretence which vanishes within the first ten years'.[27]

A literary parallel to Engels can be found forty-five years later in Gissing's *The Nether World*, where the narrator describes the suburban boundary between countryside and city 'slum' at Crouch End, on the edge of London:

> Characteristic of the locality is a certain row of one-storey cottages – villas, the advertiser calls them – built of white brick, each with one bay window on the ground floor, a window pretentiously fashioned and desiring to be taken for stone, though obviously made of bad plaster. [. . .] As you set foot in the pinched passage, the sound of your tread proves the whole fabric a thing of lath and sand. The ceilings, the walls, confess themselves neither water-tight nor air-tight. Whatever you touch is at once found to be sham.[28]

The appearance of neat white villas breaks apart on closer inspection, revealing the whole structure to be a sham, a plaster facade consisting of little more than whitewash. The porosity of the ceilings and walls – 'neither water-tight nor air-tight' – echoes the wider porosity of the boundary between city and country, which manifests itself symbolically on the map of Greater London: 'a map on which the town proper shows as a dark, irregularly rounded patch against the whiteness of suburban districts'.[29] The anxiety of Gissing's narrator is clear: the dark patch of the city is a spreading stain, creeping into the white suburban districts and rotting them from within.

Engels's 'pretence' and Gissing's 'sham' both recall Ishmael's 'mystical cosmetic', which conceals the palsied universe behind. They function also like the poor-quality Devil's-Dust cloth Engels describes, which is so badly made it is 'liable to tear or grow threadbare in a fortnight'.[30] 'Devilsdust' is the name of a character in Disraeli's *Sybil* (1845), who, abandoned as a child, enters a cotton factory, gaining employment in 'the manufacture of waste and damaged cotton, the refuse of the mills', and taking his name from this material out of which Devil's-Dust cloth is made. Devilsdust is a form of refuse himself, his name a facade with no true identity behind, as indicated at the end of the novel when he drops the nickname to give himself another, Mr Mowbray, after the town where he lives.[31] Devil's-Dust cloth recalls also the cotton dust which poisons Bessy, a factory girl in Gaskell's *North and South*. Bessy describes this material as 'fluff', or 'little bits, as fly off fro' the cotton, when they're carding it, and fill the air till it looks all fine white dust. They say it winds round the lungs, and tightens them up' (NS 102). Though this dust is ephemeral, it has a real effect, with many factory workers opposing the installation of ventilation equipment, claiming 'it made 'em hungry, at after they'd been long used to swallowing fluff, to go without it' (NS 102). The irony is that the dust the workers consume to stave off hunger is what kills them, replicating their false consciousness under capitalism, believing themselves reliant on a system that gradually suffocates them.

The use of the term 'whitewashing' in its metaphorical sense as deception, first recorded by the *OED* in 1703, is also present in Engels.[32] He writes that a Liberal report on the condition of the factories, though written 'on the side of the bourgeoisie', still 'cannot whitewash the manufacturers'.[33] The German verb here is *weißwaschen*, which is used again when Engels describes the violent response to a series of popular uprisings in 1842, after which the bourgeoisie 'tried to whitewash itself by expressing a horror of popular violence by no means consistent with its own revolutionary language of the spring'.[34] Whitewashing is thus as much a rhetorical activity as a decorative or architectural one, and in either case constitutes an attempt to cover over an unpleasant truth, making it a form of repression.

Charlotte Brontë comments on the moral implications of such repressive whitewashing in the preface to *Jane Eyre*, writing that the world finds it

> convenient to make external show pass for sterling worth – to let whitewashed walls vouch for clean shrines. It may hate him who dares to scrutinise and expose – to rase the gilding, and show base metal under it – penetrate the sepulchre and reveal charnel relics: but hate as it will, it is indebted to him.[35]

For Brontë, whitewashing is a deception, concealing a truth which is hidden because it evokes the horror of death. Whitewash for her conceals 'charnel relics', returning us to Melville's description of whiteness as a paint covering 'nothing but the charnel-house within'. Both are referring to Matthew 23.27, where scribes and Pharisees are 'like unto whited sepulchres, which indeed appear beautiful outward, but are within full of dead *men's* bones, and of all uncleanness'. This biblical association of whiteness and death is also found in *Mary Barton*, where Mrs Wilson describes Mary as 'thou whited sepulchre' (MB 220), and where Mary's 'dead whiteness' (MB 301) is emphasised. In that novel, John Barton associates the white plumes he sees on the heads of carriage horses in London with funerals (MB 98), highlighting a connection between fashion and death that interests Benjamin in the *Arcades Project*, and which is the topic of Baudelaire's 'Danse Macabre', where fashionable society consists of 'perfumed skeletons' who 'reek of death'.[36] Whiteness is implicitly linked to fashion in Baudelaire's poem through the white bones of the skeleton, and the same connection exists in Brontë, if the 'external show' that conceals death is taken to be fashion. This link is, of course, made explicit in Melville's description of whiteness as a 'mystical cosmetic'.

As these examples from Gaskell and Brontë demonstrate, the association between whitewashing and false appearance made by Engels has a wide symbolic resonance during the nineteenth century. Rather than aligning with cleanliness as in Kay, the white surface for these writers is what must be exposed as false. Despite their differences, though, Kay, Gaskell, Brontë, Engels and Gissing all position whiteness within a logic of concealment and revelation. To explore this logic further, I now turn to two moments where specifically bourgeois white surfaces function not as whitewash but as an excess of ornamentation: the Thorntons' house in Gaskell's *North and South*, and Mouret's great white sale in *Au Bonheur des Dames*.

Whiteness in the City II: Ornament and Fashion

The most striking example of spatial whiteness in Gaskell's Manchester is the house of the cotton manufacturer Mr Thornton in *North and South*.[37] Whiteness serves here to protect the bourgeois interior and its ornaments from the city through a hardening or freezing of domestic space in the face of encroaching urbanism. Modernism would later seek to dilute this hard boundary between interior and exterior, with structures such as Le Corbusier's Maison Dom-Ino, a 1914 design supposed to provide cheap European housing, removing walls altogether. Yet, as Wigley shows, in attempting to erase ornament and hence put an end to 'the parade of ephemeral fashions', modernism ends up reintroducing ornamentation in another form, through whiteness itself, which has its own embedded ideological interests.[38] By contrast, the strategy of the Thornton family is not to reject ornament, but to employ white décor and drapery as a defence of ornamentation against the dirt of the city.

As part of this strategy, whiteness is supplemented by brightness, which shifts the function of the white interior from preservation against to domination of the city. Such a strategy of exaggerating rather than underplaying whiteness reaches extravagant heights, as I will go on to show, in the great white sale held in Mouret's department store in *The Ladies' Paradise*.

Thornton's large mansion is out of place in the factory town of Milton-Northern, based on Manchester, where it stands amongst 'long rows of small houses', accessed through a lodge-door at the end of a 'long dead wall' (NS 111). Gaskell's ideal of greater closeness between workers and owners, emphasised at the end of the novel (NS 419–20), seems realised through this close proximity. This impression is illusory, however, since the factory next to the house presents a continual threat to bourgeois life within it, which can only be maintained by a rigid rejection of its surroundings and a paranoid adherence to cleanliness (NS 431–2). Although the walls are 'pink and gold' (NS 112) and the carpet carries a pattern of 'bunches of flowers' (NS 112), every piece of furniture is carefully covered over with linen, so that 'everything reflected light, nothing absorbed it' (NS 112). Margaret Hale, the southern English heroine, finds the appearance painful, so that she is 'hardly conscious of the peculiar cleanliness required to keep everything so white and pure in such an atmosphere' (NS 112). Enormous amounts of labour are employed 'solely to ornament, and then to preserve ornament from dirt or destruction' (NS 112). This drawing-room thus recalls Benjamin's account of bourgeois 'dwelling':

> [The nineteenth century] conceived the residence as a receptacle for the person, and it encased him with all his appurtenances so deeply in the dwelling's interior that one might be reminded of the inside of a compass case, where the instrument with all its accessories lies embedded in deep, usually violet folds of velvet.[39]

Such encasement is not only a protection from the external world, but a means of denying that world's existence. Yet in Thornton's house the external world is so close it touches the very threshold, with the noise of the factory proving so overwhelming that Margaret can 'hardly catch her father's voice, as they stood on the steps awaiting the opening of the door' (NS 111). These are the same steps where she later confronts a group of striking workmen, standing between them and Thornton (NS 178–9). In both cases, the steps form the narrowest of borders between classes, a border which because of this narrowness must be all the more closely policed. The dust sheets are another such border, which aims to be thin but absolute.

The Thorntons' freezing of the domestic shell in the face of the city is an alternative to the trend, observed by Benjamin, of 'the dissociation of the proprietor from the workplace'. Such dissociation is a form of alienation, and 'culminates in the emergence of the private home'.[40] Wemmick's house in *Great Expectations* is perhaps the most famous example of such dissociation, but it is also present in the failed attempt to separate business and home in *Dombey and Son* (see Chapter 2). Where Benjamin and Gaskell agree is that the bourgeois home is not in the end independent of the city, but rather what the city produces in a negative manner, as its inverse image, so that, for instance, the frozen inertia of the drawing-room is an inversion of the constant activity of the factory outside.

In this environment, encasement is not only an attempt to protect the bourgeois subject, but also serves as a constant reminder of what is rejected: the creeping encroachment of the city's dirt, which is presumably what gives the room its 'painfully spotted, spangled, speckled look' (NS 112). Significantly, the dust covers that protect the furnishings are not made of comforting velvet, as Benjamin suggests, but white linen, which seems unsettling, at least to Margaret, and restricts the inhabitants' ability to dwell in the manner described by Benjamin, which 'has to do with fashioning a shell for ourselves'.[41] If such a shell is what must be fashioned, it is also what is fashionable, constructed as a form of ornament and decoration. In this house, however, direct confrontation with the city has frozen the shell solid, revealing fashion's deathlike face. The house's air of death is not concealed below the surface as in the case of whitewashing, but emerges from the recognition that fashion is nothing but surface. This is a point made allegorically by Edgar Allan Poe's 'The Man That Was Used Up', a story of 1839 which tells of an injured former soldier who appears to be the height of fashion, with an '*air distingué* pervading the whole man'. This appearance is in fact a facade, constructed from a vast series of orthotic additions and accessories, without which there is nothing left of him but 'a large and exceedingly odd-looking bundle of something'.[42]

Although I am suggesting that the ornamentation of Thornton's drawing-room is a contrast to the clean lines of modernist architecture, there is also a similarity in the way its whiteness simultaneously replaces and becomes ornament. The difference is that the ornamentation absolutely repressed by modernism still subsists in Thornton's house, underneath the white surface laid over it, so that ornament and the absence of ornament coincide. If ornament is a staving off of social realities which cannot be denied indefinitely, as Benjamin suggests, then it must itself be protected or risk these realities breaking through. Following this logic, the white walls of modernism are not simply an opposite to Thornton's house, but a successor to it: not only a rejection of ornament, but in a peculiar way ornament's preservation. Modernist whiteness implies a hidden depth, inside which ornament might still be imagined to exist, waiting, in Gaskell's words, 'to be discovered a thousand years hence' (NS 112). This is a parallel to what Richard Dyer calls the 'white soul', an ideological construct which displaces racial whiteness from the outside to the inside, providing authority to whites but also, like the white whale for Ishmael, raising 'the desolate suspicion of non-existence'.[43] More broadly, we might say that between the nineteenth and twentieth centuries, interiority is in the process of being reimagined as a facet of individual being rather than a species of dwelling. To say this is to reformulate Benjamin's claim that, under modernity, 'dwelling has diminished'.[44] Such a displacement of dwelling onto interior subjectivity is a symptom of what Foucault calls the production of the modern soul, referring to the illusion of an interior and anterior identity that is produced by the pervasive exercise of disciplinary power.[45]

As well as merely preserving the 'soul' of ornament against the threat of the city, bourgeois whiteness and brightness can at times erupt outwards in an active assertion of power, seeking to overwhelm the surrounding city. Something of this kind takes place in Volume 1, chapter 20 of *North and South*, when Mrs Thornton, the factory owner's mother, hosts a grand reception where 'every cover was taken off' (NS 160) and 'every corner seemed filled up with ornament, until it became a weariness to the eye, and presented a strange contrast to the bald ugliness of the lookout into the great mill-yard' (NS 160). Such ornamental excess reaches greater heights in the vast white sale organised by Octave Mouret in *Au Bonheur des Dames*, where whiteness does not signify the defeat of the bourgeois interior, but its overwhelming dominance. This event is based on the *blanc* sales held in the Bon Marché department store, which evolved from an attempt to compensate for the winter off-season to become the most important sales week of the year, with sales topping 1,000,000 francs.[46] In Zola's hands, the sale becomes an opportunity for Mouret to fashion a new, artificial world that renders invisible the one outside. As the shoppers enter they are confronted with 'nothing but white, all the white goods from every department, an orgy of white, a white star whose radiance was blinding at first, and made it impossible to distinguish any details in the midst of this total whiteness' (LP 14.397). This is the logical conclusion to Mouret's earlier window displays, which were designed to 'blind' (LP 48) the customers. The galleries appear 'like a polar vista, a snowy expanse unfolding with the endlessness of steppes draped with ermine' (LP 14.397), but also harbour a 'suffocating hothouse heat' (LP 14.2.399). This impossible landscape asserts the power of the commodity to reshape nature, undoing its most fixed connections. The white sale is thus the triumph of the department store over the city that surrounds it, a denial of its dirt, cold and weather.

For Benjamin, Fourier's remarks on the phalanstery, to which Mouret's store is compared in the novel (LP 5.134), serve as a commentary on the arcades, themselves the precursors to the department store:

> Fourier on the street-galleries: 'To spend a winter's day in a Phalanstery, to visit all parts of it without exposure to the elements, to go to the theatre and the opera in light clothes and colored shoes without worrying about the mud and the cold, would be a charm so novel that it alone would suffice to make our cities and castles seem detestable'.[47]

Exposure to the elements is replaced by an interior world that creates its own weather, and by exposure to the unrestricted power of the commodity, which is both endlessly multiple and homogeneous. The white sale brings this contradictory nature of the commodity to the fore. The shared whiteness, which is also an absence of colour, implies a shared identity rooted in emptiness and lack, emphasising a sameness to the vast array of different objects, even as the appearance of endless variety unfolds: 'There was nothing but white, yet it was never the same white, but all the different tones of white, competing together, contrasting with and complementing each other, achieving the brilliance of light itself' (LP 14.397). This variety-in-sameness recalls Whistler's 'Symphony in White' paintings of the 1860s, where whiteness takes multiple forms, all of which nonetheless retain a shared character of feminine sexuality. In a similar way, Mouret's ecstatic montage-like display culminates with a white tent that is 'evocative both of the tabernacle and of the bedroom' (LP 14.398), exemplifying the religiously charged eroticism of both the sale and the store as a whole. This character was still evident in 1919, when Hope Mirrlees wrote the following in *Paris: A Poem*, her modernist tour through the city:

> All this time the Virgin has not been idle;
> The windows of les Galéries Lafayette, le Bon Marché,
> la Samaritaine,
> Hold holy bait,
> Waxen Pandoras in white veils and ties of her own
> decking;[48]

Along with other centres of Parisian consumption, the Bon Marché is associated with virginal, Christian whiteness ('white veils'), over which plays an allure of feminised and commodified sexuality ('holy bait'), reinforced by the reference to 'waxen Pandoras', Pandora being a classic representation of female vulnerability to temptation.

The idea of a 'symphony' is one Zola shares with Whistler, with the narrator describing a 'harmonic phrase' (LP 14.398) that runs throughout the display, expanding with 'the complicated orchestration of some masterly fugue' (LP 14.398). The brilliant light which seems to emerge from this symphony is another form of Ishmael's mystical cosmetic, now reimagined as the ultimate product of capitalism, as pure exchange value.[49] By contrast, the city appears, in Fourier's words, 'detestable'. Paris thus takes the role of the Lacanian real, which the white interior, as imaginary, denies. Two opposite but complementary forms of invisible architecture are in play here then: firstly the commodity, made dazzlingly, blindingly visible as a fantastical apotheosis of whiteness; and secondly the rejected, abjected city, which recedes from view.

In a similar fashion, albeit less dramatically, white linen represents resistance to the degrading effects of the city in Zola's *L'Assommoir* (1877), where the descent of Gervaise, the central character, into alcoholism and poverty is marked by her gradual transition from running a laundry proudly displaying the 'whiteness of the linen' in its window, to barely subsisting in a tiny room full of 'rubbish, dust, and muck'.[50] This fall, which takes Gervaise from cleanliness to dirt, and visibility to invisibility, results from her inability to maintain a barrier of whiteness against the city, recalling Alice Wilson's attempt to defend her cellar-dwelling against the filth of Manchester, as discussed in Chapter 1.

Fredric Jameson has argued that cleanliness in Zola represents 'something like a zero degree, what Deleuze calls a surface of inscription', against which the author's excessive descriptions necessarily unfold.[51] If this is the case, then it is not a neutral surface but a proto-modernist erasure of the existing dirt of the city, albeit one which only succeeds when it has an immense backing of capital, as in the department store. As I have suggested, though, whiteness in nineteenth-century literature is not only a background against which description and ornamentation appear, but also thoroughly imbricated with ornamentation, both as a means to preserve it and as one of its most visible and striking manifestations.

Whiteness in the City III: Targeted by Whiteness

My third approach to urban whiteness is to read it as a means of targeting and isolating subjects. In this sense it is aligned with the law, and with social regulation. Building on the ideas presented above, of whiteness as both concealing and revealing, and ornament and the absence of ornament coinciding, in this section I show how whiteness enables the identification of the subject as an ornament or stain. This typically occurs when legal and social forces aim to control or erase the subject in a Foucauldian manner. I focus specifically on a selection of passages from Charles Dickens and Charles Kingsley that deal with prisons and the police, where this dynamic becomes clear.

In Kingsley's *Alton Locke* (1850), Alton's 'prison thoughts' following his conviction for rioting testify to a process of legal isolation and observation in which whiteness plays a prominent part:

> The smooth white walls, the smooth white ceiling, seemed squeezing in closer and closer on me, and yet dilating into vast infinities [...] Oh, those smooth white walls and ceiling! If there had been but a print – a stain of dirt – a cobweb, to fleck their unbroken ghastliness! They stared at me, like grim, impassive, featureless, formless fiends; all the more dreadful for their sleek hypocritic cleanliness.[52]

The whiteness 'stares' at Alton, effectively accusing him of being the 'stain of dirt' he cannot locate on its surface. The combination of 'squeezing' and 'dilating' simultaneously pins him down and renders him insignificant. This structure is repeated in the opening section of *The Water-Babies* (1862–3), where the chimney sweeper Tom, described as filthily black (in a racialised way, as Pamela Gilbert points out) enters the aristocratic Harthover House, where 'the room was all dressed in white; white window curtains, white bed curtains, white furniture, and white walls', as a result of which he 'for the first time in his life, found out that he was dirty'.[53] Whiteness, then, is attached to both ornament (the carpet in Harthover House is 'all over gay little flowers') and lack of ornament, since it is a cleansing of waste, and it connects the wealthy and powerful with the law which protects their interests.⁵⁴

The metaphor of squeezing the imprisoned subject appears also in *Mary Barton*, where it is associated with a legendary Italian punishment:

> The supposed or real criminal was shut up in a room, supplied with every convenience and luxury; and at first mourned little over his imprisonment. But day by day he became aware that the space between the walls of his apartment was narrowing, and then he understood the end. Those painted walls would come into hideous nearness, and at last crush the life out of him. (MB 164)

This looks like an allegory for bourgeois life, but is associated by the narrator with the 'diseased thoughts' (MB 164) and 'monomania' (MB 164) of John Barton, the intended avenger of working-class suffering. The room's luxury stands in opposition to Alton's cell, but both threaten to crush the person within. When read together, their shared function short-circuits the distinction between the opulent 'painted walls' and the 'smooth white walls' of Alton's cell, collapsing the line between ornament and anti-ornament, since both are similarly constricting and constrictive. As suggested above, interiority, or dwelling, now seems to be in a state of crisis, both architecturally and as a dimension of subjectivity.

At the same time, Alton's cell dilates 'into vast infinities', echoing the expansion of the bourgeois interior that appears in Benjamin's *Arcades Project*, as in this passage quoting Adorno's commentary on Kierkegaard's *Diary of a Seducer* (1843): 'When we sit at a distance from the window, we gaze directly into heaven's vast horizon . . . Cordelia's environment must have no foreground, but only the infinite boldness of far horizons.' For Adorno, the expansion of the bourgeois interior into 'far horizons' is an effect of alienation. As he argues, 'the contents of the interior are mere decoration, alienated from the purposes they represent, deprived of their own use value, engendered solely by the isolated dwelling-space'.⁵⁵ In Alton's white prison cell there is alienation too, but it is not a feature of the commodified interior but of the imprisoned subject, who is prevented from working, suggesting Foucault's definition of madness as the 'absence of an oeuvre', so that he is deprived of his own 'use value', becoming a 'mere decoration' or stain on the white surface.⁵⁶ Whereas Gaskell's allegory and Adorno's reading present the decorated interior as either crushing or alienating, the white walls of

Alton's cell invert this dynamic by transferring both features onto the subject directly, so that he is himself designated as an isolated, unnecessary (hence ornamental) stain, in need of erasure. In the context of the novel, this process allegorises Alton's class anxieties about leaving behind his work as a tailor to become a poet, including his dual desire and inability to assimilate to fashionable middle-class life.

A related process of targeting and isolating can be observed in *Our Mutual Friend*, where the police inspector visited by Mortimer and Eugene works 'in a whitewashed office, as studiously as if he were in a monastery on the top of a mountain, and no howling fury of a drunken woman were banging herself against a cell-door in the back-yard at his elbow' (OMF 1.3.24). Whiteness is again linked to isolation here, and to lonely thoughts, and to whitewashing as erasure, since the inspector ignores the presence of the drunken woman. As well as disregarding individuals, the inspector has the power of isolating them, symbolised by the 'bull's-eye' (OMF 1.3.24) lamp he carries, which is turned on John Harmon by his 'satellite' (OMF 1.3.24), one of his officers, when Harmon is questioned. Harmon responds by adopting the false identity of Mr Julius Handford, resisting the attempt to pin him down.

White bull's-eyes also feature in Mr George's shooting gallery in *Bleak House*. This gallery, in the region of the Haymarket and Leicester Square, is reached by 'a long whitewashed passage' in a building 'composed of bare walls, floor, roof-rafters, and skylights', and contains 'two whitened targets for rifle shooting'.[57] When George conceals Gridley in a 'bare room' partitioned off from this gallery, Inspector Bucket observes them from a skylight, his gaze operating like the bull's-eye lamp in *Our Mutual Friend*, targeting the supposed criminal. Gridley's face is turned white by this pursuit, becoming 'colorless'.[58] Whiteness, in fact, seems to follow George around, since he meets Mr Bagnet, an ex-artilleryman, in a whitewashed room which 'contains nothing superfluous, and has not a visible speck of dirt or dust in it'.[59] This military association reinforces the sense of whiteness as a form of targeting that picks out the subject, in an act of Althusserian interpellation that is often coerced. Whitewashing here also alludes to bankruptcy, since in chapter 34 Phil, engaged in 'whitening the targets', suggests Mr George also whitewash himself; this was a choice made possible by the Bankruptcy Act of 1825, which allowed debtors to start their own proceedings for bankruptcy, rather than relying on creditors.[60] Dickens had earlier used this meaning in *The Pickwick Papers*, where Sam Weller is introduced to a 'whitewashed gentleman' who has been cleared of debt.[61] George's protest against escaping his debts is a moral one: 'Do you know what would become of the Bagnets in that case?' (the Bagnets being liable for his debts). Phil, meanwhile, continues with the 'allegorical scoops of his brush', an act that links whiteness and erasure, both through the act of whitewashing itself and, more subtly, through the way this allegorical brush echoes the painted Roman figure of allegory that stares down at Mr Tulkinghorn's rooms, including upon his dead body in chapter 48.[62] Being targeted by whiteness, then, involves both highlighting and erasing the subject, and includes processes of both constriction and dilation. It constructs the subject as a real or potential criminal, and in its most extreme forms threatens total obliteration.

Carker's Whiteness

To conclude this chapter, I want to consider one further instance of whiteness which brings together the characteristics of whitewashing, ornamentation and targeting discussed so far. This is the whiteness of Mr Carker in *Dombey and Son*. Though he is a character rather than a spatial or architectural feature, I read Carker's whiteness as a metaphor for the most dangerously ideological operations of invisible architecture in the nineteenth century, in particular the deceptive appearance of neutrality that it is capable of producing.

Carker is taken for granted by Mr Dombey, seen by him as an empty cipher. Yet he is one of the driving forces of the novel's narrative, bringing down both of Dombey's houses from within. In this respect, he exemplifies an eruptive potential within invisible architecture that I have discussed in various forms in earlier chapters, including the working classes who threaten to emerge from the underground cellar in Gaskell, the railway and river which open up and destabilise the city in Dickens, the overwhelming influence of the commodity in Zola's Paris, and the indeterminacy of the arabesque. All are Carker-like in emerging from or opening up the city's architectural unconscious, sometimes with sudden explosive force. In the case of Carker, an unsettling whiteness like that of the white whale is a fundamental part of his unreadability, acting as both a distinctive characteristic which picks him out against the background of the city and a barrier which prevents him being interpreted, especially by Dombey. His white body is also a site across which obscure and threatening signifiers play, repulsing Florence and Edith. This makes it like the skin of Moby Dick, but also the arabesque, Gogol's imagined street, the bourgeois Manchester streets in Engels, the river

Thames and hollow down by the flare in Dickens, and the iron and glass dream structures of Zola's store, in that it persistently implies more than it explicitly shows.

Appearing as a figure of repression, Carker is 'always closely buttoned up and tightly dressed' (DS 13.183–4), aided by the 'stiff white cravat' that he affects 'after the example of his principal' (DS 13.183). In this way, Carker simultaneously submits to Dombey's authority and intimates a desire to supplant him. In Dombey, the white cravat symbolises respectability, spotlessness and pride, as well as an ideological rejection of all that does not fit with his worldview, but in Carker it is part of a pattern of whiteness that extends across the text. Most striking are Carker's 'two unbroken rows of glistening teeth, whose regularity and whiteness were quite distressing. It was impossible to escape the observation of them, for he showed them whenever he spoke' (DS 13.183). The blankness and evenness of these teeth forms a spotlessly clean but deathlike wall, which conceals but also hints at the visceral sexual threat of Carker's body, whose appetites are registered in the text by his treatment of Alice Marwood, whom he has subjected to sexual 'ruin' (DS 34.515) and abandoned.[63]

Carker's teeth also suggest the possibility of cutting, castration or consumption, as when they seem for an instant 'prone to bite the hand they fawned upon' (DS 26.401), or when he approaches Edith 'more as if he meant to bite her, than to taste the sweets that linger on her lips' (DS 31.469). They act too like a bull's-eye lamp, being turned on Mrs Skewton 'like a light' (DS 37.554) when Carker tries to remove her from the room, and holding Rob in a state of fear, as though 'he had come into the service of some powerful enchanter, and they had been his strongest spells' (DS 42.621). Emphasising this whiteness, Carker rides a 'white-legged horse' (DS 46.671), raising him above the dirt of the street, has a 'smooth white hand', and conceives 'a natural antipathy to any speck of dust' (DS 22.316), recalling the dust covers in Mr Thornton's house or the whitewashed walls of Kay's projected Manchester. In the eighteenth century Edmund Burke characterised smoothness and delicacy as signs of beauty, but here that meaning has been inverted, so that Carker's hands become horrifying, part of an inscrutable surface that covers a cruel avarice and a desire to conquer women.[64] In his misogyny, evident in his behaviour towards Florence and Edith as well as Alice, Carker is a return of Quilp from *The Old Curiosity Shop*, except that Quilp's openly demonic nature and appearance has been repressed or sublimated behind a facade of white teeth and hands.

At the same time, Carker's appearance feminises him. For Burke, beauty was not only smooth and delicate, but representative of feminine weakness: 'the beauty of women is considerably owing to their weakness, or delicacy', he proclaims.[65] This characteristic is reinforced by Carker's description as a fastidious cat, sitting 'with a dainty steadfastness and patience at his work' (DS 22.316). Like Maxime in *La Curée*, he exhibits a combination of masculinity and femininity, linked to a sexuality which is both excessive and impotent. This is implied by his description as 'Grand Vizier' (DS 13.183) to Dombey's Ottoman Emperor, making him a eunuch figure and orientalising him, like Maxime. If Dombey's salvation is his family – he ends by building loving bonds with his grandchildren (DS 62.924–5) – it is significant that Carker not only has no children ('How could it [the child Florence] be his? You know he has none' (DS 34.518) asks Mrs Brown), but rejects the family he does have, disowning his sister with the words 'I know no Harriet Carker. There is no such person' (DS 22.318). This puts him outside the bounds of the heterosexual family unit, whose reproductive futurity he parodies by appearing as a false copy of his master, reinforcing an impression of queerness that surrounds him, despite his apparently heterosexual predation of women and girls.

To push this reading further, Carker can be read as a symptom of anxiety about British mercantile imperialism, including its relationship to race and sexuality. Though he is insistently pictured as white, his whiteness is unnaturally extreme and accompanied by an orientalised effeminacy. As the head manager of Dombey and Son's trading firm, which we know operates in the West Indies (DS 13.186), and perhaps also in China, where Walter Gay ends up travelling after a shipwreck (DS 56. 828), Carker is inevitably involved in morally dubious practices, including very probably the purchase of products of forced labour (despite slavery being formally abolished in the West Indies in 1833–4), and possibly opium trading, which Tambling identifies as a subtext to the novel.[66] In this way, Carker acts as a screen for Dombey, cleansing him of imperial guilt and leaving behind only pure whiteness. But in doing so, he is himself implicitly tainted by the racial and sexual otherness of colonised and non-European peoples. Carker thus represents an entire managerial and administrative class, which is necessary to screen the respectable bourgeoisie from its involvement in imperial exploitation, but precisely through that act of screening becomes less British, and hence compromised and threatening. As Susan Meyer has argued of *Jane Eyre*, through such processes of symbolic exchange 'all aspects of oppression [. . .] become something the British are in danger of being sullied by, something foreign and "other" to them'.[67] Carker's role in this sense is to protectively absorb the capitalist ruling class's imperial, racial and sexual sins, before being finally destroyed. It makes sense, therefore, that Carker's most powerful tool is his appearance of neutrality and blankness, which allows him to slip beneath Dombey's notice and control the transactions of the company, described by the minor character Morfin as 'a great labyrinth of which only he has held the clue' (DS 53.790). He acts at one point 'as if there were no more spots upon his soul than on his pure white linen, and his smooth sleek skin' (DS 32.496–7), simultaneously parodying and exemplifying the myth of white innocence.

Such an appearance is also what invisible architecture maintains, at least in its most thoroughly ideological forms, by erasing its own presence even while it reshapes the visible world. As I have argued in the preceding chapters, urban space in the nineteenth century is similarly predicated on a repression of elements which call the stability and unity of the city into question, and which have the power not only to maintain but also to unsettle ordered, architectural space, pulling it apart from within with the force of what it represses.

Notes

1. On the continuities between nineteenth- and twentieth-century modernities see, for instance, Kern; Jessica Feldman, *Victorian Modernism: Pragmatism and the Varieties of Aesthetic Experience* (Cambridge: Cambridge University Press, 2002); Anne-Florence Gillard-Estrada and Anne Besnault-Levita, *Beyond the Victorian/Modernist Divide: Remapping the Turn-of-the-Century Break in Literature, Culture and the Visual Arts* (New York and Abingdon: Routledge, 2018). For a critical reading of the Victorianist 'assumption that an era has a *Zeitgeist*', see John McGowan, *Democracy's Children: Intellectuals and the Rise of Cultural Politics* (Ithaca, NY: Cornell University Press, 2002), pp. 141–64. On continuing critical attachment to the term 'Victorian studies', see Amanda Anderson, 'Victorian Studies and the Two Modernities', *Victorian Studies*, 47.2 (2005), 195–203, and more recently Rojaunee Chatterjee, Alicia Christoff and Amy Wong, 'Introduction: Undisciplining Victorian Studies', *Victorian Studies*, 62.3 (2020), 369–91.
2. *White Walls*, p. 19.
3. Herman Melville, *Moby-Dick* (Harmondsworth: Penguin, 1992), p. 204.
4. *Moby-Dick*, p. 205. On racial whiteness, see for instance Birgit Brander Rasmussen et al., eds, *The Making and Unmaking of Whiteness*

(Durham, NC: Duke University Press, 2001); Richard Dyer, *White: Essays on Race and Culture* (London: Routledge, 1997). On colonial whiteness in the nineteenth and early twentieth centuries, see Katherine Ellinghaus, Jane Cary and Leigh Boucher, eds, *Re-Orienting Whiteness* (New York: Palgrave, 2009).
5. Monika Gehlawat, 'The Aesthetics of Whiteness: Melville's *Moby Dick* and the Paintings of Robert Ryman', *Soundings*, 88.3–4 (2005), 371–91 (p. 382).
6. *Moby-Dick*, p. 211.
7. *Moby-Dick*, p. 212.
8. *Seminar XI*, p. 31, p. 32.
9. See for instance Sigmund Freud, *Totem and Taboo*, trans. by James Strachey (London: Routledge, 2001), pp. 21–86.
10. Toni Morrison, 'Unspeakable Things Unspoken: The Afro-American Presence in American Literature', *Michigan Quarterly Review*, 28.1 (1989), 1–34 (p. 15, p. 16). See also Valerie Babb, *Whiteness Visible: The Meaning of Whiteness in American Literature* (New York: New York University Press, 1998), pp. 89–117.
11. Morrison, p. 16.
12. George Yancy, *Look, a White!: Philosophical Essays on Whiteness* (Philadelphia: Temple University Press, 2012), p. 161. David Lloyd, *Under Representation: The Racial Regime of Aesthetics* (New York: Fordham University Press, 2019).
13. Morrison, p. 17.
14. Louis Althusser, 'Ideology and Ideological State Apparatuses', in *Lenin and Philosophy and Other Essays*, trans. by Ben Brewster (London: Monthly Review Press, 1971), pp. 127–86.
15. *Seminar XI*, p. 53.
16. *Seminar XI*, p. 55, p. 74.
17. Kevin Goddard, '"Like Circles on the Water": Melville, Schopenhauer and the Allegory of Whiteness', *English Studies in Africa*, 51.2 (2008), 84–109 (p. 89).
18. *Seminar XI*, p. 34, p. 55. For the original context of the dream, see *Interpretation of Dreams*, p. 652.
19. *Moby-Dick*, p. 212.
20. *Moby-Dick*, p. 332.
21. Jacques Derrida, 'White Mythology: Metaphor in the Text of Philosophy', trans. by F. C. T. Moore, *New Literary History*, 6.1 (1974), 5–74 (p. 11).
22. See Chapter 2 and Lefebvre, pp. 38–40.
23. Kay, p. 18.
24. Kay, p. 45, p. 70.
25. Adolf Loos, 'Ornament and Crime' [1908], in *Crime and Ornament: The Arts and Popular Culture in the Shadow of Adolf Loos*, ed. by Bernie Miller and Melony Ward (Toronto: YYZ Books, 2002), pp. 29–36 (p. 33).

26. Engels, p. 84.
27. Engels, p. 95.
28. Gissing, p. 364.
29. Gissing, p. 364.
30. Engels, p. 103.
31. Disraeli, p. 98, p. 420.
32. *OED*, whitewash, v. *OED Online*, Oxford University Press, <www.oed.com/view/Entry/228644>. Accessed 16 May 2023.
33. Engels, p. 187.
34. Engels, p. 240.
35. Charlotte Brontë, *Jane Eyre*, 3rd edn (London: Norton, 2001), p. 1, pp. 1–2.
36. *The Flowers of Evil*, p. 199. In French: 'Vous sentez tous la mort! Ô squelettes musqués'.
37. For an extended discussion of this house, see Ben Moore, 'Invisible Architecture and Social Space in *North and South*', *Gaskell Journal*, 32 (2018), 17–35.
38. *White Walls*, p. xxii.
39. *Arcades*, p. 220.
40. *Arcades*, p. 226.
41. *Arcades*, p. 221.
42. Poe, *Selected Tales*, p. 40, pp. 46–7.
43. Dyer, p. 45.
44. *Arcades*, p. 221.
45. Michel Foucault, *Discipline and Punish*, trans. by Alan Sheridan (New York: Vintage, 1995), pp. 29–30.
46. Michael Miller, pp. 70–1.
47. *Arcades*, p. 44.
48. Hope Mirrlees, *Paris: A Poem* (Richmond: Hogarth Press, 1919), pp. 15–16.
49. Jameson comments on the ecstatic nature of the white sale and its relationship to light in *Antinomies of Realism*, pp. 56–65.
50. Émile Zola, *L'Assommoir*, trans. by Margaret Mauldon (Oxford: Oxford University Press, 1995), p. 130, p. 392.
51. *Antinomies of Realism*, p. 64.
52. Alton is imprisoned in a cathedral town that could be Ely, Lincoln or Peterborough. Charles Kingsley, *Alton Locke* (Oxford: Oxford University Press, 1983), p. 283, p. 157.
53. Charles Kingsley, *The Water-Babies* (Oxford: Oxford University Press, 2013), p. 17. Pamela Gilbert, *Victorian Skin: Surface, Self, History* (Ithaca, NY: Cornell University Press, 2019), p. 308. Interestingly, Harthover House is highly architecturally eclectic, with a combination of features ranging from the Anglo-Saxon to the Norman, Cinquecento, Elizabethan, Pure Doric and Early English, and parts copied from the Catacombs of Rome, the Taj Mahal, the caves of Elephanta near Bombay, and Brighton Pavilion. *The Water-Babies*, p. 14.

54. *The Water-Babies*, p. 16.
55. *Arcades*, p. 219, p. 220.
56. Foucault is describing both the absence of work and the absence of traces. Appendix I in *History of Madness*, ed. by Jean Khalfa (London: Routledge, 2006), pp. 541–9.
57. *Bleak House*, p. 323.
58. *Bleak House*, p. 371.
59. *Bleak House*, p. 407.
60. For an overview of the relevant legal reforms, see Michael Lobban, 'Bankruptcy and Insolvency', in *The Oxford History of the Laws of England, Volume XII: 1820–1914 Private Law*, ed. by William Cornish et al. (Oxford: Oxford University Press, 2010), pp. 779–833.
61. Charles Dickens, *The Pickwick Papers* (London: Penguin, 2003), p. 579.
62. *Bleak House*, p. 496, p. 497, p. 498, p. 614.
63. In a way that is different but not incommensurable with my reading, Bove reads Carker's mouth and teeth as signifying his status as not 'a psychologically realist character who abuses the capitalist system, but an *effigy*, a spectral embodiment of the *jouissance* of capital itself', so that the teeth 'flicker between human and nonhuman in a way that evokes an inhuman gaze within the human look and vice versa', making Carker anamorphic in a Lacanian sense. Alexander Bove, *Spectral Dickens: The Uncanny Forms of Novelistic Characterization* (Manchester: Manchester University Press, 2021), p. 122, p. 123.
64. Edmund Burke, *A Philosophical Enquiry into the Sublime and Beautiful* (Oxford: Oxford University Press, 2015 [1757]), pp. 92–4.
65. Burke, p. 94.
66. Jeremy Tambling, 'Death and Modernity in *Dombey and Son*', *Essays in Criticism*, 43.4 (1993), 308–29 (p. 311).
67. Susan Meyer, 'Colonialism and the Figurative Strategy of *Jane Eyre*', *Victorian Studies*, 33.2 (1990), 247–68 (p. 263).

Conclusion: The Invisible Architecture of New York

This book has traced the figure of invisible architecture, in its combination of the hidden, the mobile and the transparent, across a range of nineteenth-century writers, cities and spatial forms. Throughout, I have attempted to show how apparently disparate features of urban space, and the drives that accompany them, gain new significance when read together as dimensions of this larger spatial complex. I have also sought to expand the ways we might think about architecture in relation to urban space and literature, moving beyond its most straightforward and obvious manifestations. Yet although I have proposed invisible architecture as a concept associated with modernity (which is itself, of course, not a stable or singular notion), it is not only applicable to the nineteenth century, nor to the cities and writers I have discussed. In this Conclusion I offer one example of how the ideas and approaches pursued in this book might be extended to another context, that of twentieth- and twenty-first-century New York. Applications to global and historical contexts at a greater remove from the texts I have discussed would also be possible, but New York since 1900 offers a combination of literary, cultural and architectural connections to, alongside divergences from, the concerns of this book that make it a fitting place to carry my readings one step further. I take as a starting point Christoph Lindner's claim that in New York, 'the modern city does not disappear or perish in the era of globalization, but is subsumed and reconfigured'.[1] If this is so, the question becomes: which features of invisible architecture are preserved or reconfigured in an increasingly globalised New York, and in what ways? In offering a provisional response to this question, this Conclusion begins to articulate how invisible architecture might continue to be of use beyond the primary framework in which I have developed it.

The examples that follow are necessarily highly selective. If New York is, as Kenneth Goldsmith's 2015 reimagining of the *Arcades*

Project has it, the capital of the twentieth century, as Paris was of the nineteenth for Benjamin (and it has at least a reasonable claim to the title), then I cannot possibly do it justice here. I have therefore chosen to focus on a limited set of literary texts, two published in the 1910s and 1920s (Willa Cather's 'Behind the Singer Tower' and John Dos Passos's *Manhattan Transfer*), and two published in the 2010s and 2020s (Teju Cole's *Open City* and Colson Whitehead's *Harlem Shuffle*), each of which touches in some way on a scene of architectural disaster or erasure. In each case, these texts draw our attention to what has been concealed, shifted or opened up in the wake of the violent reshaping of the landscape of New York. In more or less direct ways, these examples are, I suggest, successors to Gaskell's penetration of Manchester's industrial cellars, the railway's reshaping of Camden Town in *Dombey and Son*, and Saccard's transformation of Paris in *La Curée*. I pick up where I ended in Chapter 4, with Henry James's impression of the stupefying monstrosity of New York's skyscrapers in the opening years of the 1900s.

The 1910s–20s: Cather and Dos Passos

Willa Cather's 'Behind the Singer Tower' (1912) is a short story that takes place 'the night after the burning of the Mont Blanc Hotel', a building that 'was the compete expression of the New York idea in architecture; a thirty-five story hotel that made the Plaza look modest', so that its burning also stands for the potential destruction of the city.[2] According to Lindner, Cather's 'urban panorama shares the imagery of pain and discomfort found in Henry James's earlier text [*The American Scene*]', but here 'the threat of dismemberment looming over James's skyline is gruesomely realized', questioning the 'male-inflected aura of power' that seems to define it.[3] We find here, too, an early form of the global city, since 'the hotel was full of people from everywhere'. What is most significant in the story, though, is that it dwells not on the fire that spells the end of the building (which remains as a ruin, 'massive and brutally unconcerned, only a little blackened about its thousand windows'), but a parallel disaster that took place during the building's construction.[4] The story is narrated from a boat containing six men as they look back at New York City from the harbour. Among them is Fred Hallet, an engineer who worked on the construction of the Mont Blanc. Through the story of Caesaro, or Caesarino, an Italian immigrant from the rural island of Ischia who worked with him, Hallet relays a fatal accident brought about by the negligence of Stanley Merryweather, the hotel's ruthless architect, whose depiction is touched with antisemitism. Hallet and Caesarino were working in the foundations, a hole with 'great boulders of rock and deep pits of sand and gulleys of water, with drills puffing everywhere and little crumpled men crawling about like tumble bugs under the stream from the searchlight', when 'one of the big clamshells that swung back and forth over the hole fell with its load of sand', its cabling worn out, as Hallet had previously warned. The Italian workers are crushed: 'they were all buried, Caesarino among them', his body 'all broken to pieces', and he dies in Hallet's arms.[5] Though Hallet successfully sues on Caesarino's behalf, the disaster receives no wider attention. As Hallet puts it:

> It was only a little accident, such as happens in New York every day in the year, but that one happened near me. There's a lot of waste about building a city. Usually the destruction all goes on in the cellar; it's only when it hits high, as it did last night, that it sets us thinking.[6]

Cather's story thus sets the spectacular vertical reach of the skyscraper, which corresponds with social climbing ('there was nothing for us but height. We were whipped up the ladder'), against the 'destruction that goes on in the cellar'. This form of destruction, which is made socially invisible, befalls immigrant workers and those who cannot make themselves heard (Caesarino is barely able to speak English). Unlike the Mont Blanc fire, such destruction is not in opposition to the construction of the city's skyscrapers, but rather what that construction is based upon. Recalling Gaskell and Engels's depiction of the cellar-dwelling as a hidden store of exploitable labour, Cather's story shows the city to be built upon a foundation of life that has been classed as surplus and expendable. Such life is consumed as a kind of sacrifice to what Hallet calls the 'Moloch on the Singer Tower', a skyscraper depicted as both ancient, either Hebraic or vaguely Asian, possibly 'Persian' due to its shape, and highly modern, since it makes the Statue of Liberty look like a mere 'archaeological survival'.[7] What is 'behind' the Singer Tower is therefore what is beneath or before it, what the striving verticality of New York is built upon and what it suppresses. We might think here of Benjamin's Angel of History, for whom 'where a chain of events appear before *us*, *he* sees one single catastrophe, which keeps piling wreckage upon wreckage and hurls it at his feet'.[8]

John Dos Passos's *Manhattan Transfer* (1925) also dwells on disaster, including the construction of the city as disaster. One of the most Benjaminian moments in the novel, which chronicles in a fragmented modernist style the growth of Manhattan from the late 1890s to early 1920s, comes in chapter 2, when a real-estate agent is trying to sell an empty lot beyond Manhattan to a character named Mr Perry. The scene takes place in 1898, shortly after the Greater New York Bill had brought Brooklyn, Queens and Staten Island within the City of New York. Though the land is now empty, the agent projects an accelerating future:

> We are caught up Mr Perry on a great wave whether we will or no, a great wave of expansion and progress. A great deal is going to happen in the next few years. All these mechanical inventions – telephones, electricity, steel bridges, horseless vehicles – they are all leading somewhere. It's up to us to be on the inside, in the forefront of progress . . . My God! I can't begin to tell you what it will mean . . .

But the following lines provide a stark counterpoint:

> Poking amid the dry grass and the burdock leaves Mr Perry had moved something with his stick. He stooped and picked up a triangular skull with a pair of spiralfluted horns. 'By gad!' he said. 'That must have been a fine ram.'[9]

The ram's skull casts an allegorical light on the scene. On one side, the expansion of the city can be read as 'progress', as technological revolution creating a 'storm' that sweeps the people of New York into the future. But at the foundations of the city, or before those foundations are laid, there is a death's head which reframes its history as what Benjamin calls 'a petrified, primordial landscape', a parade of the 'untimely, sorrowful, unsuccessful'.[10]

This scene is reformulated later in the same chapter, in a moment which also repeats the closing scenes of *La Curée*, discussed in Chapter 3. There, the gutted buildings next to a new boulevard 'opened to the skies their wells stripped of stairs, their gaping rooms suspended in mid-air', with squares of wallpaper 'hanging in tatters' (K 7.247–8). In *Manhattan Transfer*, a young couple in search of a new apartment walk 'up a cross street between buildinglots', where

> At a corner the rickety half of a weatherboarded farmhouse was still standing. There was half a room with a blueflowered paper eaten by brown stains on the walls, a smoked fireplace, a shattered builtin cupboard, and an iron bedstead bent double.[11]

This interior exposed to view reveals the broken pieces of a former life, a rural existence that will never again exist in the rapidly urbanising city. As in Zola, a momentary glimpse of the domestic interior in a state of ruin is opened up, devoid of life but still bearing its traces, poised on the edge of complete destruction. This moment implicitly threatens all life in the city with its own ruination, revealing it to be always fragile and impermanent.

This sense of New York as a scene of unfolding disaster is heightened in the way Dos Passos's novel, like Cather's short story, is haunted by fire. The scene with the ram's skull takes place directly after the description of a blaze in 'a narrowwindowed sixstory tenement', started intentionally by an arsonist or 'firebug', who is intoxicated by the flames.[12] Much later, the wealthy but troubled and alcoholic Stan Emery sets himself and his apartment alight, in a chapter that reuses many fragments of text which have appeared earlier in the novel. This act of self-destruction is explicitly tied to the city's skyline, most strikingly in the line 'kerist I wish I was a skyscraper', which is printed as its own paragraph, in isolation from the surrounding text. To be a skyscraper is to exist at the top of New York, to stand over and dominate it, but it is also to go up in flames. Among Stan's increasingly fractured thoughts appears the line 'skyscrapers go up like flames, in flames, flames'.[13] Flames flicker here between simile and reality. Skyscrapers are 'like flames' because they burn with the heat of progress, reaching up to the sky, but they also go up 'in flames', consumed by destruction.

Echoing Cather's Singer Tower, but also the construction of the railway as Babel in *Dombey and Son*, the same chapter imagines New York as repeating and exceeding the great cities of the ancient world, which now lie in ruins:

> There was Babylon and Nineveh, they were built of brick. Athens was goldmarble columns. Rome was held up on broad arches of rubble, In Constantinople the minarets flame like great candles round the Golden Horn ... O there's one more river to cross. Steel glass, tile, concrete will be the materials of the skyscrapers. Crammed on the narrow island the millionwindowed buildings will jut, glittering pyramid on pyramid, white cloudsheads above a thunderstorm ...[14]

New York becomes part of an architectural sequence, like Gogol's street or the historical sweep of the World Exhibitions. This passage, with its use of 'will', is written as a kind of prophecy or dream, making it like Gogol or Chernechevsky's vision of a fantastical future, but here the dream has already come to pass, giving a double temporality. Like the ram's-skull scene, it is a vision that cuts two ways: perhaps New York is the glorious culmination of a story of progress beginning with the first cities, or perhaps it is doomed to ruin like those cities, in which case it is already a sepulchral monument to death, as 'pyramid on pyramid' suggests. Although it sits high in the sky, its buildings like 'white cloudsheads', under the surface, in the foundations perhaps, a 'thunderstorm' is brewing.

The 2010s–20s: Cole and Whitehead

Around a hundred years after Cather and Dos Passos, the question of what in New York is open or closed, what is hidden and what visible, remains central to Cole's *Open City* (2011), which reinvents the figure of the flâneur as Julius, an immigrant psychiatrist in New York with mixed Nigerian and German parentage. I focus on a moment from the novel which again draws attention to the city's foundations, and to New York as a scene of catastrophe. After a section which interweaves reflections on Trinity Church, whose diminishment James had bemoaned, with thoughts on whales and whaling, including the observation that Melville was 'a sometime parishioner of Trinity Church', Julius finds himself in sight of 'the empty space that was, I now saw and admitted, the obvious: the ruins of the World Trade Center'.[15] As Julius describes it, the site is both monumental ('I remember a tourist who once asked me how he could get to 9/11: not the site of the events of 9/11 but to 9/11 itself, the date petrified into broken stones') and empty ('it was walled in with wood and chain link, but otherwise nothing announced its significance').[16] Significantly, Cole's novel records a moment when the current memorial and museum (built 2006–11) was still under construction, so that memorialisation of the event had not yet settled into a fixed architectural form. For Julius, what is erased in both the events of 9/11, as received by the general public, and the site that seeks to commemorate them, is human bodies. As he puts it:

> No bodies were visible, except the falling ones, on the day America's ticker stopped. Marketable stories of all kinds had thickened around the injured coast of our city, but the depiction of the dead bodies was forbidden. It would have been upsetting to have it otherwise.[17]

Going further than in Cather, damaged bodies are not now seen and suppressed, but never seen at all. Julius turns from this thought into a reflection on the city's lost architectural and social past, which ends by seeing it in textual terms:

> This was not the first erasure on the site. Before the towers had gone up, there had been a bustling network of little streets traversing this part of town. Robinson Street, Laurens Street, College Place: all of them had been obliterated in the 1960s to make way for the World Trade Center buildings, and all were forgotten now. Gone, too, was the old Washington Market, the active piers, the fishwives, the Christian Syrian enclave that was established here in the late 1800s. The Syrians, the Lebanese, and other people from the Levant had been pushed across the river to Brooklyn, where they'd set down roots on Atlantic Avenue and in Brooklyn Heights. And, before that? What Lenape paths lay buried beneath the rubble? The site was a palimpsest, as was all the city, written, erased, rewritten.[18]

This echoes Benjamin's observations in Convolute C of the *Arcades Project*, 'Ancient Paris, Catacombs, Demolitions, Decline of Paris'. We there read that 'Paris is built over a system of caverns from which the din of Métro and railroad mounts to the surface', and which 'since the Middle Ages, have time and again been reentered and traversed'. We also find Louis Aragon's description of the arcades as 'places that yesterday were incomprehensible, and that tomorrow will never know'.[19] Through Julius's eyes, 9/11 is reinterpreted in a similar way, as the devastating and spectacular culmination of a series of hidden erasures which are always taking place in the city. As Ankhi Mukherjee writes, 'the layers of the palimpsest are built on the erasures, not viable traces, of successive ethnoscapes'.[20] If 9/11 is a form of destruction that 'hits high', as Fred Hallet puts it, then behind it is an ongoing catastrophe that continually rewrites the urban text.

This notion of an architecture which has become invisible because it is lost, superseded and written over is also present in Colson Whitehead's *Harlem Shuffle* (2021). The novel focuses on the life of Harlem in the late 1950s and early 1960s, through the life of Ray Carney, a furniture salesman with links to the criminal underworld. Harlem is represented as a smaller black city within the larger, white-dominated Manhattan, and in this sense has its antecedent in Seneca Village, a nineteenth-century community (existing from 1825–57) of 'a couple of hundred people, mostly colored with a bit of Irish', living as free landowners with 'three churches, two schools, one cemetery', on the site of what is now Central Park.[21] As the narrator explains:

Then someone came up with the idea for a grand park in the middle of Manhattan, an oasis inside the newly teeming metropolis. Various locations were proposed, rejected, reconsidered, until the white leaders decided on a vast, rectangular patch in the heart of the island. People already lived there; no matter. The colored citizens of Seneca were property owners, they voted, they had a voice. Not enough of one. The City of New York seized the land, razed the village, and that was that.

All that remains, Carney speculates, is remnants of bodies lying below the park: 'You'll find the bones. Dig under the playgrounds and meadows and silent groves, Carney supposed, you'll find the bones.'[22] This makes the city allegorical in Benjamin's sense, as Central Park is reframed as an invisible graveyard, its apparent openness in fact part of the work of repressing the past freedoms of black citizens. Twentieth-century Harlem implicitly becomes an echo of Seneca, a comparison which again cuts two ways, indicating potential freedom and independence on the one hand, but the risk of sudden, total destruction on the other.

This notion of a hidden city within, and in tension with, the more open and visible city is extended elsewhere in the novel. It becomes a feature of character, with the narrator remarking that 'everyone had secret corners and alleys that no one else saw – what mattered were your major streets and boulevards, the stuff that showed up on other people's maps of you'.[23] This recalls Dickens's narrator in *A Tale of Two Cities* (1859), who describes 'a solemn consideration, when I enter a great city by night, that every one of those darkly clustered houses encloses its own secret; that every room in every one of them encloses its own secret'.[24] Dickens makes the enclosure of the urban interior the spatial locus of the secrets we hold, and nighttime its temporal frame. Both are significant in *Harlem Shuffle* too. Although the houses of Harlem are not literally opened up as in Zola or Dos Passos, Carney nonetheless imaginatively penetrates them like Asmodeus or Dickens's 'good spirit' (DS 47.685), in order to calculate where the goods he sells end up:

Carney imagined beyond the facades; he was looking for something. Inside, the brownstones had remained one-family homes, or been cut up into individual apartments, and their rooms were marked by different choices in terms of furniture, paint color, what had been thrown on the walls, function. Then there were the invisible marks left by the lives within, those durable hauntings. In this room, the oldest son was born on a lumpy canopy bed by the window; in that parlor the old bachelor had proposed to his mail-order bride; here the third floor had been the stage, variously, for slow-to-boil divorces and suicide schemes and suicide attempts.[25]

These 'invisible marks' or 'durable hauntings' constitute a hidden, layered history to the city that provides a counterpoint to the otherwise similar facades that line its streets. This passage appears in the section of the novel named 'Dorvay', a phonetic version of the French term *dorveille*, referring to biphasic, pre-modern sleep patterns. As Simonov, Carney's old financial accounting professor once told him:

> We've forgotten now, but until the advent of the lightbulb, it was common to sleep in two shifts. [. . .] The first started soon after dusk, when the day's labor was done – if there were no lights to see, what was the point of staying up? Then we woke around midnight for a few hours before the second phase of sleep, which lasted through the morning.[26]

According to Carney, who adopts such a schedule during this part of the narrative, 'dorvay was crooked heaven, when the straight world slept and the bent got to work. An arena for thieving and scores, break-ins and hijacks'.[27] This is an illegal counterpart to the function of nighttime in *Mary Barton*, which as discussed in Chapter 1 offers a fragile margin for working-class activity outside the sight of the bourgeoisie and the regulatory framework of industrial capitalism. In *Harlem Shuffle*, night is part of the parallel, hidden city of criminality that exists within – but also extends far beyond – Harlem. Another form of this hidden city becomes visible when Carney walks around the city with Munson, a white cop, as the latter collects bribes:

> This tour with Munson on his rounds took Carney to places he saw every day, establishments on his doorstep, places he'd walked by ever since he was a kid, and exposed them as fronts. The doorways were entrances into difference cities – no, different entrances into one vast, secret city. Ever close, adjacent to all you know, just underneath. If you know where to look.[28]

As the last sentence emphasises, to see this second city is a matter of perspective. The city 'underneath' the everyday, visible city is not exactly hidden, since it consists of places Carney has walked past all his life, but it is still invisible unless you 'know where to look'.

The last section of the book takes place in 1964, the year of both the New York World's Fair and the Harlem riot, in June of that year, which followed the killing by a white police officer of James Powell, a black teenager. Whitehead brings these events together as Carney walks down 125th Street:

> he got to thinking about the grand pavilions in Flushing, Queens. A few miles away, the World's Fair celebrated the wonders on the horizon. [. . .] In one room Bell Labs had Picturephones that showed you the face of the person on the other end of the line, in another mammoth computers talked to one another through telephone wires.

Yet at the same time:

> You didn't need to journey far, certainly didn't need three-stage rockets and manned capsules and arcane telemetry, to see what else we were capable of. If Carney walked five minutes in any direction, one generation's immaculate townhouses were the next's shooting galleries, slum blocks testified in a chorus of neglect, and businesses sat ravaged and demolished after weeks of violent protest.[29]

The dialectical structure of the city here becomes apparent. The World's Fair, a reinvention of the nineteenth century's world exhibitions, emphasises not only technological progress but growing interpersonal connection (picturephones, computers that talk to one another). In Harlem, by contrast, there is both architectural and social decline (townhouses become shooting galleries, neglected slum blocks) and disconnection, since while some blocks are entirely 'untouched', other parts of Harlem form islands of devastation.[30] The city has two faces, and neither is entirely true or entirely false.

In the novel's final pages, Carney visits the site where the World Trade Center is being constructed. This gives us the other end of the towers' lifetime from that which Julius sees in *Open City*, but the scene of destruction depicted is strikingly similar. Carney does not read the site as a sign of progress, but like Julius reflects on what has been lost in the very act of beginning this vast construction project, which serves the interests of global capital rather than the small-scale business it replaces:

> The neighborhood was gone, razed. Everything four blocks south of the New York Telephone Building and four blocks east of the miserable West Side Highway had been demolished and erased for the World Trade

Center site, down to the street signs and traffic lights. This was the aftermath of a ruinous battle. Block after teeming block of Radio Row, the textile warehouses and women's hat stores and shoe-shine stands, the greasy spoons, even the indentations in the sidewalk where the struts of the elevated tracks had been riveted to the concrete – rubble. The buildings of the old city loomed over the broken spot, this wound in itself.[31]

This site mirrors the construction of the Ladies' Paradise department store in Zola, which also destroys the small business around it, but far exceeds it in scope, scale and international reach. Carney connects this 'ruinous battle' to the Harlem riots, which are dwarfed by it: 'the devastation had been nothing compared to what lay before him now, but if you bottled the rage and hope and fury of all the people of Harlem and made it into a bomb, the results would look something like this'.[32] These lines recalls Langston Hughes's poem 'Harlem', from *Montage of a Dream Deferred* (1951), which famously asks 'what happens to a dream deferred?', ending with the lines:

Maybe it just sags
like a heavy load.

Or does it explode?[33]

The novel indirectly alludes to 'Harlem' by mentioning the 1961 film version of Lorraine Hansbury's 1959 play *A Raisin in the Sun*, which takes its title from the poem.[34] In Hughes, what this potential explosion means is ambiguous; it refers perhaps to violent protest, or to an explosion of creativity and social change, or both. In a similar way, the ending of *Harlem Shuffle* complicates the relationship between construction and destruction in New York, as well as the question of what is visible and what is invisible. The Harlem riot is brought into visibility as sheer destruction in television images, but this is not the full story, since 'despite what America saw on the news, only a fraction of the community had picked up bricks and bats and kerosene'.[35] On the one hand, the World Trade Center on the surface aligns with the World's Fair as a symbol of progress and development, but in this moment before its construction begins, after the demolition of the buildings that had stood on the site, Carney is able to instead perceive it as a 'wound' in the city. This sense of a city wounded by the process of construction is heightened by the links between real-estate capitalism, corruption and violence that run through the final section of the book.

Taken together, *Open City* and *Harlem Shuffle* draw attention to the relationship between two sides of New York, its open and hidden faces, that Cather had earlier shown to be interrelated through the construction and destruction of the Mont Blanc Hotel. Like *Manhattan Transfer*, these more recent novels continue to suggest that the making of New York is not separable from its unmaking, or from the acts of demolition and social erasures that lie under its surface. The task of seeing these two sides at once, of comprehending the connections between what is hidden in the city, what is transparent, and the mobility that mediates between the two, remains as important in these texts as in the nineteenth-century writers I have discussed over the course of this book.

Notes

1. *Imagining New York City*, p. 13. The classic definition of the global city comes from Saskia Sassen: 'Beyond their long history as centers for international trade and banking, these cities now function in four new ways: first, as highly concentrated command points in the organization of the world economy; second, as key locations for finance and for specialized service firms, which have replaced manufacturing as the leading economic sectors; third, as sites of production, including the production of innovations, in these leading industries; and fourth, as markets for the products and innovations produced. [. . .] Thus a new type of city has appeared. It is the global city.' Saskia Sassen, *The Global City: New York, London, Tokyo* (Princeton: Princeton University Press, 1991), pp. 3–4.
2. Willa Cather, 'Behind the Singer Tower', *Collier's*, 49 (18 May 1912), 16–17; 41 (p. 16). Available at Willa Cather Archive: <https://cather.unl.edu/writings/shortfiction/ss045>. Accessed 1 November 2022. On Cather as an urban writer, see Charmion Gustke, 'Willa Cather and the Metropolis', in *Palgrave Encyclopedia*, pp. 1891–7.
3. *Imagining New York City*, p. 50.
4. Cather, p. 16.
5. Cather, p. 17.
6. Cather, p. 41.
7. Cather, p. 41, p. 16.
8. *Selected Writings, Volume 4*, p. 392.
9. John Dos Passos, *Manhattan Transfer* (London: Penguin, 2000), p. 26.
10. *Selected Writings, Volume 4*, p. 392. *Origin*, p. 166.
11. Dos Passos, p. 48.
12. Dos Passos, p. 24, p. 25.
13. Dos Passos, p. 230.

14. Dos Passos, p. 229. This passage is also the epigraph to chapter 2 on p. 23.
15. Teju Cole, *Open City* (London: Faber and Faber, 2011), p. 51, p. 52.
16. Cole, p. 52.
17. Cole, p. 58.
18. Cole, p. 59.
19. *Arcades*, p. 85, p. 87.
20. Ankhi Mukherjee, *Unseen City: The Psychic Lives of the Urban Poor* (Cambridge: Cambridge University Press, 2022), p. 169.
21. Colson Whitehead, *Harlem Shuffle* (London: Fleet, 2021), p. 68.
22. Whitehead, p. 68.
23. Whitehead, p. 33.
24. Charles Dickens, *A Tale of Two Cities* (London: Penguin, 2003), pp. 14–15.
25. Whitehead, pp. 125–6.
26. Whitehead, p. 137.
27. Whitehead, p. 138.
28. Whitehead, p. 255.
29. Whitehead, p. 214.
30. Whitehead, p. 213.
31. Whitehead, p. 319.
32. Whitehead, p. 319.
33. Langston Hughes, *The Collected Poems of Langston Hughes*, ed. by Arnold Rampersad (Alfred Knopf: New York, 1996), p. 426.
34. Whitehead, p. 136.
35. Whitehead, p. 319.

Bibliography

Agathacleous, Tanya, *Urban Realism and the Cosmopolitan Imagination in the Nineteenth Century: Visible City, Invisible World* (Cambridge: Cambridge University Press, 2011)

Allen, Michael, 'Locating Tom-All-Alone's', *Dickens Quarterly*, 29.1 (2012), 32–49

Allen, Michelle, *Cleansing the City: Sanitary Geographies in Victorian London* (Athens: Ohio State University Press, 2008)

Althusser, Louis, *Lenin and Philosophy and Other Essays*, trans. by Ben Brewster (London: Monthly Review Press, 1971)

Anderson, Amanda, 'Victorian Studies and the Two Modernities', *Victorian Studies*, 47.2 (2005), 195–203

Anderson, Glaire, and Mariam Rosser-Owen, eds, *Revisiting Al-Andalus: Perspectives on the Material Culture of Islamic Iberia and Beyond* (Leiden: Brill, 2007)

Angermann, Asaf, 'Adorno and Scholem: The Heretical Redemption of Metaphysics', in *A Companion to Adorno*, ed. by Peter Gordon, Espen Hammer and Max Pensky (Hoboken, NJ: Wiley Blackwell, 2020), pp. 531–48

Armstrong, Isobel, 'Theories of Space and the Nineteenth-Century Novel', *19: Interdisciplinary Studies in the Long Nineteenth Century*, 17 (2013), 1–21

— *Victorian Glassworlds: Glass Culture and the Imagination, 1830–1880* (Oxford: Oxford University Press, 2008)

Arnold, Dana, Tore Rem and Helle Waahlberg, eds, 'Paris and London, Capitals of the Nineteenth Century', *Synergies Royaume-Uni et Irlande*, 3 (2010)

Audsley, William, and George Audsley, *Popular Dictionary of Architecture and the Allied Arts, Volume II* (New York: G. P. Putnam's Sons, 1881)

Babb, Valerie, *Whiteness Visible: The Meaning of Whiteness in American Literature* (New York: New York University Press, 1998)

Bachelard, Gaston, *The Poetics of Space*, trans. by Maria Jolas (Boston: Beacon Press, 1994)

Bakhtin, Mikhail, *Problems of Dostoevsky's Poetics*, ed. and trans. by Caryl Emerson (Minneapolis: University of Minnesota Press, 1984)

Balzac, Honoré de, *Père Goriot*, trans. by A. J. Krailsheimer (Oxford: Oxford University Press, 1991)

Barakat, Heba (author), and Muhammad Waley (editor), *The Arabesque: An Introduction* (Kuala Lumpur: Islamic Arts Museum Malaysia, 2018)

Barthes, Roland, 'The Reality Effect', in *The Rustle of Language*, trans. by Richard Howard (Berkeley and Los Angeles: University of California Press, 1989), pp. 141–8

— *Writing Degree Zero*, trans. by Annette Lavers and Colin Smith (London: Macmillan, 2012)

Baudelaire, Charles, *The Flowers of Evil*, trans. by James McGowan (Oxford: Oxford University Press, 1993)

— *The Painter of Modern Life and Other Essays*, trans. by Jonathan Mayne (London: Phaidon, 1995)

Beizer, Janet, '*Au* (delà du) *Bonheur des Dames*: Notes on the Underground', *Australian Journal of French Studies*, 38.1 (2001), 393–406

Belenky, Masha, 'Disordered Topographies in Zola's *La Curée*', *Romance Notes*, 53.1 (2013), 27–37

Bell, David, *Models of Power: Politics and Economics in Zola's Rougon-Macquart* (Lincoln: University of Nebraska Press, 1988)

Bely, Andrei, *Gogol's Artistry*, trans. by Christopher Colbath (Evanston, IL: Northwestern University Press, 2009)

Benjamin, Walter, *Selected Writings, Volume 2, Part 2: 1931–1934*, ed. by Michael Jennings, Howard Eiland and Gary Smith (Cambridge, MA: Belknap Press, 1999)

— *Selected Writings, Volume 3: 1935–1938*, ed. by Howard Eiland and Michael Jennings (Cambridge, MA: Belknap Press, 2002)

— *Selected Writings, Volume 4: 1938–1940*, ed. by Howard Eiland and Michael Jennings (Cambridge, MA: Belknap Press, 2003)

— *The Arcades Project*, trans. by Howard Eiland and Kevin McLoughlin (Cambridge, MA: Belknap Press, 1999)

— *The Origin of German Tragic Drama*, trans. by John Osborne (London: Verso, 1998)

— *The Work of Art in the Age of Its Technological Reproducibility and Other Writings on Media*, ed. by Michael Jennings, Brigid Doherty and Thomas Levin (Cambridge, MA: Belknap Press, 2008)

— *The Writer of Modern Life*, ed. by Michael Jennings (Cambridge, MA: Belknap Press, 2006)

Berg, William, *The Visual Novel: Émile Zola and the Art of His Times* (University Park: Pennsylvania State University Press, 1992)

Bergdoll, Barry, *European Architecture: 1750–1890* (Oxford: Oxford University Press, 2000)

Berman, Jacob, *American Arabesque: Arabs, Islam, and the 19th Century Imaginary* (New York: New York University Press, 2012)

Berman, Marshall, *All That Is Solid Melts into Air: The Experience of Modernity* (London: Verso, 2010)

Bernheimer, Charles, 'Cloaking the Self: The Literary Space of Gogol's "Overcoat"', *PMLA*, 90.1 (1975), 53–61

Bernstein, Michael, *Bitter Carnival: Ressentiment and the Abject Hero* (Princeton: Princeton University Press, 1992)

Bhogal, Gurminder Kaur, *Details of Consequence: Ornament, Music, and Art in Paris* (Oxford: Oxford University Press, 2013)

Bishop, Danielle, '*Au Bonheur des Dames*: A Novel of Construction, Constructors, and the Constructed', *Excavatio*, 23.1–2 (2008), 243–54

Bloch, Ernst, *The Spirit of Utopia*, trans. by Anthony Nassar (Stanford: Stanford University Press, 2000)

Bouvard, Luc, 'The Thames Persistently Revisited: Dickens on the Edge of Water', *Études Anglaises: Revue du Monde Anglophone*, 65.1 (2012), 80–95

Bove, Alexander, *Spectral Dickens: The Uncanny Forms of Novelistic Characterization* (Manchester: Manchester University Press, 2021)

Bowlby, Rachel, *Just Looking: Consumer Culture in Dreiser, Gissing and Zola* (Abingdon: Routledge, 1985)

Brander Rasmussen, Birgit, Eric Klinenberg, Irene J. Nexica and Matt Wray, eds, *The Making and Unmaking of Whiteness* (Durham, NC: Duke University Press, 2001)

Bray, Patrick, *The Novel Map: Space and Subjectivity in Nineteenth-Century French Fiction* (Evanston, IL: Northwestern University Press, 2013)

Briggs, Asa, *Victorian Cities* (London: Odhams Press, 1963)

The British Printer, vol. 12 (London: Raithby, Lawrence & Co., Ltd, 1899)

Brombert, Victor, 'Meaning and Indeterminacy in Gogol's "The Overcoat"', *Proceedings of the American Philosophical Society*, 135.4 (1991), 569–75

Brontë, Charlotte, *Jane Eyre*, 3rd edn (London: Norton, 2001)

Brooks, Peter, *Realist Vision* (New Haven: Yale University Press, 2005)

Buck-Morss, Susan, *The Dialectics of Seeing: Walter Benjamin and the Arcades Project* (Cambridge, MA: MIT Press, 1989)

Burke, Edmund, *A Philosophical Enquiry into the Sublime and Beautiful* (Oxford: Oxford University Press, 2015 [1757])

Buse, Peter, Ken Hirschkop, Scott McCracken and Bertrand Taithe, *Benjamin's Arcades: An UnGuided Tour* (Manchester: Manchester University Press, 2005)

Butt, John, and Kathleen Tillotson, *Dickens at Work* (Abingdon: Routledge, 2009 [1957])

Carlyle, Thomas, *Chartism* (London: James Fraser, 1840)

Carter, Ian, '"The lost idea of a train": Looking for Britain's Railway Novel', *Journal of Transport History*, 21.2 (2000), 117–39

Cather, Willa, 'Behind the Singer Tower', *Collier's*, 49 (18 May 1912), 16–17; 41

Cazamian, Louis, *The Social Novel in England 1830–1850*, trans. by Martin Fido (London: Routledge and Kegan, 1973 [1903])

Certeau, Michel de, *The Practice of Everyday Life*, trans. by Steven Rendall (Berkeley and Los Angeles: University of California Press, 1984)

Charley, Jonathan, ed., *The Routledge Companion on Architecture, Literature and the City* (London: Routledge, 2018)

Chatterjee, Rojaunee, Alicia Christoff and Amy Wong, 'Introduction: Undisciplining Victorian Studies', *Victorian Studies*, 62.3 (2020), 369–91

Chernychevsky, Nikolai, *A Vital Question; or, What Is to Be Done?*, trans. by Nathan Dole and S. S. Skidelsky (New York: Crowell and Co., 1886)

Clausen, Meredith, *Frantz Jourdain and the Samaritaine* (Leiden: Brill, 1987)

Cole, Teju, *Open City* (London: Faber and Faber, 2011)

Conrad, Joseph, *Heart of Darkness*, in *The Norton Anthology of English Literature*, 9th edn, vol. F, *The Twentieth Century and After*, ed. by Stephen Greenblatt (New York and London: Norton, 2012), pp. 1951–2010

Conrads, Ulrich, ed., *Programs and Manifestoes on 20th-Century Architecture*, trans. by Michael Bullock (Cambridge, MA: MIT Press, 1971)

Constantopoulos, Elias, 'Preface: On Reading Architecture', in *Reading Architecture: Literary Imagination and Architectural Experience*, ed. by Angeliki Sioli and Yoonchun Jung (New York and London: Routledge, 2018), pp. xix–xxi

Cornish, William, J. Stuart Anderson, Ray Cocks, Michael Lobban, Patrick Polden and Keith Smith, eds, *The Oxford History of the Laws of England, Volume XII: 1820–1914 Private Law* (Oxford: Oxford University Press, 2010)

Crary, Jonathan, *Techniques of the Observer: On Vision and Modernity in the Nineteenth Century* (Cambridge, MA: MIT Press, 1992)

Crysler, C. Greig, *Writing Spaces: Discourses of Architecture, Urbanism and the Built Environment* (New York: Routledge, 2003)

Debord, Guy, *The Society of the Spectacle*, trans. by Donald Nicholson-Smith (New York: Zone, 1995)

— 'Theory of the Dérive', in *Situationist International Anthology*, ed. and trans. by Ken Knabb, revised and expanded edition (Berkeley, CA: Bureau of Public Secrets, 2006), pp. 62–6

Delaney, Brigid, 'The "Colportage Phenomenon of Space" and the Place of Montage in *The Arcades Project*', *Germanic Review: Literature, Culture, Theory*, 81.1 (2006), 37–64

Deleuze, Gilles, and Felix Guattari, *A Thousand Plateaus*, trans. by Brian Massumi (London: Continuum, 2001)

Derrida, Jacques, *Acts of Literature*, ed. by Derek Attridge (London: Routledge, 1992)

— *The Ear of the Other: Otobiography, Transference, Translation*, ed. by Christie McDonald (New York: Schocken, 1985)

— *The Truth in Painting*, trans. by Geoff Bennington and Ian McLeod (London: University of Chicago Press, 1987)

— 'White Mythology: Metaphor in the Text of Philosophy', trans. by F. C. T. Moore, *New Literary History*, 6.1 (1974), 5–74

— *Writing and Difference*, trans. by Alan Bass (London: Routledge and Kegan Paul, 1978)

Dickens, Charles, *Selected Short Fiction* (London: Penguin, 1976)

— *Bleak House* (Oxford: Oxford University Press, 1999)

— *Dealings with the Firm of Dombey and Son*, no. 2 (London: Bradbury and Evans, Nov. 1846)

— *Dombey and Son* (Harmondsworth: Penguin, 1970)

— *Dombey and Son* (Oxford: Oxford University Press, 2001)

— *Dombey and Son*, ed. by Alan Horsman (Oxford: Clarendon, 1974)

— *Martin Chuzzlewit* (Oxford: Oxford University Press, 1984)

— *The Mystery of Edwin Drood* (Oxford: Oxford University Press, 1982)

— *The Old Curiosity Shop* (Oxford: Oxford University Press, 1998)

— *The Pickwick Papers* (London: Penguin, 2003)

— *Sketches by Boz* (London: Penguin, 1995)

— *A Tale of Two Cities* (London: Penguin, 2003)

Dillon, Steve, 'Victorian Interior', *Modern Language Quarterly*, 62.2 (2001), 83–115

Disraeli, Benjamin, *Sybil* (Oxford: Oxford University Press, 1998)

Donald, James, *Imagining the Modern City* (Minneapolis: University of Minnesota Press, 1999)

Doré, Gustave, and Blanchard Jerrold, *London: A Pilgrimage* (London: Grant & Co., 1872)

Dos Passos, John, *Manhattan Transfer* (London: Penguin, 2000)

Dostoevsky, Fyodor, *Crime and Punishment*, trans. by David McDuff (London: Penguin, 2003)

— *Notes from Underground/The Double*, trans. by Jessie Coulson (Harmondsworth: Penguin, 1972)

Downes, Daragh, '"Excellent Monsters": The Railway Theme in Dickens's Novels', *English*, 61.235 (2012), 382–93

Duggett, Tom, *Gothic Romanticism: Architecture, Politics and Literary Form* (New York: Palgrave, 2010)

Dyer, Richard, *White: Essays on Race and Culture* (London: Routledge, 1997)

Edwards, Sarah, and Jonathan Charley, eds, *Writing the Modern City: Literature, Architecture, Modernity* (Abingdon: Routledge, 2012)

Eisenstein, Sergei, *Selected Works, Volume 2: Towards a Theory of Montage*, trans. by Michael Glenny (London: BFI, 1991)

— *Nonindifferent Nature*, trans. by Herbert Marshall (Cambridge: Cambridge University Press, 1987)

Elfenbein, Andrew, 'Managing the House in *Dombey and Son*: Dickens and the Uses of Analogy', *Studies in Philology*, 92.3 (1995), 361–82

Eliot, George, *The Essays of George Eliot*, ed. by Nathan Sheppard (New York: Funk and Wagnells, 1883)

— *The Lifted Veil and Brother Jacob* (Oxford: Oxford University Press, 1999)

Ellinghaus, Katherine, Jane Cary and Leigh Boucher, eds, *Re-Orienting Whiteness* (New York: Palgrave, 2009)

Ellison, David, 'Mobile Homes, Fallen Furniture, and the Dickens Cure', *South Atlantic Quarterly*, 108.1 (2009), 87–114

Engels, Friedrich, *The Condition of the Working Class in England* (London: Penguin, 2009)

Eskilson, Stephen, *The Age of Glass: A Cultural History of Glass in Modern and Contemporary Architecture* (London and New York: Bloomsbury, 2018)

Éveno, Bertrand, 'Jung's "Multicolored Arabesques": Their Renderings and Intentions in the Pictorial Vocabulary of *The Red Book*', trans. by Leslie de Galbert, *Psychological Perspectives*, 58.1 (2015), 5–33

Fanger, Donald, *The Creation of Nikolai Gogol* (Cambridge, MA: Belknap Press, 1979)

Feldman, Jessica, *Victorian Modernism: Pragmatism and the Varieties of Aesthetic Experience* (Cambridge: Cambridge University Press, 2002)

Finger, Anke, and Danielle Follett, eds, *The Aesthetics of the Total Artwork* (Baltimore: Johns Hopkins University Press, 2011)

Flam, Jack, *Matisse on Art* (Berkeley and Los Angeles: University of California Press, 1995)

Flaubert, Gustave, *The Letters of Gustave Flaubert 1830–1857*, ed. and trans. by Francis Steegmuller (Cambridge, MA: Belknap Press, 1979)

Forster, John, *The Life of Charles Dickens* (Oxford: Benediction Classics, 2011 [1872–4])

Foster, Hal, *The Art-Architecture Complex* (London: Verso, 2011)
Foucault, Michel, *Discipline and Punish*, trans. by Alan Sheridan (New York: Vintage, 1995)
— *History of Madness*, ed. by Jean Khalfa (London: Routledge, 2006)
— *The Order of Things*, trans. by Alan Sheridan (Abingdon: Routledge, 1989)
Frazier, Melissa, 'Arabesques, Architecture and Painting', in *Russian Subjects: Empire, Nation and the Culture of the Golden Age*, ed. by Monika Greenleaf and Stephen Moeller-Sally (Evanston, IL: Northwestern University Press, 1998), pp. 277–95
Frede, Victoria, *Doubt, Atheism and the Nineteenth-Century Russian Intelligentsia* (Madison: University of Wisconsin Press, 2011)
Freedgood, Elaine, *The Ideas in Things: Fugitive Meaning in the Victorian Novel* (Chicago: University of Chicago Press, 2006)
Freeman, Michael, *Railways and the Victorian Imagination* (New Haven: Yale University Press, 1999)
Frenk, Joachim, and Lena Steveker, *Charles Dickens as an Agent of Change* (Ithaca, NY: Cornell University Press, 2019)
Freud, Sigmund, *The Standard Edition, Volume XII (1911–1913)*, ed. by James Strachey (London: Vintage, 2001)
— *The Standard Edition, Volume XIV (1914–1916)*, ed. by James Strachey (London: Vintage, 2001)
— *The Standard Edition, Volume XVII (1917–1919)*, ed. by James Strachey (London: Vintage, 2001)
— *The Standard Edition, Volume XVIII (1920–1922)*, ed. by James Strachey (London: Vintage, 2001)
— *The Standard Edition, Volume XX (1925–1926)*, ed. by James Strachey (London: Vintage, 2001)
— *The Standard Edition, Volume XXI (1927–1931)*, ed. by James Strachey (London: Vintage, 2001)
— *The Interpretation of Dreams*, trans. by James Strachey (London: Penguin, 1976)
— *Totem and Taboo*, trans. by James Strachey (London: Routledge, 2001)
Fusso, Susanne, and Priscilla Meyer, eds, *Essays on Gogol: Logos and the Russian Word* (Evanston, IL: Northwestern University Press, 1992)
Fyfe, Paul, *By Accident or Design: Writing the Victorian Metropolis* (Oxford: Oxford University Press, 2015)
Gallagher, Catherine, *The Body Economic: Life, Death, and Sensation in Political Economy and the Victorian Novel* (Princeton: Princeton University Press, 2006)
— *The Industrial Reformation of English Fiction: Social Discourse and Narrative Form, 1832–1867* (Chicago: University of Chicago Press, 1985)

Garratt, James, *Music, Culture and Social Reform in the Age of Wagner* (Cambridge: Cambridge University Press, 2010)

Gaskell, Elizabeth, *Mary Barton* (Oxford: Oxford University Press, 2006)

— *North and South* (Oxford: Oxford University Press, 1998)

Gaylin, Ann, *Eavesdropping in the Novel from Austen to Proust* (Cambridge: Cambridge University Press, 2002)

Gehlawat, Monika, 'The Aesthetics of Whiteness: Melville's *Moby Dick* and the Paintings of Robert Ryman', *Soundings*, 88.3–4 (2005), 371–91

Giedion, Sigfried, *Building in France, Building in Iron, Building in Ferroconcrete*, trans. by J. Duncan Berry (Chicago: University of Chicago Press, 2014)

— *Space, Time and Architecture: The Growth of a New Tradition*, 5th edn (Cambridge, MA: Harvard University Press, 1967)

Gilbert, Pamela, *Victorian Skin: Surface, Self, History* (Ithaca, NY: Cornell University Press, 2019)

Gillard-Estrada, Anne-Florence, and Anne Besnault-Levita, *Beyond the Victorian/Modernist Divide: Remapping the Turn-of-the-Century Break in Literature, Culture and the Visual Arts* (New York and Abingdon: Routledge, 2018)

Gilman, Charlotte Perkins, *The Yellow Wallpaper and Selected Writings* (London: Virago, 2009)

Ginsburg, Michal, 'House and Home in *Dombey and Son*', *Dickens Studies Annual*, 36 (2005), 57–73

Gippius, V. V., *Gogol*, trans. by Robert Maguire (Durham, NC: Duke University Press, 1989 [1924])

Gissing, George, *The Nether World* (Oxford: Oxford University Press, 1992)

Goddard, Kevin, '"Like Circles on the Water": Melville, Schopenhauer and the Allegory of Whiteness', *English Studies in Africa*, 51.2 (2008), 84–109

Goethe, Johann Wolfgang von, *Essays on Art and Literature*, ed. by John Gearey, trans. by Ellen von Nardroff and Ernest von Nardroff (Princeton: Princeton University Press, 1986)

— *Sämtliche Werke*, vol. 30 (Stuttgart: J. G. Cotta, 1895)

Gogol, Nikolai, *The Collected Tales of Nikolai Gogol*, trans. by Richard Pevear and Larissa Volokhonsky (London: Granta, 1998)

— *Arabesques*, trans. by Alexander Tulloch (Ann Arbor: Ardis, 1982)

Goldsmith, Kenneth, *Capital: New York, Capital of the Twentieth Century* (London and New York: Verso, 2016)

Gong, Haomin, *Uneven Modernity: Literature, Film, and Intellectual Discourse in Postsocialist China* (Honolulu: University of Hawai'i Press, 2012)

Gordon, Rae Beth, *Ornament, Fantasy, and Desire in Nineteenth-Century French Literature* (Princeton: Princeton University Press, 1992)

Gorham, Deborah, *The Victorian Girl and the Feminine Ideal* (London: Croom Helm, 1982)

Graham, Joseph, ed., *Difference in Translation* (Ithaca, NY and London: Cornell University Press, 1985)

Grewe, Cordula, *The Arabesque from Kant to Comics* (Abingdon and New York: Routledge, 2021)

Hamon, Philippe, *Expositions: Literature and Architecture in Nineteenth-Century France*, trans. by Katia Sainson-Frank and Lisa Maguire (Berkeley and Los Angeles: University of California Press, 1992)

Havik, Klaske, *Urban Literacy: Reading and Writing Architecture* (Rotterdam: nai0I0, 2014)

Havik, Klaske, Jorge Mejía Hernández, Mike Schäfer, Mark Proosten and Susana Oliveira, eds, *Writingplace: Investigations in Architecture and Literature* (Rotterdam: nai010, 2016)

Hegel, G. W. F., *Aesthetics: Lectures on Fine Art, Volume II*, trans. by T. M. Knox (Oxford: Clarendon, 1975)

Helfer, Martha, ed., *Rereading Romanticism* (Amsterdam: Rodopi, 2000)

Hemmings, F. W. J., *The Life and Times of Émile Zola* (London: Elek, 1977)

Hennessy, Susie, 'Consumption and Desire in *Au Bonheur des Dames*', *French Review*, 81.4 (2008), 696–706

Hewitt, Martin, *Making Social Knowledge in the Victorian City: The Visiting Mode in Manchester, 1832–1914* (Abingdon: Routledge, 2020)

Heynen, Hilde, *Architecture and Modernity: A Critique* (Cambridge, MA: MIT Press, 1999)

Hofer-Robinson, Joanna, *Dickens and Demolition: Literary Afterlives and Mid-Nineteenth-Century Urban Development* (Edinburgh: Edinburgh University Press, 2018)

Hoffenberg, Peter, *An Empire on Display: English, Indian, and Australian Exhibitions from the Crystal Palace to the Great War* (Berkeley and Los Angeles: University of California Press, 2001)

Hogarth, William, *The Analysis of Beauty* (London: W. Strahan, 1772)

Hollier, Denis, *Against Architecture: The Writings of Georges Bataille*, trans. by Betsy Wing (Cambridge, MA: MIT Press, 1989)

Horowitz, Evan, 'London: Capital of the Nineteenth Century', *New Literary History*, 41.1 (2010), 111–28

Hughes, Langston, *The Collected Poems of Langston Hughes*, ed. by Arnold Rampersad (Alfred Knopf: New York, 1996)

Hugo, Victor, *Notre Dame de Paris*, trans. by Alban Krailshelmer (Oxford: Oxford University Press, 1993)

Hund, Wulf D., 'Advertising White Supremacy: Capitalism, Colonialism, and Commodity Racism', in *Colonial Advertising and Commodity Racism*, ed. by Wulf D. Hund, Michael Pickering and Anandi Ramamurthy (Zurich and Berlin: LIT Verlag, 2013), pp. 21–69

Hutchisson, James, ed., *Edgar Allan Poe: Beyond Gothicism* (Newark: University of Delaware Press, 2011)

Hwang, Haewon, *London's Underground Spaces: Representing the Victorian City, 1840–1915* (Edinburgh: Edinburgh University Press, 2013)

Irwin, Robert, *The Alhambra* (London: Profile Books, 2004)

James, Henry, *Complete Stories 1892–1898* (New York: Library of America, 1996)

— *The American Scene* (London: Chapman and Hall, 1907)

— *The American Scene*, ed. by Peter Collister (Cambridge: Cambridge University Press, 2019)

— 'Emile Zola', in *Documents of Literary Realism*, ed. by George Becker (Princeton: Princeton University Press, 1963)

Jameson, Fredric, *Antinomies of Realism* (London and New York: Verso, 2013)

— *Archaeologies of the Future: The Desire Called Utopia and Other Science Fictions* (London: Verso, 2005)

Jaouad, Hédi, *Browning upon Arabia: A Moveable Feast* (Cham: Palgrave, 2018)

Jespersen, John, 'Originality and Jones' *The Grammar of Ornament* of 1856', *Journal of Design History*, 21.2 (2008), 143–53

Jones, Owen, *The Alhambra Court in the Crystal Palace* (London: Crystal Palace Library and Bradbury & Evans, 1854)

— *The Grammar of Ornament* (New York: Van Nostrand Reinhold, 1972 [1856])

Kant, Immanuel, *Critique of Judgement*, trans. by James Creed Meredith, ed. by Nicholas Walker (Oxford: Oxford University Press, 2007)

Kanzler, Katja, 'Architecture, Writing, and Vulnerable Signification in Herman Melville's "I and My Chimney"', *Amerikastudien/American Studies*, 54.4 (2009), 583–601

Karlinsky, Simon, *The Sexual Labyrinth of Nikolai Gogol* (Chicago: University of Chicago Press, 1996)

Kaufmann, David, 'Beyond Use, Within Reason: Adorno, Benjamin and the Question of Theology', *New German Critique*, 83 (2001), 151–73

Kay, James Phillips, *The Moral and Physical Condition of the Working Classes Employed in the Cotton Manufacture in Manchester* (London: James Ridgeway, 1832 [1st edn])

Kayser, Wolfgang, *The Grotesque in Art and Literature*, trans. by Ulrich Weisstein (Gloucester, MA: Peter Smith, 1968)

Kern, Stephen, *The Culture of Time and Space 1880–1918* (Cambridge, MA: Harvard University Press, 1983)

Keyes, William, 'Meditations on Form and Meaning in Gogol's "On Present-Day Architecture"', *Russian History*, 37 (2010), 378–88

Kilcup, Karen, ed., *Soft Canons* (Iowa City: University of Iowa Press, 1999)

Kingsley, Charles, *Alton Locke* (Oxford: Oxford University Press, 1983)

— *The Water-Babies* (Oxford: Oxford University Press, 2013)

Klotz, Michael, ʻ*Dombey and Son* and the "Parlour on Wheels"', *Dickens Studies Annual*, 40 (2009), 61–79

Kochhar-Lindgren, Gray, *Urban Arabesques: Philosophy, Hong Kong, Transversality* (London: Rowman and Littlefield, 2020)

Kohlmaier, George, *Houses of Glass: A Nineteenth-Century Building Type*, trans. by Barna von Sartory (Cambridge, MA: MIT Press, 1986)

Koolhaas, Rem, *Delirious New York: A Retroactive Manifesto for Manhattan* (New York: Monacelli Press, 1994)

Koolhaas, Rem, Bruce Mau and OMA, *S, M, L, XL*, 2nd edn (New York: Monacelli Press, 1998)

Krauss, Rosalind, *The Optical Unconscious* (Cambridge, MA: MIT Press, 1993)

Lacan, Jacques, *The Seminar of Jacques Lacan, Book XI: The Four Fundamental Principles of Psychoanalysis*, trans. by Alan Sheridan (London: Norton, 1981)

Larkin, Brian, 'The Politics and Poetics of Infrastructure', *Annual Review of Anthropology*, 42 (2013), 327–43

Leckie, Barbara, *Open Houses: Poverty, the Novel, and the Architectural Idea in Nineteenth-Century Britain* (Philadelphia: University of Pennsylvania Press, 2018)

Lefebvre, Henri, *The Production of Space*, trans. by Donald Nicholson-Smith (Oxford: Blackwell, 1991)

Lehan, Richard, *The City in Literature: An Intellectual and Cultural History* (Berkeley and Los Angeles: University of California Press, 1998)

Lenman, Robin, *Artists and Society in Germany: 1850–1914* (Manchester: Manchester University Press, 1997)

Leonard, Anne, ed., *Arabesque Without End: Across Music and the Arts, from Faust to Shahrazad* (New York: Routledge, 2022)

Lewis, Linda, *Dickens, His Parables, and His Reader* (Columbia: University of Missouri Press, 2011)

Liggins, Emma, *George Gissing, the Working Woman, and Urban Culture* (Abingdon: Routledge, 2017 [2006])

Lincoln, Bruce, *Sunlight at Midnight: St Petersburg and the Rise of Modern Russia* (New York: Basic Books, 2000)

Lindner, Christoph, *Fictions of Commodity Culture: From the Victorian to the Postmodern* (Aldershot: Ashgate, 2003)

— *Imagining New York City* (Oxford: Oxford University Press, 2015)

Lloyd, David, *Under Representation: The Racial Regime of Aesthetics* (New York: Fordham University Press, 2019)

Loeb, Lori Anne, *Consuming Angels: Advertising and Victorian Women* (Oxford: Oxford University Press, 1994)

Loos, Adolf, 'Ornament and Crime' [1908], in *Crime and Ornament: The Arts and Popular Culture in the Shadow of Adolf Loos*, ed. by Bernie Miller and Melony Ward (Toronto: YYZ Books, 2002), pp. 29–36

Lowe, Brigid, 'Elizabeth Gaskell', in *The Cambridge Companion to English Novelists*, ed. by Adrian Poole (Cambridge: Cambridge University Press, 2009), pp. 193–209

Lukács, Georg, *Writer and Critic*, ed. and trans. by Arthur Kahn (London: Merlin, 1970)

Mabbott, T. O., ed., *The Collected Works of Edgar Allan Poe, Vol. 1: Poems* (Cambridge, MA: Belknap Press, 1969)

McCombie, Elizabeth, *Mallarmé and Debussy: Unheard Music, Unseen Text* (Oxford: Oxford University Press, 2003)

McGowan, John, *Democracy's Children: Intellectuals and the Rise of Cultural Politics* (Ithaca, NY: Cornell University Press, 2002)

McKee, Patricia, *Reading Constellations: Urban Modernity in Victorian Fiction* (Oxford: Oxford University Press, 2014)

MacPhee, Graham, *The Architecture of the Visible: Technology and Urban Visual Culture* (London: Continuum, 2002)

Mancini, Michelle, 'Demons on the Rooftops, Gypsies in the Streets: The "Secret Intelligence" of *Dombey and Son*', *Dickens Studies Annual*, 30 (2001), 113–40

Marcus, Sharon, *Apartment Stories: City and Home in Nineteenth-Century Paris and London* (Berkeley, Los Angeles and London: University of California Press, 1999)

Marcus, Steven, *Dickens: From Pickwick to Dombey* (London: Chatto and Windus, 1965)

Marriott, John, *The Other Empire: Metropolis, India and Progress in the Colonial Imagination* (Manchester: Manchester University Press, 2003)

Martin, Amy, 'Blood Transfusions: Constructions of Irish Racial Difference, the English Working Class, and Revolutionary Possibility in the Work of Carlyle and Engels', *Victorian Literature and Culture*, 32.1 (2004), 83–102

Marx, Karl, *Economic and Political Manuscripts*, in *Early Writings*, trans. by Rodney Livingstone and Gregor Benton (Harmondsworth: Penguin, 1975), pp. 279–400

— *Capital*, ed. by David McLellan (Oxford: Oxford University Press, 1995)

— *Der historische Materialismus*, vol. 1, ed. by Siegfried Landshut and Jacob Peter Mayer (Leipzig: Kröner, 1932)

Matus, Jill, *Shock, Memory and the Unconscious in Victorian Fiction* (Cambridge: Cambridge University Press, 2009)

Melville, Herman, 'I and My Chimney', in *Billy Budd, Sailor and Selected Tales* (Oxford: Oxford University Press, 1997), pp. 248–78

— *Moby-Dick* (Harmondsworth: Penguin, 1992)

Menninghaus, Winfried, *In Praise of Nonsense: Kant and Bluebeard*, trans. by Henry Pickford (Stanford: Stanford University Press, 1999)

Meyer, Susan, 'Colonialism and the Figurative Strategy of *Jane Eyre*', *Victorian Studies*, 33.2 (1990), 247–68

Miller, Andrew, *Novels Behind Glass: Commodity Culture and Victorian Narrative* (Cambridge: Cambridge University Press, 1995)

Miller, J. Hillis, 'The Figure in the Carpet', *Poetics Today*, 1.3 (1980), 107–18

— 'The Topography of Jealousy in *Our Mutual Friend*', in *Dickens Refigured: Bodies, Desires and Other Histories*, ed. by John Schad (Manchester: Manchester University Press, 1996), pp. 218–36

Miller, Michael, *The Bon Marché: Bourgeois Culture and the Department Store, 1869–1920* (Princeton: Princeton University Press, 1981)

Mirrlees, Hope, *Paris: A Poem* (Richmond: Hogarth Press, 1919)

Moore, Ben, 'Architecture', in *The Edinburgh Companion to Charles Dickens and the Arts*, ed. by Juliet John and Claire Wood (Edinburgh: Edinburgh University Press, forthcoming 2024)

— 'The Eyes of the Other: Mary Shelley's *Frankenstein* and the Uncanny', in *The Bloomsbury Handbook to Literature and Psychoanalysis*, ed. by Jeremy Tambling (London: Bloomsbury, 2023), pp. 35–48.

— 'Invisible Architecture and Social Space in *North and South*', *Gaskell Journal*, 32 (2018), 17–35

— '"When I went to Lunnon town sirs": Transformation and the Threshold in the Dickensian City', *Dickens Quarterly*, 29.4 (2012), 336–49

Moretti, Franco, *Atlas of the European Novel 1800–1900* (London: Verso, 1998)

— *Signs Taken for Wonders*, trans. by David Forgacs (London: Verso, 2005)

Morrison, Toni, 'Unspeakable Things Unspoken: The Afro-American Presence in American Literature', *Michigan Quarterly Review*, 28.1 (1989), 1–34

Mukherjee, Ankhi, *Unseen City: The Psychic Lives of the Urban Poor* (Cambridge: Cambridge University Press, 2022)

Murphy, Douglas, *The Architecture of Failure* (Alresford: Zero Books, 2012)

Nelson, Brian, *Zola and the Bourgeoisie: A Study of Themes and Techniques in Les Rougon-Macquart* (Totowa, NJ: Barnes and Noble, 1983)

Nesbet, Anne, 'Gogol, Belyi, Eisenstein and the Architecture of the Future', *Russian Review*, 65 (July 2006), 491–511

Nietzsche, Friedrich, *The Genealogy of Morals*, trans. by Douglas Smith (Oxford: Oxford University Press, 1996 [1887])

Nord, Deborah Epstein, *Walking the Victorian Streets: Women, Representation, and the City* (Ithaca, NY: Cornell University Press, 1995)

Panerai, Philippe, Jean Castex, Jean-Charles Depaule and Ivor Samuels, *Urban Forms: The Death and Life of the Urban Block*, trans. by Olga Samuels (Oxford: Architectural Press, 2004)

Parkinson-Bailey, John J., *Manchester: An Architectural History* (Manchester: Manchester University Press, 2000)

Phillips, Samuel, *Guide to the Crystal Palace and Park* (London: Crystal Palace Library and Bradbury and Evans, 1854)

Philpotts, Trey, 'Dickens, the Metropolis and the Railway: Displacement or Progress?', *Dickens Quarterly*, 31.4 (2014), 334–42

Piggott, Gillian, *Dickens and Benjamin: Moments of Revelation, Fragments of Modernity* (Farnham: Ashgate, 2012)

Piggott, Jan, *Palace of the People: The Crystal Palace at Sydenham 1854–1936* (London: Hurst and Company, 2004)

Pike, David, *Subterranean Cities: The World Beneath Paris and London, 1800–1945* (Ithaca, NY: Cornell University Press, 2005)

Pile, Steve, 'Sleepwalking in the Modern City: Walter Benjamin and Sigmund Freud in the World of Dreams', in *A Companion to the City*, ed. by Gary Bridge and Sophie Watson (Oxford: Blackwell, 2000), pp. 75–86

Poe, Edgar Allan, *Selected Tales* (Oxford: Oxford University Press, 1998)

— 'The Philosophy of Furniture', *Burton's Gentleman's Magazine*, 6.5 (May 1840), 243–5

Poovey, Mary, *Making a Social Body: British Cultural Formation, 1830–1864* (Chicago: University of Chicago Press, 1995)

Potter, Jonathan, *Discourses of Vision in Nineteenth-Century Britain: Seeing, Thinking, Writing* (Palgrave: Cham, 2018)

Pugin, Augustus Welby, *Contrasts: or, A Parallel between the Noble Edifices of the Fourteenth and Fifteenth Centuries and Similar Buildings of the Present Day; Shewing the Present Decay of Taste* (London: n.p., 1836)

Purkiss, Diane, *The Witch in History: Early Modern and Twentieth-Century Representations* (London: Routledge, 1996)

Puskar, Jason, *Accident Society: Fiction, Collectivity, and the Production of Chance* (Palo Alto: Stanford University Press, 2012)

Rancière, Jacques, *Aisthesis: Scenes from the Aesthetic Regime of Art*, trans. by Zakir Paul (London and New York: Verso, 2013)

— *The Future of the Image*, trans. by Gregory Elliott (London: Verso, 2007)

— *Mute Speech*, trans. by James Swenson (New York: Columbia University Press, 2011)

— *The Politics of Aesthetics: The Distribution of the Sensible*, ed. and trans. by Gabriel Rockhill (London and New York: Bloomsbury, 2004)

Rancière, Jacques, Gavin Arnall, Laura Gandolfi and Enea Zaramella, 'Aesthetics and Politics Revisited: An Interview with Jacques Rancière', *Critical Inquiry*, 38.2 (2012), 289–97

Rennie, Nicholas, 'Benjamin and Zola: Narrative, the Individual and Crowds in an Age of Mass Production', *Comparative Literature Studies*, 33.4 (1996), 396–413

Reynolds, Nicole, *Building Romanticism: Literature and Architecture in Nineteenth-Century Britain* (Ann Arbor: University of Michigan Press, 2010)

Richards, Thomas, *The Commodity Culture of Victorian England: Advertising and Spectacle, 1851–1914* (London: Verso, 1991)

Rowe, William, *Through Gogol's Looking Glass: Reverse Vision, False Focus, and Precarious Logic* (New York: New York University Press, 1976)

The Royal Commission for the Chicago Exhibition 1893: Official Catalogue of the British Section (London: William Clowes and Sons, n.d.)

Royle, Nicholas, *The Uncanny* (Manchester: Manchester University Press, 2003)

Ruskin, John, *The Correspondence of John Ruskin and Charles Eliot Norton*, ed. by John Bradley and Ian Ousby (Cambridge: Cambridge University Press, 1987)

— *The Stones of Venice, Volume I* (London: Smith, Elder and Co., 1851)

— *The Stones of Venice, Volume II* (Boston: Estes and Lauriat, 1851)

Salingaros, Nikos, *Anti-Architecture and Deconstruction* (Solingen, Germany: Umbau-Verlag, 2004)

Salotto, Eleanor, '*Frankenstein* and Dis(re)membered Identity', *Journal of Narrative Technique*, 24.3 (1994), 190–211

Sassen, Saskia, *The Global City: New York, London, Tokyo* (Princeton: Princeton University Press, 1991)

Schivelbusch, Wolfgang, *The Railway Journey: The Industrialization of Time and Space in the Nineteenth Century* (Berkeley and Los Angeles: University of California Press, 1986)

Schlegel, Friedrich, *The Aesthetic and Miscellaneous Works of Frederick von Schlegel*, trans. by E. J. Millington (London: Henry G. Bohn, 1849)

— *Gespräch über die Poesie* (Stuttgart: J. B. Metzlersche, 1968)

Schwarzbach, F. S., *Dickens and the City* (London: Athlone Press, 1979)

Scott, Walter, 'On the Supernatural in Fictitious Composition; and Particularly on the Works of Ernest Theodore William Hoffman', *Foreign Quarterly Review*, 1 (July 1827), 60–98

Sealts, Merton, 'Herman Melville's "I and My Chimney"', *American Literature*, 13.2 (1941), 142–54

Sen, Sambudha, *London, Radical Culture and the Making of the Dickensian Aesthetic* (Columbus: Ohio State University Press, 2012)

Sennet, Richard, *The Conscience of the Eye: The Design and Social Life of Cities* (New York: Norton, 1990)

Shapiro, Gavriel, *Nikolai Gogol and the Baroque Cultural Heritage* (University Park: Pennsylvania State University Press, 1993)

Shelley, Mary, *Frankenstein* (London: Norton, 2012 [1818])

Shelston, Alan, 'Nell, Alice and Lizzie: Three Sisters Amidst the Grotesque', in *Master Narratives: Tellers and Telling in the English Novel*, ed. by Richard Gravil (Aldershot: Ashgate, 2001), pp. 148–73

Sherwin, Paul, '*Frankenstein*: Creation as Catastrophe', *PMLA*, 96.5 (1981), 883–903

Slater, Isaac, *A Plan of Manchester and Salford with Vicinities* (1848), Manchester City Council archive

Smith, Grahame, *Dickens and the Dream of Cinema* (Manchester: Manchester University Press, 2003)

Spivak, Gayatri Chakravorty, *An Aesthetic Education in the Era of Globalization* (Cambridge, MA: Harvard University Press, 2012)

Spurr, David, *Architecture and Modern Literature* (Ann Arbor: University of Michigan Press, 2012)

Star, Susan Leigh, 'The Ethnography of Infrastructure', *American Behavioral Scientist*, 43.3 (1999), 377–91

Steebert, Alf, '"Steam of Consciousness": Technology and Sensation in Dickens' Railway Sketches', *Philament*, 14 (2009), 91–115

Steinlight, Emily, *Populating the Novel: Literary Form and the Politics of Surplus Life* (Ithaca, NY: Cornell University Press, 2018)

Surridge, Lisa, *Bleak Houses: Marital Violence in Victorian Fiction* (Athens: Ohio University Press, 2005)

Tambling, Jeremy, 'Death and Modernity in *Dombey and Son*', *Essays in Criticism*, 43.4 (1993), 308–29

— *Dickens, Violence and the Modern State* (Houndmills: Macmillan, 1995)

— *Going Astray: Dickens and London* (London: Pearson, 2009)

—, ed., *The Palgrave Encyclopedia of Urban Literary Studies* (Palgrave: Cham, 2022).

Thornton, Sara, *Advertising, Subjectivity and the Nineteenth-Century Novel: Dickens, Balzac and the Language of the Walls* (Houndmills: Palgrave Macmillan, 2009)

Tillotson, Kathleen, *Novels of the Eighteen-Forties* (London: Clarendon Press, 1954)

Tucker, Janet, 'Genre Fragmentation in Nikolai Gogol's "The Overcoat"', *Canadian–American Slavic Studies*, 46 (2012), 83–97

Unwin, Simon, *Analysing Architecture*, 2nd edn (London: Routledge, 2003)

Vanoosthuyse, François, 'Zola dans l'Optique d'Eisenstein', *Les Cahiers Naturalistes*, 87 (2013), 311–29

Vidler, Anthony, *The Architectural Uncanny: Essays in the Modern Unhomely* (Cambridge, MA: MIT Press, 1992)

Walls, Alison, *The Sentiment of Spending: Intimate Relationships and the Consumerist Environment in the Works of Zola, Rachilde, Maupassant, and Huysmans* (New York: Peter Lang, 2008)

Wetherill, P. M., 'Flaubert, Zola, Proust and Paris: An Evolving City in a Shifting Text', in *Émile Zola*, ed. by Harold Bloom (Broomall, PA: Chelsea House, 2004), pp. 151–64

Whitehead, Colson, *Harlem Shuffle* (London: Fleet, 2021)

Whiteley, Giles, *The Aesthetics of Space in Nineteenth-Century British Literature, 1843–1907* (Edinburgh: Edinburgh University Press, 2020)

Wigley, Mark, *White Walls, Designer Dresses: The Fashioning of Modern Architecture* (Cambridge, MA: MIT Press, 1995)

Williams, Raymond, *The Country and the City* (London: Hogarth Press, 1985)

— *Culture and Society: 1780–1950* (London: Chatto and Windus, 1967)

— *Marxism and Literature* (Oxford: Oxford University Press, 1977)

Wohlfarth, Irving, '"Construction Has the Role of the Subconscious": Phantasmagorias of the Master Builder (with Constant Reference to Giedion, Weber, Nietzsche, Ibsen, and Benjamin)', in *Nietzsche and the Architecture of Our Minds*, ed. by Alexandre Koskka and Irving Wohlfarth (Los Angeles: Getty Research Institute, 1999), pp. 141–98

Wolff, Janet, 'Manchester, Capital of the Nineteenth Century', *Journal of Classical Sociology*, 13.1 (2013), 69–86

Wolfreys, Julian, *Literature, in Theory: Tropes, Subjectivities, Responses and Responsibilities* (London: Continuum, 2010)

Woollen, Geoff, 'Zola's Halles, A *Grande Surface* Before Their Time', *Romance Studies*, 18.1 (2000), 21–30

Wright, Frank Lloyd, *An Organic Architecture: The Architecture of Democracy* (Cambridge, MA: MIT Press, 1970)

Wyman, Alina, 'The Specter of Freedom: *Ressentiment* and Dostoevskij's *Notes from Underground*', *Studies in East European Thought*, 59.1–2 (2007), 119–40

Yancy, George, *Look, a White!: Philosophical Essays on Whiteness* (Philadelphia: Temple University Press, 2012)

Zemka, Sue, 'Brief Encounters: Urban Street Scenes in Gaskell's Manchester', *ELH*, 76.3 (2009), 793–819

Zola, Émile, *The Belly of Paris*, trans. by Brian Nelson (Oxford: Oxford University Press, 2007)

— *The Kill*, trans. by Brian Nelson (Oxford: Oxford University Press, 2004)

— *L'Assommoir*, trans. by Margaret Mauldon (Oxford: Oxford University Press, 1995)

— *La Bête Humaine*, trans. by Roger Pearson (Oxford: Oxford University Press, 1996)
— *The Ladies' Paradise*, trans. by Brian Nelson (Oxford: Oxford University Press, 1995)
— *The Masterpiece*, trans. by Thomas Walton (Oxford: Oxford University Press, 1993)

Index

Adorno, Theodor, 23, 24, 88–9, 219
advertising, 23, 102, 143–6, 157, 185, 210
arabesque, 11, 13, 21, 26, 28, 118, 133, 136, 157, 204, 221
arabesque city, 4, 167, 172–98
Aragon, Louis, 234
architecture
  Alexandrian, 158
  and anti-architecture, 2, 68–9, 89, 96, 102, 122
  and arabesque, 133, 172, 175, 176–7, 181–2; *see also* arabesque
  and capital, 37, 43, 50–1, 94–5, 110, 113, 118–19, 126–7, 131, 134, 160, 165–6, 237–8
  and engineering, 3, 6–7, 70, 75, 159, 229
  and exclusion, 43–9, 51, 63, 77, 109, 124
  and language, 18–19, 21, 92, 160, 162, 184, 187, 196, 198, 234
  and literature, 3–4, 5, 10, 11–19, 25–7, 69, 110, 116, 122, 156–9, 165, 172, 228
  and urban literary studies, 20–8
  Arabian, 155, 158
  architectural uncanny *see* Vidler, Anthony
  architectural unconscious *see* unconscious

bourgeois domestic architecture, 60–1, 69, 75, 90–5, 116–22, 186, 212–15
Byzantine, 154, 158
commodity architecture, 109, 121–2, 126, 131, 134–6, 160
Egyptian, 19, 147, 153–5, 158, 176, 181, 232–3
ferrovitreous, 3, 4, 7, 9, 13, 15, 75, 109, 115, 125, 126, 127–8, 133, 142, 156, 159, 222, 232; *see also* Crystal Palace; department store; Zola, Émile
Gothic *see* Gothic
Greek, 118, 154, 158, 232
in Hegel, 62, 175, 176–7, 184
invisible architecture, 1–11, 13, 22, 25, 27, 28, 37–8, 42, 50, 90, 92, 95, 96, 103, 111, 125, 133, 136–7, 142–3, 146, 150, 153, 157, 173, 178, 184–5, 198, 203, 207–8, 217, 221, 224, 228, 234–6; (in)visible architecture, 38
Japanese, 147
modern *see* modernism
Moorish, 181, 183, 187, 188
Norman, 161
Persian, 230
Roman, 148, 155, 158, 232
Second Empire style, 110, 111, 118–19

architecture (*cont.*)
  Turkish, 155, 232
  see also cathedral; cellars; Gogol, Nikolai; Haussman, Baron Georges-Eugène; phalanstery; railway; Semper, Gottfried; skyscraper; World Exhibitions
Agathacleous, Tanya, 22
Alhambra, 179–84, 186, 188
Althusser, Louis, 45, 206, 220
Arabian Nights, 113–14, 119
Armstrong, Isobel, 79
Art Nouveau see Jugendstil
Asmodeus, 12, 18, 20, 21, 77, 235
assemblage, 2, 159, 161, 164
Atget, Eugène, 123

Babel, tower of, 72, 73, 75, 133, 232
Bachelard, Gaston, 21, 22, 49–50, 60, 62–3, 186
Bakhtin, Mikhail, 16
Balzac, Honoré de, 85
  Père Goriot, 113
Barthes, Roland, 11
Bataille, Georges, 160
Baudelaire, Charles, 2, 22–3, 25, 71, 114, 115, 143, 192
  'Danse Macabre', 212
  'Le Cygne', 159–60
  'Le Soleil', 115
Baudrillard, Jean, 166
Belenky, Masha, 117
Bely, Andrei, 149, 196
Benjamin, Walter, 22–5, 26, 27, 45, 60–1, 62–3, 74, 79, 81, 86–9, 93, 123, 143, 174, 175, 182, 190, 191, 213, 214–15, 231
  and allegory, 14, 235
  and aura, 102
  and fashion, 125, 214
  and film, 86–8, 158
  and fore-history, 71, 121, 174
  and the dialectical image, 52, 86, 152, 164, 183
  and the flâneur, 116, 130, 158, 192
  and the fragment, 20, 123
  and the monad, 71, 75, 133
  Arcades Project, 12–14, 17, 22–3, 52, 59, 69, 72, 75, 112–13, 114, 116–18, 119, 125–6, 133, 134, 149, 155, 212, 216, 219, 228–9, 234
  'Hashish in Marseilles', 25
  'On the Concept of History', 24–5, 230
  optical unconscious see unconscious
  The Origin of German Tragic Drama, 95, 231
Berg, William J., 112
Bergdoll, Barry, 141–2
Berman, Marshall, 15, 16, 23, 52
Bernard, Claude, 160
Bernheimer, Charles, 195, 196
Bloch, Ernst, 166
  The Spirit of Utopia, 147–9
Boileau, L. A., 127
Bowlby, Rachel, 131
Briggs, Asa, 1, 20
Brombert, Victor, 195, 196
Brontë, Charlotte, *Jane Eyre*, 211–12, 223–4
Brooks, Peter, 11, 122
Browne, Hablot, 90, 99
Bryullov, Karl, *The Last Day of Pompeii*, 146–7
Burke, Edmund, 222–3
Byron, Lord George Gordon, 157

Calvino, Italo, 4
Carlyle, Thomas, 42
  Chartism, 48–9
cathedral, 18–19, 26, 157, 160
  Cologne, 151–2, 156–7, 158, 162

Strasbourg, 151
Rochester, 161
see also Gothic
Cather, Willa, 'Behind the Singer Tower', 229–30, 239
cellars, 2, 16, 26, 49, 60, 89, 186, 221, 229, 230
  cellar-dwelling, 4, 11, 37, 46–63, 117, 210, 217, 230
  and garrets, 20–1, 48
Certeau, Michel de, 20–1, 22, 113, 166
Cervantes, Miguel de, 175, 179, 196
Cézanne, Paul, 146
Chadwick, Edwin, 40
Chapman, John Gadsby, 190
Chartism, 47–9
Chernychevsky, Nikolai, *What Is to Be Done?*, 14–16, 232
Chomsky, Noam, 187
Cole, Teju, *Open City*, 229, 233–4, 237
colportage, 81, 117, 121, 156;
  see also montage
Conrad, Joseph, *Heart of Darkness*, 17
Crary, Jonathan, 96
Cruikshank, George, 12
Crystal Palace, 7, 11, 12, 13–14, 14–16, 75
  at Sydenham 5–11, 14, 15, 152, 179, 181–4
Cubism, 148

Danaë, 114
Darwin, Charles, 4
Debord, Guy, 130
  and the spectacle, 120–1, 127, 131, 136
Debussy, Claude, 178
Deleuze, Gilles, 177, 217
Deleuze, Gilles, and Felix Guattari
  de- and re-territorialisation, 112
  the molar, 1

department store, 2, 11, 75, 119, 122, 125–7, 136, 155, 216
  Bon Marché, 126, 127, 215, 217
  Samaritaine, 128, 217
  see also Zola, Émile
Derrida, Jacques, 72, 80, 160, 207
  the parergon, 91–2, 94, 95, 158, 191
Dickens, Charles, 2, 21, 48, 59, 63, 68–9, 102–3, 109, 186, 218, 221
  'A Flight', 74, 76
  A Tale of Two Cities, 235
  Bleak House, 16, 220–1
  Dombey and Son, 6, 27–8, 39, 42, 53, 59, 63, 68–79, 84, 89–90, 90–5, 100, 115, 123, 124, 131, 133, 177, 178, 186, 198, 214, 221–4, 229, 232, 235
  'George Silverman's Explanation', 47, 49–50, 54
  Great Expectations, 214
  Hard Times, 100
  Martin Chuzzlewit, 74
  Our Mutual Friend, 27–8, 63, 68–9, 80–90, 95–102, 125, 152, 161, 206, 220, 221–2
  The Mystery of Edwin Drood, 160–1
  The Old Curiosity Shop, 88–9, 98–9, 222
  The Pickwick Papers, 220
Diderot, Denis, 175
Disraeli, Benjamin, *Sybil*, 47, 55, 210
Doesburg, Theo van, 13
Doré, Gustave, 6, 72, 77, 184
Dos Passos, John, *Manhattan Transfer*, 229, 230–3, 235, 239
Dostoevsky, Fyodor
  Crime and Punishment, 197
  Notes from Underground, 14–16, 21, 46, 173, 195

dreams, 3, 48, 49, 61, 74, 80, 82, 83, 92–3, 238
  and awakening, 25, 175, 238
  and cinema, 88
  and unintelligibility, 72, 74–5
  city as dreamworld, 22–3, 59, 81, 112, 114, 116, 119–20, 121, 124, 131, 132–3, 136, 181, 222, 232–3
  collective dream, 147
  daydreaming, 21, 197
  dreamlike, 2, 74, 112, 131, 136, 178, 191
  dream-vision, 161
  see also utopia
Dyer, Richard, 215

Egg, Augustus, 76
Eiffel, Gustave, 127
Eiffel Tower, 151, 162
Eisenstein, Sergei, 119–20
  and montage, 110–11, 114, 119, 129, 130, 136
  Nonindifferent Nature, 133, 149, 153
Elfenbein, Andrew, 91
Eliot, George, 4, 28, 179, 181, 184–8, 190
  'The Lifted Veil', 187–8
Ellison, David, 90,
Emerson, Ralph Waldo, 18
Engels, Friedrich, 27, 37, 39, 43–6, 47, 48, 50, 52, 55, 57, 208, 209–11, 212, 221, 230
Eskilson, Stephen, 13
Éveno, Bertrand, 178
Expressionism, 148

Fanger, Donald, 149
Ferry, Kathryn, 181
flâneur *see* Benjamin, Walter
Flaubert, Gustave, 19, 160
Foster, Hal, 3

Foucault, Michel, 4, 18, 40, 70, 215, 218, 219
  The Order of Things, 111
Fourier, Charles, 134, 216–17; *see also* phalanstery
Fra Angelico, 153
Frazier, Melissa, 176
Freedgood, Elaine, 53
Freud, Sigmund, 43, 45, 55, 56, 59, 74, 80–3, 87, 92, 97, 205
  and Rome, 96
  and trauma, 156
  see also unconscious
Friedrich Wilhem IV, 152
Fuller, Loie, 178
Fusso, Susanne, 156, 176

Garratt, James, 146
Gaskell, Elizabeth, 2, 4, 27, 37, 38, 50, 134, 186, 221, 229, 230
  Mary Barton, 38, 47–9, 51–2, 52–63, 97, 109, 117, 136, 186, 211–12, 217, 219, 236
  North and South, 46, 90, 210–11, 212–15, 222
Gautier, Théophile, 17
Gehlawat, Monika, 204
Gesamtkunstwerk, 13, 146–7
Giedion, Sigfried, 3, 5, 11, 13, 25, 70, 75, 112, 117, 127, 159; *see also* unconscious
Gilbert, Pamela, 218
Gilman, Charlotte Perkins, 28, 188
  'The Yellow Wallpaper', 192–4, 196
Ginsburg, Michal, 94
Gissing, George, *The Nether World*, 5–11, 14, 210, 212
Glacier Window Decoration, 143–6
Goddard, Kevin, 206
Goethe, Johann Wolfgang von, 52, 151, 172
  'von Arabesken', 175

Gogol, Nikolai, 28, 119, 181, 188
  Arabesques, 142, 146, 149, 156, 166–7, 172, 176, 195
  'On Present-Day Architecture', 132–3, 142, 149–56, 157–8, 160, 161, 163, 166–7, 181, 221, 232
  'The Overcoat', 176, 194–8
Goldsmith, Kenneth, 228–9
Gong, Haomin, 174
Gordon, Rae Beth, 177
Gothic, 3, 196
  architecture, 133, 141–67, 191, 204
  cathedral, 2, 7, 11, 13, 18–19, 26–7, 28, 142–3, 147–8, 150–3, 156–7, 160, 161; see also cathedral
  nationalism, 142
  tale, 195
Graphic (newspaper), 143
Great Exhibition see Crystal Palace; World Exhibitions
Gropius, Walter, 203
grotesque, 122, 173–4, 188, 189–91, 193, 196; see also arabesque
Guattari, Felix see Deleuze, Gilles, and Felix Guattari
Gutenberg, Johannes, 157

Hamon, Philippe, 25–6, 72, 112, 116
Hansberry, Lorraine, 238
Haussmann, Baron Georges-Eugène, 11, 69, 109, 111, 113, 118, 125–6, 160
Havik, Klaske, 27
Hegel, Georg Wilhelm Friedrich, 62, 160
  Aesthetics, 176–7, 184
Heidegger, Martin, 186
Hennessy, Susie, 129

Hewitt, Martin, 40
Heynen, Hilda, 174
Hoffman, E. T. A., 189, 196
Hogarth, William, 173
Holbein, Hans, 86
Hollier, Denis, 71–2, 102
Hong Kong, 177, 178
Hughes, Langston, 238
Hugo, Victor, 28, 142, 156, 166
  Notre Dame de Paris, 18–19, 156–60, 164
Huysmans, J. K., 173
Hwang, Haewon, 20

ideology, 1, 2, 3, 5, 12, 28, 38, 41–2, 45, 76, 109, 110, 129, 132, 134–6, 203, 205–6, 207, 212, 215, 221–2, 224; see also utopia
imperialism, 8, 9, 186, 205, 223–4
and literature, 17
Impressionism, 148
infrastructure, 2
invisible architecture see architecture
Irwin, Robert, 183–4

James, Henry, 28
  The American Scene, 142, 162–6, 229, 233
  'The Figure in the Carpet', 178–9, 193–4
Jameson, Fredric, 11, 111, 217
Jerrold, Blanchold, 72
Jones, Owen, 28
  The Grammar of Ornament, 174, 179–89
Jourdain, Frantz, 128
Jugendstil, 22, 71, 175
Jung, Carl, 178

Kandinksy, Wassily, 21
Kant, Immanuel, 172–3, 175, 176, 185, 187, 194, 196

Kay, James, 27, 37–43, 44, 45, 46, 50, 51, 56, 123, 208–9, 212, 222
Kayser, Wolfgang, 174
Kern, Stephen, 71
Kierkegaard, Søren, 196, 219
Kimball, Francis, 165
Kingsley, Charles
  Alton Locke, 218–20
  The Water-Babies, 218
Klotz, Michael, 75, 76, 77, 78
Kochhar-Lingren, Gray, 177
Koolhaas, Rem, 153, 166

Lacan, Jacques, 80, 82, 205
  and the gaze, 85–90, 101–2, 161
  and the real, 206, 208, 217
Lao Tze (Laozi), 148
Le Corbusier, 15, 117, 181, 203, 212
Leckie, Barbara, 11, 117
Lefebvre, Henri, 21, 37–8, 40, 43–4, 46, 54, 109, 142, 148, 186
Lehan, Richard, 112
Lenman, Robin, 151–2
Leo X (Pope), 174
Leonard, Anne, 177
Les Halles, 115, 159–60, 164
Lewes, G. H., 185
Lindner, Christoph, 57–9, 166, 228, 229
Loeb, Lori, 145
London, 2, 5, 6, 12, 20, 21, 26, 27–8, 39, 53, 70, 72, 141, 191, 210, 212
  and the Alhambra, 182, 184
  as Darkest London, 16–17
  see also Dickens, Charles
Loos, Adolf, 148
Louvre, 9, 119
Lukács, Georg, 110, 120
Lyobomudry circle, 150

Macaulay, Thomas, 72
McCaw, Stevenson and Orr *see* Glacier Window Decoration
Mckee, Patricia, 25, 81, 86
MacPhee, Graham, 22, 120
Manchester, 27, 37–63, 123, 131, 136, 208–10, 213, 217, 221, 222
  and the Irish, 42–3
  as 'shock city', 37, 153
  see also Gaskell, Elizabeth; Engels, Friedrich; Kay, James
Marcus, Sharon, 12, 117
Marcus, Steven, 70
Marx, Karl, 24, 39, 41, 50–2, 62–3, 89, 95, 160
Marxist, 23, 24, 93, 147
medievalism, 13, 141–2, 143–6, 152, 153, 155
  the medieval church, 156
  see also Gothic
Matisse, Henri, 178
Melville, Herman, 233
  'Bartleby the Scrivener', 196
  'I and My Chimney', 97
  Moby-Dick, 203–8, 210, 211, 215, 217, 221
Menninghaus, Winfried, 172
Meyer, Susan, 223–4
Mies van der Rohe, Ludwig, 7
Miller, J. Hillis, 80, 178–9
Miller, Michael, 127–8
Mirrlees, Hope, 216–17
modernism
  in architecture, 3, 5, 7, 15, 19, 26, 28, 72, 117, 133, 147, 203, 212, 214–15
  in literature, 19, 26, 111, 216–17, 231
modernity, 2, 14, 16, 18, 21, 22, 26–7, 28, 61, 69–70, 72, 74, 205, 215, 228, 230
  and Gothic, 13, 141–67

and postmodernity, 153
in art, 122–3, 146–7, 159–60, 192
uneven modernity, 174, 186, 198
Monet, Claude, 114
montage, 110–11, 114, 117, 121, 129, 136, 216, 238; see also colportage; Eisenstein, Sergei
Moore, Thomas, 190
moresque, 174; see also arabesque
Moretti, Franco, 84–5
Morris, William, 181
Morrison, Toni, 205–6, 207
Muhammad I (of Granada), 182
Mukherjee, Ankhi, 234
Murphy, Douglas, 13–14, 181

Narcissus, 130
naturalism, 110, 159–60
Nelson, Brian, 126
New York, 228–39
　Greater New York Bill, 231
　Harlem, 234–8
　Manhattan, 153, 231
　in Henry James, 162–6
Nietzsche, Friedrich, 207

Pandora, 217
Panofsky, Erwin, 142, 163
panorama, 21, 81, 95, 96, 149, 158, 229
Pantheon (Rome), 148
parergon see Derrida, Jacques
Paris, 11, 12, 20, 26, 27–8, 112–13, 142, 150–1, 155, 158, 160, 216–17, 229
　Paris Commune, 119
　see also Benjamin, Walter; Haussman, Baron Georges-Eugène; Zola, Émile
Paxton, Joseph, 6–7, 9

phalanstery, 26, 131, 133, 216
Phillips, Samuel, *Guide to the Crystal Palace and Park*, 6–7, 181
Philpot, Glyn, 153–4, 164
Philpotts, Trey, 70–1
Phiz see Browne, Hablot
picturesque, 156
Piggott, Gillian, 74
Pike, David, 20
Piranesi, Giovanni Battista, 133
Poe, Edgar Allan, 28, 188, 193
　'Ligeia', 191–2
　Tales of the Grotesque and Arabesque, 189
　'The Lake', 190
　'The Man That Was Used Up', 214
　'The Man of the Crowd', 191–2
　'The Philosophy of Furniture', 189–91, 192
　'The Raven', 190
Poovey, Mary, 39, 114
Potter, Jonathan, 22
Pugin, A. N. W., 141, 150
Purkiss, Diane, 55

railway, 2, 3, 6–7, 11, 26, 27, 53, 56, 152
　in Dickens, 63, 68–9, 70–9, 80, 89, 90, 93–4, 95, 103, 115, 133, 221, 229, 232
　in Zola, 131
Rancière, Jacques, 11, 17–19, 26, 111, 129, 142, 160
Raphael, 174, 175, 188
realism, 19
　in art, 85, 159–60
　in literature, 11, 19, 111
Rennie, Nicholas, 129
Reynolds, Nicole, 26
Riegl, Alois, 181
Rippl, Gabrielle, 189, 192–3

river, 2, 11, 26, 27, 232, 234
  Irk, 57, 62
  Lethe, 98
  of commodities, 130, 132
  Seine in Zola, 113
  Thames in Dickens, 63, 68–9, 75, 80–90, 95, 97–9, 102–3, 161, 221–2
Romano, Giulio, 188, 189, 192
Royal Institute of British Architects, 75
Royle, Nicholas, 161
Ruskin, John, 4, 19, 70–1, 147, 155
  The Stones of Venice, 141, 157

St Petersburg, 46, 195, 197
Sainte-Eustache Church, 159–60, 164, 166
Schelling, Friedrich von, 18, 80
Schlegel, Friedrich, 166, 172, 175, 187, 194, 196, 204
  Gespräch über die Poesie, 175–6, 179
  'Principles of Gothic Architecture', 150–1
Scott, Walter, 189–90, 196
Semper, Gottfried, 97, 135
Sen, Sambudha, 12, 21, 85
Shakespeare, William, 157
  Hamlet, 68
Shapiro, Gavriel, 196
Shelley, Mary, *Frankenstein*, 51–2
skyscraper, 15, 16, 143, 153, 162–6, 229, 230–4
Southey, Robert, 161
Spurr, David, 26–7
stained glass, 13
Stanfield, Clarkson, 190
Statue of Liberty, 230
Steebert, Alf, 74
Sterne, Lawrence, 175, 179, 195–6, 197
Stone, Marcus, 100–1

Strathausen, Casper, 196
Surridge, Lisa, 91

Tambling, Jeremy, 70, 78, 80, 223
Tatlin's tower, 133
Taylor, William Cook, 1
Thackeray, William Makepeace, 85
The British Printer, 143, 146
Tillotson, Kathleen, 70
Titov, Vladimir Pavlovich, 150
Trinity Church (New York), 162–6, 233
Tucker, Janet, 195

uncanny, 3, 28, 69, 80–3, 90–1, 95, 97–8, 102, 166, 205
  architectural uncanny *see* Vidler, Anthony
unconscious
  architectural unconscious, 3, 37, 59–60, 63, 70, 75, 79, 89, 103, 115, 159, 221, 224
  historical unconscious, 9
  in psychoanalysis, 1, 16, 20, 43, 45, 48–9, 56, 80–2, 87–8, 92–3, 96, 97, 161, 178, 178, 187, 205; *see also* Freud, Sigmund; Lacan, Jacques
  optical unconscious, 45, 86–7, 88, 96; *see also* Benjamin, Walter
  spatial unconscious, 43–6, 89, 191
utopia, 1, 2, 10, 15–16, 22, 129, 134, 136, 147–9, 203; *see also* ideology

Vidler, Anthony, *The Architectural Uncanny*, 3, 25, 97, 166

Wagner, Wilhelm Richard, 146
Walls, Alison, 113
Wetherill, P. M., 113

Whistler, James McNeil, 216–17
Whitehead, Colson, *Harlem Shuffle*, 229
Whiteley, Giles, 161, 163
whiteness
    and race, 122, 132, 205–6, 207, 215, 223–4
    in the city, 28, 198, 203–24
    whitewash, 208–12, 220
Wigley, Mark, 203, 212
Wilhelm I, Emperor, 152
Williams, Raymond, 2, 56, 70, 78
Winnicott, Donald, 278
Wohlfarth, Irving, 24
Wolfreys, Julian, 90–1
World Trade Center, 233–4, 237–8
World Exhibitions, 11, 13–14, 16, 22, 112–13, 116, 122, 126, 133, 149, 155, 232, 237
    Chicago World's Fair, 143
    Exposition Universelle of 1889, 151
    New York World's Fair, 237
    see also Crystal Palace

Wright, Frank Lloyd, 13, 133, 146–7, 166, 181
    'Organic Architecture', 146
Wyatt, Matthew Digby, 188, 192

Yancy, George, 205

Zeus, 114
Zola, Émile, 2, 4, 26, 28, 109–11, 142, 156, 161, 164–6, 178, 221
    Au Bonheur des Dames, 28, 94, 109, 113, 118, 120, 121, 122, 125–36, 160, 164, 165, 191, 212, 213, 215–18, 222, 238
    L'Argent, 125, 164
    L'Assommoir, 9, 217
    L'Oeuvre, 146
    La Bête Humaine, 119–20, 131
    La Curée, 27, 28, 109, 111–25, 126, 136, 223, 229, 231–2, 235
    La Débâcle, 119
    Le Roman Experimental, 160
    Le Ventre de Paris, 111, 122, 159–60, 164, 165–6
    Nana, 122
    Pot-Bouille, 117, 164

EU representative:
Easy Access System Europe
Mustamäe tee 50, 10621 Tallinn, Estonia
Gpsr.requests@easproject.com

www.ingramcontent.com/pod-product-compliance
Lightning Source LLC
Chambersburg PA
CBHW050213240426
43671CB00013B/2316